New **Patterns in Global Television**

New Patterns in Global Television

Peripheral Vision

Edited by John Sinclair, Elizabeth Jacka,
and Stuart Cunningham

OXFORD UNIVERSITY PRESS
1996

Oxford University Press, Great Clarendon Street, Oxford OX2 6DP

Oxford New York
Athens Auckland Bangkok Bogota Bombay Buenos Aires
Calcutta Cape Town Dar es Salaam Delhi Florence Hong Kong
Istanbul Karachi Kuala Lumpur Madras Madrid Melbourne
Mexico City Nairobi Paris Singapore Taipei Tokyo Toronto Warsaw

and associated companies in
Berlin Ibadan

Oxford is a trade mark of Oxford University Press

Published in the United States
by Oxford University Press Inc., New York

First published 1996

British Library Cataloguing in Publication Data
Data available

Library of Congress Cataloging in Publication Data
New patterns in global television: peripheral vision/edited by John Sinclair, Elizabeth Jacka, and Stuart Cunningham.
1. Television broadcasting—Developing countries. 2. Television broadcasting—Canada. 3. Television broadcasting—Australia.
I. Sinclair, John, 1944– . II. Jacka, Elizabeth.
III. Cunningham, Stuart.
PN1992.3.D44N48 1996
302.23'45—dc20 95-30432
ISBN 0-19-871122-0
ISBN 0-19-871123-9 (Pbk.)

3 5 7 9 10 8 6 4 2

Printed in Great Britain on acid-free paper by
Bookcraft Ltd.
Midsomer Norton, North Somerset

Preface

When the debate about the international 'flows' of television systems and programmes first emerged in the 1970s, its sites were the metropolitan centres of Europe and the USA, and its protagonists came to be known as the camps of the 'North' versus the 'South'.

This is a source of some ironic amusement to the editors of this book for, as Australians, there are very few people in the world who live further to the south than we do, and although our nation has been referred to as 'the poor white trash of Asia' by one leader in our region, it is not usually classified along with the erstwhile 'Third World' countries of the South. Yet that does not mean that it has nothing but geographical location in common with them—the palm trees of our botanical gardens and other historical sites are testament to a time when we were bound in to the British Empire, along with several countries in Asia, and others which are represented in this book: India, Egypt, and Canada.

Correspondingly, Australia's traditional understanding of itself as a 'Western' nation is becoming transformed as the membership of the OECD broadens and the two nations with which we have most closely identified ourselves become more deeply enmeshed with their respective regional trading blocs—Britain in the EU and the USA in NAFTA.

It is the view afforded from the periphery of both North and South which has given us the concept of this book. Rather than the self-absorption which now characterizes most communication research in Europe as it undergoes the privatization and regional integration of its television systems, and the traditional insularity of mainstream US work, a more outward-looking and truly international vantage-point is possible from Australia. Derivative as we might be of theoretical paradigms and research styles from Europe and the USA, we have the advantage of being in a position to weigh these against one another and, with the clarity of distance, to assess their relevance in different contexts. Furthermore, we are able to incorporate and help articulate, for an English-speaking audience, how the world looks from the perspective of the several key sites outside the metropolitan centres of the North which have become significant production centres both for television programmes and services, and for academic research about them.

We would like to thank Andrew Lockett of Oxford University Press for his crucial role in helping us develop this concept and realize it with the present book, and our respective institutions for providing the conditions under which the work could proceed. Of course, the expertise and co-operation of the contributors from the different regions was essential to the character of the book, and we acknowledge that with the greatest appreciation for the quality of their work and effort, and their durable faith in the project.

More particularly, John Sinclair would like to make some personal acknowledgements: Bill Melody, who provided material support and encouragement during his time as the director of CIRCIT (Centre for International Research on Communication and Information Technologies) in Melbourne; fellow researchers Kent Wilkinson and Ingrid Schleicher for their assistance with the most recent data on Latin America; and John Downing and Emile McAnany for their hospitable collegiality at the University of Texas.

For some of the material that appears in Chapter 7, Elizabeth Jacka and Stuart Cunningham would like to acknowledge an Australian Research Council Large Grant awarded to them and colleague Helen Wilson in 1992–4, for a project entitled 'Global Trends in Audiovisual Media—Effects on Australian Industrial and Cultural Development'. For research assistance with Chapter 3, Elizabeth Jacka would like to thank Amanda Hickie.

Joseph Man Chan wishes to acknowledge a grant from the South China Research Program at the Chinese University of Hong Kong for making possible the research reported in Chapter 5, and to thank Chien-san Fang, Georgette Wang, Chin-Chuan Lee, and Lily Liu for their valuable help at the stage of data collection.

John Sinclair, Victoria University of Technology, Melbourne
Elizabeth Jacka, University of Technology, Sydney
Stuart Cunningham, Queensland University of Technology, Brisbane

Contents

List of Tables

About the Editors

John Sinclair has published several articles about television in Latin America over recent years in *Media, Culture and Society* as well as US and Australian journals. He is also known for his book on the international advertising industry, *Images Incorporated*, published in the UK, USA, and Australia in 1987. He is an Associate Professor in the Faculty of Arts at Victoria University of Technology, Melbourne, and a Senior Research Associate with the Centre for International Research on Communication and Information Technologies.

Elizabeth Jacka is one of Australia's best-known researchers on the film and television industries, and on the impact of government policies on the media. She has co-authored and edited two volumes of *The Screening of Australia*, and *The Imaginary Industry*. She is the author of *The ABC of Drama*, several recent papers on the globalization of television, and also editor of *Continental Shift: The Globalisation of Culture*. She is Professor of Communication Studies in the Faculty of Humanities and Social Sciences, University of Technology, Sydney.

Stuart Cunningham is a prominent researcher and writer on film and television in Australia, as well as an experienced analyst and adviser on media policy. As well as numerous articles in several books and leading journals in Australia, he has also published journals such as *Screen* and *Cultural Studies*. He is the author of *Featuring Australia* and *Framing Culture*, co-author of *Contemporary Australian Television* and *Australian Television and International Mediascapes*, and co-editor of *The Media in Australia*. He is an Associate Professor in the School of Media and Journalism at Queensland University of Technology, Brisbane.

Sinclair, Jacka, and Cunningham are all editors of the leading communication media journal in Australia, *Media International Australia*.

About the Contributors

Hussein Y Amin is an Associate Professor in Journalism and Mass Communication at the American University in Cairo. First trained as a professional broadcaster, he has published book and journal articles on a wide range of media topics in Egypt, in both English and Arabic, and has presented several conference papers overseas. His most recent work is on the globalization of television in Egypt and the Arab world.

Paul Attallah is Associate Director of the School of Journalism and Communication at Carleton University, Ottawa. He is the author of two volumes on communication theory, *Histoire, Contexte, Pouvoir* and *Sens, Sujets, Savoir*, and of numerous articles on the institutional aspects and genres of North American television. These have appeared in European and Australian as well as Canadian journals.

Joseph Man Chan is a Senior Lecturer and Chair of Journalism and Communication at the Chinese University of Hong Kong. His research interests include the political, developmental, and international aspects of communication, and the social impact of information technology. He has published extensively in international journals, and is co-author of *Mass Media and Political Transition: The Hong Kong Press in China's Orbit*.

Manjunath Pendakur is a Professor and Chair of Radio/Television/Film at Northwestern University in Chicago, and Director of the Program on Communication and Development Studies. He has published numerous articles on the media in international journals, and is author of a book on the Canadian film industry, *Canadian Dreams and American Control*, and the forthcoming *Indian Cinema: Industry, Ideology, and Consciousness*.

Manas Ray is a Fellow in Sociology and Social Bases of Culture at the Centre for Studies in Social Science in Calcutta, and a visiting faculty member in the Film Studies Department of Jadavpur University, Calcutta. He completed his Ph.D. in cultural theory at Griffith University in Brisbane, Australia.

Radha Subramanyam writes on film and is completing her Ph.D. dissertation on Indian women film-makers at Northwestern University in Chicago. She edits *Directions*, the journal of the Program of Communication and Development Studies, with Manjunath Pendakur, and is review editor of *Asian Cinemas*.

1

Peripheral Vision

John Sinclair, Elizabeth Jacka,
and Stuart Cunningham

A sea-change in television systems around the world began in the late 1970s. An integral element in the various complex phenomena usually captured under the rubric of 'globalization', this transformation has forced the West to confront the television cultures of the more 'peripheral' regions of the world. Shifting geopolitical patterns within the world system, most notably the partial dismantling of national boundaries in Europe, the demise of communism, and the rise of the Asian economies, are having a profound effect on cultural ecologies and the consequent receptiveness of many regions of the world to new cultural influences, including new sources and kinds of television. Alongside this, and related to it, the last ten years have seen major changes in the television cultures of many countries as technological innovation, industrial realignments, and modifications in regulatory philosophy have begun to produce a new audiovisual landscape.

The Transformation of the Audiovisual Landscape

All these changes in turn have been part of a broader movement in the Western world, spearheaded by the USA and the UK, towards a 'post-Fordist' mode of organization of the economy, composed of four major elements—globalization, trade liberalization, increased national and international competition, and a decrease in the centrality of the state as a provider of goods and services. These tendencies in the advanced Western economies were all reflected in the arena of communications and the cultural industries, but with the added factor of a revolution in technology which promised, at least according to its enthusiasts, to provide many more channels than had ever been possible on the traditional bandwidth, and bring about a new era of diversity and choice in broadcasting services.

At the forefront of the technological changes in broadcasting technology was the satellite, which abolished distance and allowed for the first time the linking of remote territories into new viewing communities. There is no doubt that the satellite has acted as a kind of 'Trojan horse' of media liberalization. Although evidence from Europe and elsewhere indicates that satellite services originating outside national borders do not usually attract levels of audience that would really threaten traditional national viewing patterns, the ability of satellite delivery to transgress borders has been enough to encourage generally otherwise reluctant governments to allow greater internal commercialization and competition.

Until the late 1970s only three regions of the world (North America, Latin America, and Australia) had mixed systems of broadcasting, that is, some combination of public and private sectors. The ITV sector in the UK, though technically a privately owned commercial system, was so heavily regulated and protected from competition up until 1992 that to all intents and purposes it operated as a second public service network after the BBC. Everywhere else state-owned broadcasting dominated, either in the traditional public service version characteristic of Europe, or the state-controlled model common in Asia and the Middle East. As the 'Fordist' mode of capitalist economic and political organization began to crumble, this pattern began to change. First in Italy in the late 1970s, then in the mid- to late 1980s in other European countries, including Germany, France, The Netherlands, and the UK, privately owned commercial competitors to the public service monopoly were introduced. This process often proceeded in a back-door and rather chaotic fashion and the regulatory repercussions are still being felt. The process in Europe was enormously complicated by the contemporaneous move towards a united Europe with its parallel set of regulatory requirements (Silj 1992).

The result of these upheavals was a very large increase in the number of channels available, and a consequent spreading of audience and revenue across a much greater range of services. This led to a shortage of product at the same time as the capacity of each service to pay for programmes was strained. In the early stages of the new services there was heavy dependence on USA imports, but it also led to a demand for programmes from new sources, including some formerly peripheral regions, such as Australia and Canada. Similarly, Latin American *telenovelas* began to enjoy popularity in southern Europe. At the same time, new satellite and cable delivery systems permitted the opening up of viable international channels for minority audiences, such as services available in Europe which carry entertainment and news programming from India and the Middle East.

By the beginning of the 1990s similar changes had begun to occur in Asia. The rapid development and opening up of Asian economies has not excluded the media industries. Advances in telecommunications are an inherent component of economic development, and the commercial entertainment possibilities of convergent telecommunication and television technologies have proved attractive to Asian entrepreneurs. However, as is evident in Joseph Man Chan's chapter on the Greater China region (Chapter 5), this development has produced an intense contradiction, harder and harder to reconcile, between liberalization at the economic level and a continued desire for political control and censorship at the cultural level. The same pattern of privately owned, entertainment-driven media that appeared in Europe in the 1980s can be seen in most of the emergent economies of Asia in the 1990s. Thus, the hunger for programmes seen in Europe also operates in the Asian market, and while the traditionally strong production industries of Hong Kong and India will continue to be major sources of product, programming from other sources, especially in the English language, will also be important. Furthermore, the emergence of new media services in countries like Malaysia, Indonesia, Singapore, and Korea has stimulated indigenous production industries in those countries, so that in the future they in turn might develop an export capacity, even if it were to remain a regional rather than a global one.

The most significant innovation has undoubtedly been the advent of STAR TV, the pan-Asian satellite service which operates from Hong Kong. Asian television cultures traditionally have been heavily controlled politically and protected from a high level of Western programming, but STAR TV has introduced them to new sources of programming, especially from the West, and exposed them to diverse sources of news reporting. Although the advent of STAR TV seems to demonstrate that attempts to control the national television space are fruitless, some Asian governments still seek to maintain bans on satellite receiver dishes, notably China, Malaysia, and Singapore.

In the Americas, where the privately owned commercial model has been the norm since television's inception in the 1950s, the 1980s have also brought significant changes, again stimulated by the potential of the new technologies and a more deregulatory mood. In the USA cable technology has facilitated the proliferation of new specialist channels which cater for all sorts of minorities, including ethnic minorities. This has created new viewing sub-communities on both a national and a transnational basis. While some programming for these services is produced inside the USA, a great amount of it is imported from those countries from which the immigrant and exile communities are drawn, including many countries of Asia and Latin America. As John Sinclair demonstrates in Chapter 2, the strongest television economy of Latin America, Mexico, has not been slow to exploit the possibilities offered by the very sizeable Spanish-speaking population of the largest and richest television market in the world, and has benefited from both its programme exports to the USA and its ownership of the major Spanish-language network within it.

Even in the Middle East, which is undoubtedly the most closed and controlled television region in the world, the satellite has brought transnational services which cross borders within the Arab world. As Hussein Amin notes in Chapter 4, this is a cause of some friction between countries which share a common language but have distinct political and cultural orientations. Furthermore, comparable to some international Asian services, the existence of sizeable Arab populations outside the Middle East, mainly in Europe, North America, and Asia, opens up new overseas markets for Arab-language programming.

What emerges from this sketch of changes in world television is indeed an extremely complex picture, better described by Michael Tracey's image of a 'patch-work quilt' (1988: 24), than by Kaarle Nordenstreng and Tapio Varis's 'one-way street' metaphor of the 1970s (1974). In this new vision, global, regional, national, and even local circuits of programme exchange overlap and interact in a multi-faceted way, no doubt with a great variety of cultural effects, which are impossible to conceptualize within the more concentric perspective appropriate to previous decades. Instead of the image of 'the West' at the centre dominating the peripheral 'Third World' with an outward flow of cultural products, this book sees the world as divided into a number of regions which each have their own internal dynamics as well as their global ties. Although primarily based on geographic realities, these regions are also defined by common cultural, linguistic, and historical connections which transcend physical space. Such a dynamic, regionalist view of the world helps us to analyse in a more nuanced way the intricate and multi-directional flows of television across the globe.

New Patterns of Television Flow

Public discourse about television and the media-studies literature are both replete with anxiety about the supposed cultural effects of the global spread of programmes like *Dallas* (Silj 1988: 22–58) or, more recently, *Beverly Hills 90210*. The unquestioned basis for this anxiety is expressed in the orthodox critical paradigm for analysing the connection between international power relations and the media, the thesis of 'cultural imperialism', or more particularly, 'media imperialism'. According to this view, world patterns of communication flow, both in density and in direction, mirror the system of domination in the economic and political order. Thus, world centres like New York, Los Angeles, London, and Tokyo are major nodes for international telecommunications traffic, as well as for other kinds of flows, such as television programmes. The media imperialism perspective more particularly sees that the major world sources for programme exports are located in the USA and secondarily in Europe, mainly the UK, and that these centres act as nodes through which all flows of cultural products must pass, including those from one peripheral part of the world to another.

The *locus classicus* of the cultural imperialism thesis is found in the work of Herbert Schiller. As recently as 1991, in an article tellingly entitled 'Not Yet the Post-Imperialist Era', he has restated his position in the following way: 'The role of television in the global arena of cultural domination has not diminished in the 1990s. Reinforced by new delivery systems—communication satellites and cable networks—the image flow is heavier than ever. Its source of origin also has not changed that much in the last quarter of the century' (p. 15). The classic study for UNESCO by Nordenstreng and Varis in 1974 cited earlier documented the dominance of the USA in world television programme exports at that time. Television programme flows became an integral issue for the New World Information Order movement and its debate within UNESCO. As this continued into the 1980s, the cultural imperialism view of international domination stood challenged only by those who were seen as apologists for the USA and its demand for a 'free flow' international regime for trade in cultural products. Neither critics nor apologists questioned the oft-quoted factoid that entertainment is second only to aerospace as an export industry for the USA (Carveth 1992: 707).

Indeed, as long as the flows of television programme exports seemed to continue along the 'one-way street' from the West (and the USA in particular) to the rest of the world, the critical discourse of cultural imperialism was a plausible theoretical response, at least in its more subtle variations, notably that of 'cultural dependence' (Salinas and Paldán 1974), and 'media imperialism' (Boyd-Barrett 1977). In an essential respect, the cultural imperialism perspective was the then-current neo-Marxist analysis of capitalist culture projected on to an international scale: the 'dominant ideology' thesis writ large. As such, it had the all-embracing appeal of a comprehensive theory, and also provided the high moral ground from which the international activities of USA networks and the ideological content of their television programmes could be analysed, and then denounced.

However, by the mid-1980s it became evident that the cultural imperialism discourse had serious inadequacies, both as theory and in terms of the reality which the theory purported to explain. Actual transformation of the world television system made it less and less sustainable on the empirical level, and shifting theoretical paradigms, including postmodernism, postcolonialism, and theories of the 'active' audience, made its conceptual foundations less secure (Sinclair 1990; Tomlinson 1991, McAnany and Wilkinson 1992; Naficy 1993). To take the empirical aspect first, Jeremy Tunstall had long since pointed out that the 'television imperialism thesis' of such writers as Schiller (1969) and Wells (1972) was based on the quite incorrect assumption that the high levels of USA programme imports into Latin America in the 1960s were a permanent condition rather than a transitional stage in the development of television in these regions (1977: 38–40). The other empirical development which ought to have given pause to theorists of cultural imperialism was the research reported by Varis as an update of the original 'one-way street' project, in which he noted 'a trend toward greater regional exchanges', in spite of continued USA and European dominance in television programme flows (1984). This finding was reinforced by other studies around the same time which, although absurdly exaggerated in their estimation of how far the flows had formed new patterns, were able nevertheless to document just how one such regional market was taking shape, in the case of Latin America (Rogers and Antola 1985).

Thus, even in Latin America, virtually the cradle of the theorization of cultural imperialism, USA imports were prominent only in the early stages. As the industry matured in Latin America, and as it developed 'critical mass', USA imports were to some extent replaced by local products, a pattern that can be found repeated many times over around the world, and which is currently shaping Europe's new privately owned services. Of course, not all countries in Latin America have the capacity to develop sizeable indigenous television production industries. Rather, the pattern in Latin America, as in Asia and the Middle East, is that each 'geolinguistic region', as we shall call them, is itself dominated by one or two centres of audiovisual production—Mexico and Brazil for Latin America, Hong Kong and Taiwan for the Chinese-speaking populations of Asia, Egypt for the Arab world, and India for the Indian populations of Africa and Asia. The Western optic through which the cultural imperialism thesis was developed literally did not see these non-Western systems of regional exchange, nor understand what they represented. Yet by the late 1980s, Tracey could observe that the 'very general picture of TV flows . . . is not a one-way street; rather there are a number of main thoroughfares, with a series of not unimportant smaller roads' (1988: 23).

We have noted how, as theory, the cultural imperialism critique tended to identify the USA as the single centre of a process of mediacentric capitalist cultural influence which emanated out to the rest of the world in the form of television programmes. It also assumed that these programmes had an inevitable and self-sufficient ideological effect upon their helpless audiences in the periphery. Although this rationale established a theoretical connection between US television programmes and 'consumerism', it did not address the question of just how such a mechanism of effect might work, nor how it could be observed in action upon actual audiences. In the discourse of cultural imperialism, the mystique of television entertainment's multivalent appeal for its audiences, and how specific audiences responded to it, were never on the agenda.

Other shortcomings arose from the theory's emphasis on external forces from the USA, and the corresponding disregard for the internal sociological factors within the countries seen to be subject to them. In its eagerness to hold US companies, and behind them, the US government, responsible for regressive sociocultural changes in the 'Third World', the cultural imperialism critique neglected the internal historical and social dynamics within the countries susceptible to their influence. This left out of consideration the strategic social structural position of the individuals and interest groups who benefited from facilitating US market entry or even from taking their own initiatives. Some of these have subsequently built up their own international media empires, as will be evident from Chapter 2 on Mexico and Brazil. Other players have more recently joined the game, such as the Saudi investors mentioned in Chapter 4, while investment in the new channels in India by expatriates, noted by Manas Ray and Elizabeth Jacka (Chapter 3), shows that media entrepreneurism also can be widespread on a small scale. The cultural imperialism theory failed to see that, more fundamental than its supposed ideological influence, the legacy of the USA in world television development was in the implantation of its systemic model for television as a medium—the exploitation of entertainment content so as to attract audiences which could then be sold to advertisers. American content may have primed this process, but as the experience of many parts of the peripheral world shows, it is not required to sustain it.

We should also note that with its dichotomized view of 'the West' versus the 'Third World', the cultural imperialism theory was unable to give an adequate account of semi-peripheral settler societies such as Australia and Canada, where the experience of colonialism, and postcolonialism, has been quite distinct from that of nations in other former colonized zones, a distinctiveness manifest in the television systems which they developed.

The basic assumption of Western domination via television is worth further comment. Paradoxically, even though the cultural imperialism thesis has been articulated in the name of defending the 'Third World' against domination by audiovisual products from the USA, it is more inclined to reinforce Western cultural influence by taking it as given, when it should be challenging it. A more postcolonial perspective in theory has forced us to realize that USA domination always was limited, either by cultural or political 'screens', or both. A related weakness or 'blind spot' of the cultural imperialism thesis has been its over-emphasis on the significance of imported *vis-à-vis* local television. Television has always been more of a local than a global medium, and remains so, although the increasingly multichannel and globalized nature of the industry may alter the balance at the margin in the longer term. According to figures from 1989, the volume of purely domestic material in national markets is twenty-nine times higher than that which is traded (O'Regan 1992). Television is still a gloriously hybrid medium, with a plethora of programming of an inescapably and essentially local, untranslatable nature.

Although US programmes might lead the world in their transportability across cultural boundaries, and even manage to dominate schedules on some channels in particular countries, they are rarely the most popular programmes where viewers have a reasonable menu of locally produced material to choose from. And even where there is imported content, it is no longer acceptable to read off from that fact alone any presumed effects of a cultural or political kind. Hamid Naficy captures this vividly in his brilliant study of television amongst Iranian exiles in Los Angeles. Describing how his exclusively English-speaking Iranian daughter, Shayda, and his exclusively German-speaking Iranian niece, Setarah, communicated through the Disney film, *The Little Mermaid*, he goes on to comment:

> The globalization of American pop culture does not automatically translate into globalization of American control. This globalized culture provides a shared discursive space where transnationals such as Setarah and Shayda can localize it, make their own uses of it, domesticate and indigenize it. They may think with American cultural products but they do not think American. (Naficy 1993: 2)

If the discourse of cultural imperialism has proven inadequate to understand the more complex international patterns of television production, distribution, and consumption as they became evident in the 1980s, and the responses which audiences make to the television available to them, what new theories have become available which might serve these purposes? As Richard Collins has observed, there has been no adequate replacement for the fallen 'dominant ideology paradigm' in which cultural imperialism theory had grounded its view of the world (1990: 4–5). One important reason for this is that in the process by which postmodernism has succeeded neo-Marxism as the master paradigm in social and cultural theory, the new orthodoxy has taught us to be sceptical of such 'grand narratives' or totalizing theories as that of cultural imperialism.

Yet, it must also be said that within postmodernism itself there is no clear theoretical model with which to understand the international trade in television programmes. On the contrary, postmodernism has tended to valorize the fractured cultural meanings of all images and goods, and to conflate the actual processes by which they are produced, distributed, and consumed. In this context, it is ironic to recall the exhortation of Jorge Schement and his colleagues more than a decade ago that we disengage from the 'grand theory' of both the 'free flow' and the 'American hegemony' paradigms in favour of Robert Merton's 'theory of the middle range' (1984), yet this now appears to be just the level of abstraction to which we should now climb down the ladder.

Home on the Middle Range: Geolinguistic Regions

Germane amongst theories at this more modest rung of explanation is the classical economists' notion of 'comparative advantage', which now has been renovated as 'competitive advantage' (Porter 1986), and applied to explain the traditional dominance enjoyed by the USA in the international trade in audiovisual products. Colin Hoskins and Stuart McFadyen argue that of the several comparative advantages enjoyed by audiovisual producers in the USA, the most crucial is their 'unique access to the largest market' (1991: 211–12). The US domestic market, while heterogeneous in terms of its cultural mix, is more or less homogeneous in terms of language, and so represents the largest English-language market in the world. The economies of scale and scope offered by the huge size of the domestic market can be exploited as a platform for audiovisual exports to the rest of the English-speaking world.

In this respect, Collins's observations on English as 'the language of advantage' are fundamental:

> Works in English enjoy enormous advantages, for not only are anglophones the largest and richest world language community—excluding non-market economies . . . but English is the dominant second language of the world. The size and wealth of the anglophone market provides producers of English language information with a considerable comparative advantage *vis-à-vis* producers in other languages. But it is important to recognize that this is a *potential* advantage which may or not be realizable. (1990: 211)

He goes on to point out that the converse also holds, that is, that the USA and other anglophone markets exhibit resistance against imported programmes in languages other than English. Of course, such a 'cultural discount' (Hoskins and Mirus 1988) is also applied against English-language programmes in non-anglophone markets, but nowhere near as much. Language is thus a natural protective barrier as well as a basic source of advantage in the process by which the USA has built up its pre-eminence within what we can call the 'geolinguistic region' of English. This includes not only the anglophone countries, but also those where English is widely used as a second language, or perhaps just by a particular social stratum. It is worth emphasizing Collins's point that language of production is a potential rather than necessary advantage, but as Paul Attallah (Chapter 8) and Stuart Cunningham and Elizabeth Jacka (Chapter 7) show, it is clearly one which has been exploited with increasing success by both Canada and Australia respectively, in spite of the relative disadvantages of their small market size and their semi-peripheral, postcolonial, and derivative status within the world that speaks English.

An even more striking feature of the new international media landscape beyond the traditional anglophone centre, however, is the consolidation of the trend to regional markets. As noted above, these also are geolinguistic rather than just large, geographically contiguous regions, as international satellite networks enable the television production centres of the major domestic markets in the world's largest language regions to beam programmes across the world to the 'imagined communities' of their diasporic concentrations and former colonial masters in the metropolises of Europe and the USA. It is worth noting, too, how far these new regional centres have been built upon already existing centres of film production identified with characteristic popular tradeable 'hybrid' genres of their own, such as the Hong Kong action movie or Hindi musical. Manjunath Pendakur and Radha Subramanyam show in Part 1 of Chapter 3 the considerable extent to which this has been true in the case of India in particular. Latin America, which the 'geolinguistic region' explanation fits particularly well, also has had its film production centres, but its tradeable hybrid became the *telenovela*, a commercial television serial genre, reflecting the long-standing commercialization of Latin American broadcasting.

Although some of these regions appear to have been victims of cultural imperialism in the past, at least in terms of their heavy importation of US films or television programmes, the pattern which had emerged by the mid-1970s was that the 'countries which are strong regional exporters of media tend themselves to be unusually heavy importers of American media' (Tunstall 1977: 62). This suggests a process of indigenization in which the US generic models, in establishing themselves as 'international best practice', also invite domestic imitation. However, the substitute products become adapted to the local culture in the process, whether for market reasons, for the sake of diversity, or to diminish foreign influence, and new 'hybrid' genres are created.

The resulting situation is not the passive homogenization of world television which cultural imperialism theorists feared, but rather its heterogenization. Within the anglophone world, Australia and Canada, and even the UK, produce programmes which have assimilated the genre conventions of US television, but with their own look and feel. Outside of it, US genres (such as the MGM musical and the soap opera) have been adapted beyond recognition in a dynamic process of cultural syncretism. For it is cultural similarities in general, not just language in particular, that binds geolinguistic regions into television markets. Pan-Sino cultural elements allow programmes produced in Cantonese to cross easily into Mandarin, just as

Spanish and Portuguese readily translate into each other in 'Latin' markets. Religion, music, humour, costume, nonverbal codes, and narrative modes are all elements in what Joe Straubhaar calls 'cultural proximity'. He hypothesizes that audiences will first seek the pleasure of recognition of their own culture in their programme choices, and that programmes will be produced to satisfy this demand, relative to the wealth of the market. Similar to Tunstall's prediction of the growth of a level of hybrid programme choice between the global and the local, Straubhaar argues that, in general:

> audiences will tend to prefer that programming which is closest or most proximate to their own culture: national programming if it can be supported by the local economy, regional programming in genres that small countries cannot afford. The U.S. continues to have an advantage in genres that even large Third World countries cannot afford to produce, such as feature films, cartoons, and action-adventure series. (1992: 14–15)

This is consistent with Hoskins and McFadyen's prognosis that US production will continue to increase, finding its strength especially in the prosperous 'North American/West European/ Australasian market', but that it will also 'constitute a smaller share of an expanding market' in world terms as regional and national production also expands (1991: 221). This expansion will occur to the extent that competitors also develop comparative advantages such as the USA has enjoyed historically. As well as dominance of the largest market within a geolinguistic region, these include economies of scale, high levels of commercialization, and 'first mover advantage', especially where that is based on technical and stylistic innovation. Thus, with the important proviso that the flow of peripheral production is not so much displacing US production as finding its own intermediate level, the way is open to enquire into how these levels might be impacting upon the cultural identification and restratification of television audiences on a global scale. First, however, we should consider some other middle range theories which strive to account for the rise of peripheral nations' television export markets.

Cross-Cultural Textual and Audience Analysis

Just as the cultural imperialism thesis has governed the analysis of industrial, technological, and linguistic factors which underpin peripheral nations' export activity, so has it informed how we should grasp the cross-cultural implications of such activity. John Tomlinson, in his careful examination of the discourse of cultural imperialism, contends that 'there is a definite sense of . . . "the moment of the cultural" being forever deferred' (1991: 40) in favour of the more solid evidence that seems to be delivered by a political economy approach. By this he means that factual accounts of media production and distribution too often have stood in place of an attempt to analyse exactly how domination, resistance, and negotiation work in the transfer and 'consumption' of cultural meaning by actual audiences. In his wide-ranging overviews of the idea of dominance in international television culture, Michael Tracey (1985, 1988) caustically draws attention to the 'curious . . . way the level of analysis employed for understanding the implications of the mass media at the international, as opposed to the national and individual level, has remained frozen at the stage of intellectual development achieved by communications research in the first three or four decades of this century' (1985: 44). In other words, cultural imperialism theory has been dogged by the outdated notion of an automatic media effect that, paradoxically, it shares with traditional US social science. Tracey submits that these crude models of cultural transmission and of the assumed cultural impact of economic and political influence are patently inadequate for the task of tracking cultural transfer.

Part of the reason for this inadequacy is that traditional grand theories have not given sufficient attention to the middle range factors that ought to be taken into account in explaining the relationship between the world television trade, the changing character of transmission technologies, and questions of cultural proximity and cultural screens. Current explanations for the popularity and success of imported television drama in particular range from arguments about textual form and content, to fortuitous placement in programme schedules. There is also the approach, most closely associated with John Fiske (1987), which focuses on the use to which particular programmes might be put by audiences—the pleasures they might gain and the cognitive, intersubjective and social experiences that might be generated around particular programmes.

In all these approaches the programmes that have attracted the most attention have been those which have had the greatest success in terms of ratings, high industrial or critical regard, or number of territories into which they have been sold. Commercial success is not a necessary precondition for choosing programmes for audience use studies, although in practice the two have gone together. It is generally more feasible and perhaps of more significance to study cross-cultural audience use of programmes with high and lasting international visibility. For these reasons, in the English-speaking literature it has been American programmes, almost without exception, which have been the object of critical or ethnographic audience studies.

We must ask what precisely it means, and how might it be possible, to carry out research on how audiences respond to television programmes from other cultures, and not just the dominant ones. Methodological protocols central to this line of investigation need modification to account for peripheral programme reception. When studies are restricted to reporting and analysis of the self-understanding of selected audience respondents, wider factors affecting the impact of programmes are often bracketed out, or treated superficially as just 'background'. Instead, the middle range research advocated here looks at the broader context of viewer reception set by the social environment; the professional practices of trading in, marketing, and scheduling television programmes; and the strategic role played by the 'gatekeepers' of the television industries, including owners, managers, and programme buyers.

In recent years a tradition of micro-situational audience analysis, influenced in some measure by 'ethnographic' anthropological methodologies, has been used to demonstrate the great variety of ways in which programmes are interpreted by different audiences in different 'places'. The best-known of these is undoubtedly the Tamar Liebes and Elihu Katz (1990) study of the reception of *Dallas*, the series which became 'the perfect hate symbol' of cultural imperialism critics in the 1980s (Mattelart *et al.* 1984: 90). While this line of investigation is welcome as far as it goes, we want to argue that, just in itself, a micro approach is also inadequate to track the fortunes of the television exports of peripheral nations.

However, it is worth giving some attention to this landmark study to show why we believe this to be the case. It is an investigation of cross-cultural audience decodings of *Dallas* on three continents, in which the authors argue that the key reasons for the international popularity of US prime-time television, and especially serial/soap formats like *Dallas*, lie in:

> (1) the universality, or primordiality, of some of its themes and formulae, which makes programmes psychologically accessible; (2) the polyvalent or open potential of many of the stories, and thus their value as projective mechanisms and as material for negotiation and play in the families of man [*sic*]; and (3) the sheer availability of American programmes in a marketplace where national producers—however zealous—cannot fill more than a fraction of the hours they feel they must provide. (1990: 5)

However, it is clear that universality and primordiality are features of the genre as a whole rather than peculiar to US soap opera; even a cursory examination of, for example, Mexican and Brazilian *telenovelas* or Egyptian soap opera makes this clear. This criticism also holds for the second reason given. Thus, universality cannot account for the international success of US serials. The third reason that Liebes and Katz adduce is the one they least explore, yet it is far more significant than they allow. Indeed, there is something strangely decontextualized about the detailed recording and elegant analyses of their selected respondents in Israel, Japan, and the USA. 'Vigorous marketing', they say, 'is certainly a reason for the international success of *Dallas*' (1990: 4), but they pay almost no attention to this level of explanation.

This treatment should be compared with the analyses of the

programme's introduction into foreign markets presented by Jean Bianchi (1984), and the *East of Dallas* research team led by Alessandro Silj (1988), which indicate that factors like scheduling, programme philosophy, and the cultural environment prior to the programme's reception militated against its success in countries such as Peru, or, for unexpected and surprising reasons, enhanced its success in countries such as Algeria. In the latter, a one-party nation with one television station (state-owned), *Dallas* was a popular success. 'One wonders', says Silj, 'why the television of an anti-imperialist, anti-capitalist state, the guardian of a social and family morality deeply marked by the Islamic religion, a pioneer of collective values . . . should wish to put on a programme so imbued with antagonistic, "American" values' (1988: 36).

In the Peruvian case, where *Dallas* was not successful—it ran for less than a year—Silj's mode of explanation is industrial and cultural. *Dallas* became the losing card in a ratings battle between the two leading commercial channels when it was pitted against a local comedy programme. This seems to bear out Straubhaar's hypothesis, that successful local programming will tend to relegate US material to second or lower place. However, Silj is careful to remind us that the situation in Peru was a contingent one—had the local programme been of lesser quality the outcome may well have been reversed. Bianchi's and Silj's conclusions are that viewer reception is a dynamic process governed by the cultural identities of audiences and the 'sedimentation of other social practices' (Silj 1988: 40); which we can take to mean, amongst other factors, the industrial and institutional conditions obtaining prior to any audience seeing any foreign programme.

'Gatekeepers' and Cultural Industry Factors in Television Flows

Many cross-cultural studies emphasize the diverse, localized character of international audience responses, and are imbued with a sense of the viability and integrity of the cultures of peripheral or 'small' nations. So it is somewhat ironic, because of the dominance of American programmes at highly visible though only provisionally premium places in schedules, that such studies should focus on US programmes almost exclusively. As Ellen Seiter argues strongly with regard to the theoretical field from which this position draws, 'in our concern for audiences' pleasures . . . we run the risk of continually validating Hollywood's domination of the worldwide television market' (Seiter *et al.* 1989: 5).

Far more than for the USA, the success or otherwise of peripheral nations' exports is contingent on factors other than those captured by established modes of audience study. This explains why so little audience reception research has been able to be conducted on their products in international markets, and why we need instead middle range analysis to do so. In the middle range between political economy approaches and reception analysis, a number of factors are mediating. How are programmes acquired overseas? Who engages in their appraisal and acquisition and what perceptions have they formed of peripheral programming? This 'primary audience' is the major source of informed 'gatekeeping' which regulates (in the widest sense) the flow of peripheral programming in international markets. And what are the characteristics of the major territories which influence the success or failure of such programmes internationally? All these mediating factors embody legitimate, indeed central, aspects of cultural exchange, as virtually all the significant research on non-dominant nations' television production and reception indicates (Lee 1980; Silj 1988; de la Garde *et al.* 1993).

The actual structure of major international television trade markets is central to middle range analysis. There is an ever-wider variety of modes of contracting for international programme production and exchange: offshore, co-production, official co-production, co-venture (including presales), and straight purchase of territorial rights for completed programmes in the major trade markets such as MIP-TV and MIPCOM. These run on annual cycles suited to the programming and scheduling patterns of the major northern hemisphere territories, but a notable shift in the patterns of global television traffic was indicated in 1994 when the first

MIP-Asia was held, a trade market specifically for the Asian region. At such events, programming is often bought (or not bought) on the basis of company reputation or distributor clout, in job lots and sight-unseen. Very broad, rough-and-ready genre expectations are in play; judgements may seem highly 'subjective' and arbitrary.

Universalist explanations such as those of Liebes and Katz may prove useful in accounting for the international successes of historically universal forms like US series drama, but there is solid evidence that cultural specificities, along with other middle range industrial factors, are unavoidable and, at times, enabling factors for international success in peripheral countries' export activity. Studies which compare viewers' engagement with US as against other sources of television programming confirm that there tends to be a more distanced realm of 'pure entertainment' within which US programmes are processed—as markers of modish modernity, as a 'spectacular' world—compared to more culturally specific responses made to domestic and other sources (Biltereyst 1991).

The capacity for peripheral countries to export their programmes across diverse markets is to some extent based on their substitutability or non-substitutability for US material, although this also depends in part on the type of channel they are purchased for, as indicated by the case-studies in Chapter 7. Australian productions have provided useful models from which the protocols of commercial popularity may be learnt in rapidly commercializing European broadcasting environments, but the fact that Australian programmes are perceived as imitations of US formats constitutes a problem for both commentators and regulators in Europe (de Bens *et al.* 1992).

To be sure, the structure of content and the form of internationally popular serial drama in particular are widely shared and may even be 'borrowed' from US practice, as the *telenovela* was decades ago. But the 'surface' differences, nevertheless, almost always are consequential, and contribute to the acceptance or rejection of non-US material, depending on whether the 'primary audience' of gatekeepers and the viewing audience respond positively or negatively to those differences. As Anne Cooper-Chen (1993) has shown, even that most transparently internationalized of television formats, the game show, contains significant differences in the widely variant cultures in which it is popular. After looking at popular game shows in fifty countries, she regards them as having at least three structural variants—the East Asian, Western, and Latin models—and innumerable surface particularities. Hamid Mowlana and Mehdi Rad (1992) show that the Japanese programme *Oshin* found acceptance in Iran because its values of perseverance and long suffering were compatible with cultural codes prevalent in what might appear a distinctly different society. The evidence for the popularity of *Neighbours* in Britain demonstrates that, while Australian soaps arguably were brought into the market as substitutes for US material, their popularity built around textual factors based on projections and introjections of Australian 'life-style'. Australia has served in many ways as a kind of 'other' to Britain—the younger, more upstart and hedonistic vision of how the British might like to see themselves.

The 'export of meaning' is not just a matter of viewer reception. Many nations, both core and peripheral, place special importance on the international profile they can establish with their audiovisual exports. These are fostered both as a form of cultural diplomacy, and for intrinsic economic reasons, although national cultural objectives and audiovisual industry development are not always compatible, as Australia and Canada have long been aware, and some Asian countries are now learning. In the case of the Middle East, one commentator has observed that the popularity of Egyptian television exports in the Arab states has a number of cultural and even political 'multiplier effects'. This popularity was preceded by the success of Egyptian films, and carries with it a potential acceptance and recognition of Egyptian accents and performers that can operate as 'a soft-sell commercial for Egyptian values' which then carries over into indirect political leverage (M. Viorst, quoted in Tracey 1988: 12). While it might be difficult to isolate and measure them, it is not unreasonable to infer cultural, trade, and political multiplier effects from what can be seen of peripheral nations' products on the world's television screens.

'Globalization': More than Meets the Eye

While it is fundamental that we recognize the new patterns of television programme exchange and service distribution to be global in their scale, this does not mean that we must therefore conceive of them in any facile framework of 'globalization'. As Marjorie Ferguson has so vigorously pointed out, the concept of globalization is shrouded in myth, and it is not at all clear that its protagonists all mean the same thing by it (1992). At best, it is no more than a catch-all category to refer to various trends towards more complex patterns of international circulation, not only of media products, but also of technologies, finance, people, and ideas (Appadurai 1990). At worst, it is the ideological gloss which the beneficiaries of these trends put upon them—the global village, at your service. Ien Ang has argued that talk about globalization may have been 'part of a short-lived rhetoric which coincided with a precise historical moment' during the late 1980s and early 1990s. This was a period when news of major political transformations, notably the end of the Cold War, and events such as Tiananmen Square and the Gulf War, were carried to the world by media with instantaneous global reach, such as CNN. These produced 'an apocalyptic sense of globalised reality', but she suggests that our present and immediate future is better characterized as a '*post*-globalised world rife with regional realignments and fracturings, nationalist and ethnic separatisms, and, in parallel, a proliferation of overlapping and criss-crossing media vectors which undermine a unified and singular notion of the "global"' (1994: 325). Thus, globalization has already become a cliché that it is time to move beyond, and analysis of the new patterns discernible in global television show a useful way in which this can be done.

Discussions of globalization often counterpose the global with the local, and the local is in turn equated with the national. However, as we have already suggested, in the analysis of television production and distribution on a world scale it is important to distinguish not just the local from the national, but the regional from the global. Of these distinct but related levels, it is the local and the regional which have been most neglected in the literature to date. This book redresses this imbalance to the extent that it outlines the local characteristics of the television industries of significant non-metropolitan countries that have built a presence outside their own borders. This includes the phenomenon of 'contra-flow' (Boyd-Barrett and Kishan Thussu 1992), where countries once thought of as major 'clients' of media imperialism, such as Mexico, Canada, and Australia, have successfully exported their programmes and personnel into the metropolis—the empire strikes back.

The book also is concerned to give emphasis to the regional level, and the national within the context of the regional, where 'region' must now be understood to be geolinguistic and cultural as well as geographic. A regional perspective on the development of television markets brings to light national similarities, such as the widespread adoption of commercial television in Latin America, or to take a familiar example from the old metropolis, the wave of privatization and new services which has transformed television in Europe since the mid-1980s. A regional, rather than a global, perspective elucidates the connections between trade and culture, particularly in the potential impact which the formation of regional free-trade zones might have upon programme exchange, and in the clash of free-trade rhetoric with national cultural objectives. Again, the prominent example of a regional position is the EU's refusal to allow their audiovisual industries to be opened up to free trade under the GATT trade-in-services agreement, and instead seek to implement a European content quota. An instance which emphasizes the tension of the national and regional is NAFTA (North American Free Trade Agreement), in which Canada's insistence that its audiovisual industries be excluded contrasted with Mexico's position in which the protection of these industries was never an issue.

So long as television remained a terrestrial technology, there was less distance between the local and the national levels on one hand, and the national and the global on the other. However, satellite distribution has opened up regional and transcontinental geolinguistic markets, as we have argued, while terrestrial broadcasting and videocassettes have provided an additional but less immediate means for the distribution of television products to diasporic communities, notably those of Chinese, Arab, and Indian origin. Attention to this regionalization of markets gives greater insight into what is happening in the world than does the hollow rhetoric of globalization. Two instances of trends elucidated by a regional perspective are the rise of the regional entrepreneurs, and the restratification of audiences into 'imagined communities' beyond national boundaries.

Although Rupert Murdoch severed his national ties with Australia by taking up US citizenship in 1986, it remains the case that his rise to become perhaps the world's most spectacular media entrepreneur was based upon his initial accumulation of media assets in Australia, where he still controls almost 70 per cent of the daily press. From this base, literally on the periphery of the English-speaking world, he launched his ventures into the largest countries of that geolinguistic region, first Britain and then the USA. Even more peripheral in origin were the two generations of Azcárragas whose dominance of the world's largest Spanish-speaking market in an erstwhile 'Third World' country has been turned into a platform for extensive operations in the USA as well as South America, and a toehold in Spain. In this respect, 'El tigre' (the tiger) Azcárraga is not 'Mexican' any more than Murdoch is Australian. If the term 'globalization' is to mean anything, it must take account of such deracination of corporations and entrepreneurs from 'their' nation-states, and furthermore, the more recent moves of these entrepreneurs in particular even beyond their geolinguistic regions. With Murdoch's purchase of STAR TV and Azcárraga's return to partnership in the PanAmSat international satellite corporation, we see both of them ratcheting up the scale of their operations so as to establish a strong presence in Asia, expected to be the fastest-growing regional media market of the next century. Also of note is the strategic alliance which they have made to exchange programming from each other's regions.

Benedict Anderson's concept of 'imagined communities' has been one of the most influential tropes in theories of national consciousness for more than a decade (1983), but as satellite television distribution transcends the borders of the nation-state, there is some value in applying it to the new audience entities which that process creates. Similarly, in the decades since Nordenstreng and Varis first drew attention to the transnational media's action upon 'the nonhomogeneity of the national state' (1973), there have arisen international services which stratify audiences across national boundaries not just by class and education, but by 'taste culture' and age—the ostensible international youth culture audience for MTV, for example. Of more interest to us in this book are the imagined communities of speakers of the same language and participants in similar cultures which form the geolinguistic regions exploited by the media entrepreneurs, especially the diasporic communities of émigrées on distant continents.

Even amongst the globalization theorists, it is becoming a commonplace to observe that the globalizing forces towards 'homogenization', such as satellite television, exist in tension with contradictory tendencies towards 'heterogenization', conceived pessimistically as fragmentation, or with post-modernist optimism, as pluralism. Thus, 'identity and cultural affiliation are no longer matters open to the neat simplifications of traditional nationalism. They are matters of ambiguity and complexity, of overlapping loyalties and symbols with multiple meanings' (Castles *et al.* 1990: 152). To the extent that we can assume that television is in fact a source of identity, and that audiences for the same programme derive similar identities from it, it becomes possible to think of identities which are multiple, although also often contradictory, corresponding to the different levels from which the televisual environment is composed in a given market. An Egyptian immigrant in Britain, for example, might think of herself as a Glaswegian when she watches her local Scottish channel, a British resident when she switches over to the BBC, an Islamic Arab expatriate in Europe when she tunes in to the satellite service from the Middle East, and a world citizen when she channel surfs on to CNN. In both the positivist mainstream and critical traditions of communication theory in the past, disregard for actual content, disdainful stereotypes of 'lowest common denominator' programming, and dichotomous thinking about tradition and modernity, all have prevented this more pluralistic conception of audience identity to surface. What it has required has been, firstly, the more recent theorization of multiple social identities being overlaid in the individual subject, and then the perception argued for here, that these identities are related to the local, national, regional, and global levels at which cultural products such as television programmes circulate.

Staking Out the Periphery

The countries and their regions represented in this book have been chosen with a number of criteria in mind. First, there is their relevance to the geolinguistic region hypothesis, that is, the broad proposition that export markets will develop amongst countries which share a similar language and culture. While this applies most obviously to exchange amongst neighbouring countries in a region, such as Greater China or the Middle East, the geolinguistic region in these cases goes far beyond the immediate geographic clustering to include the respective diasporic communities on other continents. As well as the Chinese and Arab diasporas, there is also the Indian, which has created substantial markets in Europe, North America, Africa, Asia, and the Pacific. This reminds us that to discuss television flows in the age of the international satellite and the VCR is no longer just a matter of tracking the traditional mode of exchange, the sale of broadcast rights for programmes. We must also take into account direct satellite services, and ever more frequently, local cable retransmission of such services, as well as the rise of videocassette distribution of television and film products. In this way the book attempts to provide an account of the impact of such transborder technologies as the satellite and the VCR, but in an empirically grounded manner.

A second common element to the countries and/or regions selected is their historical background as colonies. While both the past and the present of the former 'white settler' colonies of

Australia and Canada are vastly different to those of the British colonies of Asia and the Middle East (actually west of where this is being written), the colonial legacy has been formative of and consequential for contemporary markets for cultural products. For example, British migration to Australia and other colonial ties have helped to foster a receptiveness to Australian television series in the UK. Even more fundamentally, colonialism has been decisive in the patterning of language use in the world. This is just as true for the former 'Latin' American colonies of Spain and Portugal as it is for the more dispersed former British colonies.

Thirdly, countries have been selected as much for certain unique characteristics as well as common ones. Like India and Egypt, Hong Kong is of interest because of the export market which already had been achieved for its films during the decades prior to the rise of television exports in the 1970s, but also because of its predestined return to mainland China in 1997, with all the questions that raises for the subsequent development of television in the region. Canada is like Australia with its small population and its peripheral status within the English-speaking world, and like Mexico in its long border with the USA, but quite distinct in its combination of both cultural and geographical proximity to what is still the world's most successful audiovisual exporter.

A comparison of particular chapters reveals further differences within the similarities. Australian and English-speaking Canadian productions have in common their substitutability for American programmes in schedules around the world. That is, their status as English-language producers means that Australia and Canada are different to most other countries in the book, in that they both export outside of their geolinguistic region. However, where they differ is that Canada's proximity to the USA, coupled with its failure, until recently, to produce sufficient audience-drawing indigenous programming in popular genres, has meant that Canada has not produced the same volume and range of exportable programmes as Australia has done over the years. There are also differences between as well as within geolinguistic regions. Whereas programmes move across borders with relatively ready acceptance within the Latin world, the geolinguistic region *par excellence* outside of the English-speaking world, political differences and variable forms of adherence to Islam impose limits upon the amount of integration which is achievable within the Arabic geolinguistic region. Another case again is the hegemony which Hindi enjoys over the other languages of India as the 'language of advantage' in audiovisual production and export.

Thus, the countries and regions to which the following chapters are devoted are the major nodes of television programme export and service expansion outside of the traditional sources of television flows. Of course there are certain other countries which some readers might have thought deserved inclusion in a book about peripheral nations' television export activity. Japan has had considerable success in exporting mainly children's animation throughout the world; indeed, it is a world leader in this genre. It has also found a wide variety of markets for some of its drama (Mowlana and Rad 1992), and has increasingly entered into fruitful co-production arrangements with Western and other Asian nations, especially those with public broadcasters, to make programmes in such international genres as documentary and children's programming. However, while the story of Japanese programme export is one of relatively recent and increasing success, it could hardly be asserted that Japan is a peripheral nation in the world audiovisual trade, any more than it is in broader political and economic terms. With the second biggest broadcaster (NHK) and five other broadcasters in the world's top twenty (TBI 1994), as well as its leading role in entertainment hardware export and major investments in production companies throughout the world, Japan is very definitely a heavyweight.

New Zealand has provided a radical model of rapid transition from a wholly public service-based broadcasting ecology in the few years since the late 1980s. It is now aggressively outward-looking, with an increased presence in the South Pacific and Asia; it has its own prime time soap opera, *Shortland Street*, which is incorporated into its co-production partner Grundys' world sales catalogue of 'programmes that work'; and its small but enterprising film industry has attracted international attention. However, it is still rather early to assess adequately the extent and vitality of New Zealand's television export 'career'. While English-language production has compensated for small domestic markets in the Australian and Canadian cases, New Zealand's three and a half million population would seem to stretch that tendency to its limit.

The small European countries are often pointed to as examples of nations within and yet peripheral to a metropolitan constellation of considerable power and dynamism. However, these countries must be excluded from our optic because of their very low export viability (Lange and Renaud 1989). Additionally, there is already a substantial and rapidly growing literature on the European audiovisual scene. Rather, our purpose here is to provide a series of timely overviews of the major regions of television production and distribution beyond the metropolitan centres of the North Atlantic region: a peripheral vision.

References

ANDERSON, BENEDICT (1983), *Imagined Communities: Reflections on the Origin and Spread of Nationalism* (Verso, London).

ANG, IEN (1994), 'Globalisation and Culture', *Continuum*, 8/2: 323–5.

APPADURAI, ARJUN (1990), 'Disjunction and Difference in the Global Cultural Economy', *Public Culture*, 2/2: 1–24.

BIANCHI, JEAN (1984), *Comment comprendre le succes international des séries de fiction a la television?—Le cas 'Dallas'*, Laboratoire CNRS/IRPEACS, Lyon.

BILTEREYST, DANIEL (1991), 'Resisting American Hegemony: A Comparative Analysis of the Reception of Domestic and US Fiction', *European Journal of Communication*, 7: 469–97.

BOYD-BARRETT, OLIVER (1977), 'Media Imperialism: Towards an International Framework for the Analysis of Media Systems', in J. Curran, M. Gurevitch, and J. Woollacott (eds.), *Mass Communication and Society* (Edward Arnold, London), 116–35.

—— and KISHAN THUSSU, DAYA (1992), *Contra-flow in Global News: International and Regional News Exchange Mechanisms* (John Libbey, London).

CARVETH, ROD (1992), 'The Reconstruction of the Global Media Marketplace', *Communication Research*, 19/6: 705–23.

CASTLES, STEPHEN, KALANTZIS, MARY, COPE, BILL, and MORRISSEY,

MICHAEL (1990), *Mistaken Identity: Multiculturalism and the Demise of Nationalism in Australia* (2nd edn., Pluto Press, Sydney).

COLLINS, RICHARD (1990), *Television: Policy and Culture* (Unwin Hyman, London).

COOPER-CHEN, ANNE (1993), 'Goodbye to the Global Village: Entertainment TV Patterns in 50 Countries', paper presented to the conference of the Association for Education in Journalism and Mass Communication, Kansas City, August.

DE BENS, ELS, KELLY, MARY, and BAKKE, MARIT (1992), 'Television Content: Dallasification of Culture?', in K. Siune and W. Treutzschler (eds.), *Dynamics of Media Politics: Broadcast and Electronic Media in Western Europe* (Sage, London).

DE LA GARDE, ROGER, GILSDORF, WILLIAM, and WECHSELMANN, ILJA (eds.) (1993), *Small Nations, Big Neighbour: Denmark and Quebec/Canada Compare Notes on American Popular Culture* (John Libbey, London).

FERGUSON, MARJORIE (1992), 'The Mythology about Globalization', *European Journal of Communication*, 7: 69–93.

FISKE, JOHN (1987), *Television Culture* (London, Routledge).

HOSKINS, COLIN, and MCFADYEN, STUART (1991), 'The U.S. Competitive Advantage in the Global Television Market: Is it Sustainable in the New Broadcasting Environment?', *Canadian Journal of Communication*, 16/2: 207–24.

—— and MIRUS, ROGER (1988), 'Reasons for the US Dominance of International Trade in Television Programmes', *Media, Culture and Society*, 10/4: 499–515.

KPMG Management Consulting (1992), *A History of Offshore Production in the UK: A Report for the Australian Film Commission*, April.

LANGE, ANDRÉ, and RENAUD, JEAN-LUC (1989), *The Future of the European Audiovisual Industry*, Media Monograph No. 10, European Institute for the Media, Dusseldorf.

LEE, CHIN-CHUAN (1980), *Media Imperialism Reconsidered: The Homogenizing of Television Culture* (Sage, London).

LIEBES, TAMAR, and KATZ, ELIHU (1990), *The Export of Meaning: Cross-Cultural Readings of 'Dallas'* (Oxford University Press, New York).

MATTELART, ARMAND, DELCOURT, XAVIER, and MATTELART, MICHÈLE (1984), *International Image Markets* (Comedia, London).

MCANANY, ÉMILE, and WILKINSON, KENTON (1992), 'From Cultural Imperialists to Takeover Victims? Questions on Hollywood's Buyouts from the Critical Tradition', *Communication Research*, 19/6: 724–48.

MOWLANA, HAMID, and RAD, MEHDI MOHENSIAN (1992), 'International Flow of Japanese Television Programs: The "Oshin" Phenomenon', *KEIO Communication Review*, 14: 51–68.

NAFICY, HAMID (1993), *The Making of Exile Cultures: Iranian Television in Los Angeles* (University of Minnesota Press, Minneapolis).

NORDENSTRENG, KAARLE, and VARIS, TAPIO (1973), 'The Nonhomogeneity of the National State and the International Flow of Communication', in G. Gerbner, L. Gross, and W. Melody (eds.), *Communications Technology and Social Policy* (Wiley, New York), 393–412.

—— and —— (1974), *Television Traffic—A One-Way Street?* (UNESCO, Paris).

O'REGAN, TOM (1992), 'New and Declining Audiences: Contemporary Transformations in Hollywood's International Market', in Elizabeth Jacka (ed.), *Continental Shift* (Local Consumption Publications, Sydney), 74–98.

PORTER, MICHAEL (1986), *Competition in Global Industries* (Harvard Business School Press, Boston).

ROGERS, EVERETT, and ANTOLA, LIVIA (1985), '*Telenovelas*: A Latin American Success Story', *Journal of Communication*, 35/4: 24–35.

SALINAS, RAQUEL, and PALDÁN, LEENA (1974), 'Culture in the Process of Dependent Development: Theoretical Perspectives', in K. Nordenstreng and H. Schiller (eds.), *National Sovereignty and International Communication* (Ablex, Norwood, NJ), 82–98.

SCHEMENT, JORGE, GONZÁLEZ, IBARRA, LUM, PATRICIA, and VALENCIA, ROSITA (1984), 'The International Flow of Television Programmes', *Communication Research*, 11/2: 163–82.

SCHILLER, HERBERT (1969), *Mass Communications and American Empire* (Augustus M. Kelley, New York).

—— (1991), 'Not Yet the Post-Imperialist Era', *Critical Studies in Mass Communication*, 8: 13–28.

SEITER, ELLEN, BORCHERS, H., KREUTZNER, G., and WARTH, E. (eds.), (1989), *Remote Control* (Routledge, London), 'Introduction', 1–15.

SILJ, ALESSANDRO (1988), *East of Dallas: The European Challenge to American Television* (British Film Institute, London).

—— (1992), *The New Television in Europe* (John Libbey, London).

SINCLAIR, JOHN (1990), 'Neither West nor Third World: The Mexican Television Industry Within the NWICO Debate', *Media Culture and Society*, 12/3: 343–60.

STRAUBHAAR, JOSEPH (1992), 'Assymetrical Interdependence and Cultural Proximity: A Critical Review of the International Flow of TV Programs', paper presented to the conference of the Asociación Latinoamericana de Investigadores de la Comunicación, São Paulo, August.

TBI (Television Business International) (1994), 'The 1994 TBI 100', *Television Business International* (March), 22.

TOMLINSON, JOHN (1991), *Cultural Imperialism* (Johns Hopkins University Press, Baltimore).

TRACEY, MICHAEL (1985), 'The Poisoned Chalice? International Television and the Idea of Dominance', *Daedalus*, 114/4: 17–56.

TRACEY, MICHAEL (1988), 'Popular Culture and the Economics of Global Television', *Intermedia*, 16/2: 9–25.
TUNSTALL, JEREMY (1977), *The Media Are American* (Constable, London).
VARIS, TAPIO (1984), 'The International Flow of Television Programmes', *Journal of Communication*, 34/1: 143–52.
WELLS, ALAN (1972), *Picture-Tube Imperialism? The Impact of U.S. Television on Latin-America* (Orbis, Maryknoll, NY).

2

Mexico, Brazil, and the Latin World

John Sinclair

We think of the development of television on a global scale as primarily an 'American' phenomenon, and so it has been in important ways, but as this chapter will demonstrate there is also a Latin American version of that story to be told. To most English-speakers, 'America' means the USA, even though that is just one zone within the two continents of America that join to form a virtual hemisphere, almost from one pole to the other. We also need to remind ourselves that the legacy of the Iberian colonization of America which began more than half-a-millennium ago includes the fact that the majority of the inhabitants of those continents speak Spanish or Portuguese. Not only do South and Central America, including Mexico, present a unique world region of contiguous nations with a common language, with the notable exception of Brazil, but now close to a tenth of the US population is Spanish-speaking. In significant respects, it has been Latin American corporations which have been best placed to perceive and exploit the commercial possibilities of the region's demographics for television. Their comparative advantage in that regard has been the basis upon which they have built a major world market, one which the US television programme and service providers have begun to take seriously in only recent years.

Media Transnationals of the 'Third World'

In particular, two major media conglomerates have arisen in

the 'Latin' world: Televisa, based in Mexico, the largest and most influential media corporation amongst all those countries of the world that speak Spanish; and Globo, rooted in Brazil, the predominant network amongst the Portuguese-speaking nations. They have been called 'Third World multimedia groups' in the sense that they are defined by their vertically and horizontally integrated ownership of the major audiovisual and other media in their home countries. Another label is 'multinationals of the Third World' or, as is now preferred, 'transnationals', by virtue of the scale and organization of their intercontinental television operations, and the relatively autonomous relationships they bear to their respective national governments. Yet, at the same time, their global activities are conditioned by the fact that their domestic markets are in 'newly industrialized' countries wracked with debt and other classic symptoms of underdevelopment and dependence (Mattelart *et al.* 1984: 51–7). Although they have to be seen in relation to the other important networks and production centres of the Latin world (a concept which is used here to embrace the Spanish-speaking and Portuguese-speaking populations of the USA and Europe as well as Latin America), it is Televisa and Globo which have made the most strenuous and consequential efforts to internationalize themselves, and which present the most striking challenge to the former critical orthodoxies of cultural and media imperialism.

'The language of advantage'

With both Televisa and Globo, it is evident that their international expansion and the niches they each have come to occupy within the present structure of global communication have been built upon the comparative advantage they enjoy in dominating their domestic markets. These are not only substantial in themselves, and compare with European markets, for example, but are also the largest home markets in the Spanish- and Portuguese-speaking worlds respectively: Mexico contains nearly a quarter of the world's Spanish speakers, and three-quarters of all Portuguese speakers are in Brazil (Dunnett 1990: 194). Mexico is a nation of 91 million people, and contains 15.3 million television households; Brazil has a population of over 157 million, with 38.5 million television households, of which Globo maintains a 76 per cent average share over its competitors SBT, Bandeirantes, Manchete, and provincial networks (BIB 1993: A168, 287). Its share at prime time is 80 per cent. Television in Brazil received at least 55 per cent, and up to 61 per cent, of total advertising revenues for the decade up to 1992 (Mattos 1992: 18), and Globo garnered around 60 per cent of that (Marques de Melo 1992: 5).

Televisa dominates its market against much less competition than Globo: it obtains an 80 per cent share of all television advertising, with the rest going to the government's former networks, but its audience share in peak hours is estimated to be as high as 98 per cent (Warburg 1992: 1). The other significant indicator to note is the exceptional amount of original production: unlike networks in the English-speaking world, both Televisa and Globo produce most of their own programmes, and do so across a wide range of television genres, some of them quite 'tradeable', or successful as exports. Televisa produces 78 per cent of all the programmes it broadcasts (Warburg 1992: 4), while the corresponding figure for Globo is a comparable 80 per cent (BIB 1993: A287).

With both companies, the buildup of productive capacity made to meet the expansion of their domestic networks has been exploited by a related shift into the export of programming, with the first export markets being those countries with the same language as that in which the programmes were made. In this respect, they have been capitalizing upon comparative advantages quite similar to those long enjoyed by US producers within the much larger, and richer, English-speaking markets of the world. However, no single network dominates the world's largest English-speaking market to the degree that Televisa and Globo have each secured their domestic markets, the world's largest national markets in their respective languages. While English remains 'the language of advantage' (Collins 1989) as the most widely spoken Western European language in the world with its 450 million speakers, it is important to bear in mind that Spanish comes next, with 352 million, and then Portuguese with 175 million (*World Almanac* 1991: 573–4). Furthermore, Spanish has been assessed as the fifth wealthiest linguistic population in the world, with Portuguese as the eighth (Wildman and Siwek 1988: 85).

Such 'unique access to the largest market', fortified by linguistic-cultural barriers, is conducive to economies of scale and hence the competitive advantage of lower costs when the higher volume of production for export markets absorbs the fixed costs of production expended in the domestic market: this has been called 'domestic opportunity advantage' (Wildman and Siwek 1988: 68). In conjunction with 'first mover advantage' and geographical proximity of export markets (Hoskins and McFadyen 1991: 209–11, 217–18), we can see how Televisa and Globo have been able to make themselves the centres of their respective international regions. It is worth taking this point further: where there is satellite access available to remote external markets, such as Televisa's direct link to Spain via PanAmSat, then geographical proximity is less important than linguistic similarity and 'cultural proximity' (Straubhaar 1991). This exemplifies the phenomenon of 'geolinguistic regions', or world-wide markets based on linguistic and cultural similarities, in this case, a 'Latin audiovisual space' (Mattelart *et al.* 1984). Although Televisa and Globo sell their programmes all over the world, it will be seen that their prime export markets are all 'Latin': the various nations of Latin America; the Spanish-speaking USA; and Spain, Portugal, and Italy. Furthermore, as well as programme exports, this geolinguistic 'space' is now also constituted by direct satellite transmission services and investment in foreign broadcasters.

Entrepreneurs and Investors

In the present age, when European countries are only now learning to come to terms with commercial television as a social institution, it is instructive to review the Latin American experience, where television in most countries was commercial from the outset. Even those countries which first opted for what was then thought of as the 'European' state-operated model had shifted to a commercial 'American' model by the early 1960s (Muraro 1985: 79; Fox 1991: 6–9).

However, the 'cultural imperialism' framework, which over recent decades has been the dominant paradigm for thought about international media influence, has characterized the adoption of broadcasting in Latin American countries as a form of cultural imposition. Consequently, this view has ignored the degree to which local entrepreneurs not only co-operated with US networks in the spread of commercial radio and television, but actively sought their support so as to build a media system in which those entrepreneurs could entrench themselves and expand their own interests. An international pressure group of Latin American radio network owners with US links, the Asociación Interamericana de Radiodifusión (Interamerican Association of Broadcasting) or AIR, was founded in Mexico in 1946 with the purpose of fostering the commercial model of broadcasting and minimizing government regulation throughout the region. The lenient government controls on the commercialization of television found throughout Latin America today can be attributed to the effectiveness of this group, which is still in operation (Muraro 1985: 80; Fernández 1987: 36–43; *Fox* 1991: 3–8).

Prominent in the beginnings of AIR was the Mexican radio entrepreneur Emilio Azcárraga Vidaurreta, who also was to become the principal figure in the development of Mexican television and the eventual formation of Televisa. He successfully prevailed upon the Mexican president of the time, Miguel Alemán Valdés, to permit television to develop on a private commercial basis. Beginning on 1 September 1950, Mexico was the first Latin American nation to establish television. Azcárraga was one of the first licensees. By 1955, however, the still-weak market for television at that stage motivated the competing licencees to unite themselves into a federation, Telesistema Mexicana, the immediate corporate ancestor of Televisa. Televisa itself was not formed until 1972, with Azcárraga's son Emilio Azcárraga Milmo succeeding him in control on his death that year (Sinclair 1986: 88–90; Mejía Barquera 1987: 24; Sinclair 1990: 94).

In the case of Brazil, Straubhaar has argued against the

orthodox assumption that it was US influence which ensured that television began on the commercial model. In fact, he cites evidence that when Francisco de Assis Chateaubriand Bandeira de Melo began Brazil's first television channel TV Tupi Difusora (commencing on 18 September 1950 in São Paulo and, the following year, in Rio de Janeiro), he acted in spite of advice from US consultants that the advertising base was too small to support commercial television (Ferraz Sampaio 1984: 199; Straubhaar 1984: 222). As with Mexico, it should be borne in mind that commercial radio was already flourishing in Brazil, under the conventional commercial system where the state had nominal control over the airwaves but granted concessions to private licensees. Chateaubriand was an established owner of newspapers and radio stations, and was prepared to invest his own capital to secure a ground-floor entrance for himself with the new medium (de Lima 1988: 117; Vink 1988: 22; Mattos 1992: 5).

Yet again, as in Mexico, the first decade of television in Brazil was not profitable. The television market was indeed too small and too élite, and since the era of transnational investment in consumer industries had not yet begun, prospective advertisers were still few. TV Tupi's first biggest advertisers were all Brazilian (Mattos 1992: 3). While Chateaubriand's stations remained dominant in such market as there was, the small advertising pool could not adequately sustain the number of stations which continued to appear. Furthermore, while some transnational advertising agencies had arrived during the radio days of the 1930s, the new wave of agencies, with their experience of television and marketing techniques fresh from the USA, was yet to come.

It would have been for these reasons that the US networks clearly preferred to form affiliations with local entrepreneurs and provide technical assistance rather than make direct investments at this stage. It was not until the end of the 1950s that the US networks began to make direct investments. Constitutional restrictions on foreign ownership of broadcasting in several countries also limited the foreign networks' options and so favoured participation through the local entrepreneurs. Unlike Mexico, then, it would appear that

Brazilian television was financed by Brazilian capital throughout this first phase, that is, until 1965 with the advent of Globo and its controversial relationship with Time-Life.

On the other hand, the foreign advertisers that were interested in television fostered the development of the same kind of 'sponsorship' system as still characterized commercial radio everywhere and which was at first inherited by television in the USA. In both Brazil and Mexico, foreign advertisers and their agencies, such as Ford via J Walter Thompson, would import programmes from the USA as well as commission local productions on US models. It was not until 1960, after the sponsorship system came under challenge in the USA, that Telesistema Mexicana brought programming under its own control. However, in Brazil sponsorship (as distinct from the sale to advertisers of spot time in programmes produced or commissioned by the network itself) lasted up until the end of 1970, from which time can be traced the rise of Globo as a producer (Straubhaar 1982: 145; Sinclair 1986: 90; Mattos 1992: 4–6).

The beginning of the end of the sponsorship system, which would take programme production out of the control of advertising agencies and put it into the hands of independent producers and the networks, was only one of several changes in the character of television as a business which can be dated from around the year 1960. It is also from that time that the push strengthens towards the internationalization of US companies, including consumer goods manufacturers, communication companies, and advertising agencies: the beginning of the era of the 'transnational corporation'.

Within the television industry itself, there was rapid exploitation of the technical innovation of videotape, which became available from about 1958. Whereas previous television recording technology was so costly and poor in quality that it was little used, video recording meant that there no longer had to be as much live broadcasting as in the early 1950s. Rather, new programme genres and forms of schedule could be cultivated to reach new audiences. In particular, there emerged the *telenovela* or Latin American 'soap opera', strip-programmed daily, that is, shown at the same time every day. Above all, videotape also meant that an export trade could be developed for such programmes (Mattos 1992: 7). In time, the *telenovela* was to become the most popular and frequently traded genre throughout the region. On the other hand, in 1960 Brazil also adopted technology for dubbing imported programmes into Portuguese before they were broadcast, which the government had made mandatory. This gave television stations access to large amounts of foreign programmes at low cost, mostly series, films, and cartoons from the USA (Straubhaar 1984: 223–4; Vink 1988: 24). By this time Mexico was already established as the dubbing centre for such foreign programmes into Spanish for the Latin American market.

Given the lacklustre prospects of television as a commercial medium during the 1950s and these new possibilities of the 1960s, it is understandable that Roberto Marinho, who was to found the Globo network and thus become the Brazilian counterpart to Azcárraga and Televisa, did not enter the field until quite late. Significantly, the licence for the first Globo station was granted before the end of 1957, but it was April 1965 before it was put to air. Marinho was the director of *O Globo*, the major national daily newspaper based in Rio de Janeiro, established in 1925 and subsequently integrated with magazine and radio interests, backed by Brazilian rather than foreign capital (de Lima 1988: 122; Marques de Melo 1988: 13).

However, when the Globo channel was launched it was in collaboration with Time-Life, with whom Globo had signed a contract in 1962. For legal reasons this agreement had to be terminated in 1968, but what Globo gained over the period was not just the finance to build the basis of a national network, but also the management techniques and experience derived from commercial television in the USA. By Straubhaar's account, however, when it came to programming Globo had more success with their own Brazilian managers than with the Time-Life advisers. Certainly Globo was able to broaden the appeal of television to a mass market in Brazil, and so deliver the kind of audiences which the transnational consumer industries and their agencies wanted. The finance enabled Globo to leap entry barriers and open up a competitive advantage over the other networks which it could then go on to consolidate in subsequent decades. Whatever Time-Life expected to gain would have been frustrated by the cancellation of the agreement, but that had in any case coincided with the period in which Time-Life and other US communications corporations were withdrawing from their Latin American ventures (Straubhaar 1984: 228–9; Fox 1991: 9–10).

Just as Globo and Time-Life sought to exploit the new commercial television environment of the 1960s, so did ABC, the most active of the US networks in Latin America, in conjunction with Telesistema Mexicana. With an investment of 25 per cent from ABC, Teleprogramas de Acapulco was created as a production subsidiary. Under the management of Miguel Alemán Velasco, son of the former president, it successfully produced television programmes for export as well as for the domestic market (Mejía Barquera 1987: 28–9). However, the Mexicans had not just waited for ABC: in 1954, even before Azcárraga had joined in the formation of Telesistema Mexicana, he had established a programme-export arm. The creation of an additional market for Mexican programmes became the motive factor in the subsequent establishment of a network of stations in the USA, an important platform for later international development, as will be discussed below.

'Savage capitalism'

In their assessment of Latin American television markets, Rogers and Antola argue that 'favourable government policies' assisted Televisa and Globo to monopolize their domestic markets and so build an export base (1985: 27). It is important to understand the precise sense in which this might be true, since government policies can determine media development at least as much by their failure as by their success, and by their absence as by their presence. In this section, the behaviour of successive governments towards Televisa and Globo in their respective countries will be reviewed and assessed on a comparative basis with regard to frameworks of regulation, infrastructural provision and other points of contact between government and media.

State Control of Television

For its first decades in Mexico television was allowed to operate under a minimal regime of regulation. However, in the 1970s the Echeverría presidential administration became critical of the quality of television content with regard to national culture, public health, and moral concerns. Rather than try belatedly to regulate the private licencees, the government confronted them with the launch of its own national network, Channel 13, funded by advertising as well as state subsidies. It was this move which generated the formation of Televisa at the end of 1972: Telesistema Mexicana merged with its competitor, Televisión Independiente de México, to form a united front against the government's challenge. Thus was created the 'Mexican formula': a mixed system with all private licences under one monopoly, and a state network competing weakly with it and giving unintended legitimation to its dominance (Sinclair 1986). Over two decades of this regime came to an end in 1993 when the government channels were sold to a private owner and relaunched as TV Azteca (Paxman 1993).

Commentators agree that in Brazil there was a quite different situation, however, in which Globo was in fact favoured by the military regime which ruled Brazil through the five successive presidential administrations from the coup of 1964 until 1985. The regime was of the 'bureaucratic-authoritarian' type, which sought to put civilian technology and big business in the service of state-directed capitalism (Guimarães and Amaral 1988: 123). Even so, the conflict which eventually developed between the government and the network was resolved in favour of the private broadcaster as in Mexico, and with more decisive consequences.

In the first place, there was the question of the government's attitude to Globo's initial deal with Time-Life. This was judged to be illegal in 1963, but it was not until 1968 that it was cancelled. This tardiness lends weight to the view that, at least in its early years, the marshals saw Globo as an exemplary model of the modern, national capitalist enterprise which they were trying to cultivate in Brazil, as well as a reliable ally in their efforts to legitimize their rule and to manage information and public opinion. The Brazilian dictatorship could not assert the total ideological control it wanted because it also was intent on creating a free market for consumer capitalism, and Globo was the beneficiary of this contradiction (de Lima 1988: 118–123; Mattelart and Mattelart 1990: 30–1; Marques de Melo 1992: 5).

Yet Globo seems to have been complicit with the state only to the extent that it was serving its own interests, and when the regime recognized that it had allowed Globo to build itself into an economic, political, and ideological institution in its own right, it sought to break the monopolistic advantages upon which the network's power rested. In 1980 the government cancelled the ailing TV Tupi's licences, and divided them between two new competitors. These were SBT (Sistema Brasileiro de Televisão), owned by the performer and entrepreneur Silvio Santos, which began broadcasting in 1982; and the Manchete network, then owned by the Bloch group, which began a year later. The redistribution had little immediate effect on Globo's market share, but the dictatorship's action provoked Roberto Marinho into withdrawing Globo's support for its candidate in the 1985 election and building up the candidacy of the civilian Sarney, who subsequently was elected as president of the 'New Republic' (de Lima 1988: 121; Guimarães and Amaral 1988; Vink 1988: 29). The era of Globo's identification with dictatorship was over.

We have seen how in Mexico the state challenged an oligopolistic structure of private television ownership, only to see it consolidate itself into a monopoly, while in Brazil the state's attempt to strengthen competition cost it the public support of the major network and subsequent electoral loss. In other words, these are cases where the state has had the political will to move against market dominance by one or two players, but without success. Certainly, the dictatorship in Brazil was able to assert control over the content of television in a way that the Mexican government could not, but apart from that, and the failed attempts to create competition, it can be said that the state has put few regulations in the way of broadcasters in either Mexico or Brazil. This kind of unregulated environment has been called 'savage capitalism' in at least two main aspects: the lack of control over cross-media ownership, and the regulation of advertising (Mattelart 1991: 96; Straubhaar 1991: 48).

In both countries the state has allowed not just 'horizontal integration' of media holdings, but also 'vertical integration'. What makes Televisa and Globo so distinct from television networks elsewhere is the considerable degree to which they produce as well as distribute their own programmes, a practice which is specifically proscribed in the USA, by contrast, as anticompetitive. *Laissez-faire* broadcasting regulation in both Mexico and Brazil has fostered the consolidation of the fundamental commercial model, but as well, has sanctioned the growth of cross-owned media conglomerates beyond the point at which the state can control them by reasonable means.

As far as advertising regulation is concerned, the picture is more complex. Regulation in both countries allows a degree of commercialization of television content and time that also would be unacceptable in the USA. In Brazil, for example, the statutory fifteen minutes of commercials per hour is much enhanced by unregulated product placement, or 'merchandizing'. This involves an advertiser paying to have a product appear in a programme: to have it scripted into a *telenovela* for example (Litevski 1982: 15–16).

'Communication is integration'

Another crucial area in which government policies have conditioned the development of television in Mexico and Brazil is in the provision of technological infrastructure. It becomes apparent that both Televisa and Globo have been major private beneficiaries of public expenditure on telecommunications. In Brazil the state supported the growth of the television industry in general and Globo in particular to the extent that, through its Brazilian Telecommunications Enterprise (Embratel), it was the provider of the telecommunications facilities (microwave, satellite, and cable) which enabled the major stations in São Paulo and Rio to establish themselves as national networks. This was fundamental to the full commercialization of television in Brazil, for it enabled the cultivation of audiences on a national scale to which advertisers could be sold access.

It also has been claimed that, whereas in 1964 'Brazil was a cultural archipelago made up of semi-autonomous geo-economic regions', national networks meant not just an increase in the size of audiences, but also the growth of more 'popular' programme styles and the binding of diverse regional populations into a sense of identity as 'Brazilians' (Marques de Melo 1992: 1–2). For example, there could be no national television news before 1969 when the satellite infrastructure was first established, and made possible Globo's *Jornal Nacional*. Of course, such national integration was in the interests of the dictatorship's modernization and 'national security' project as well as those of the television industry, but Globo and its national advertisers have been the ones able to reap the ultimate benefits. The same could be said of the introduction of colour television in 1972. As Embratel's motto goes, 'Communication is integration' (Mattelart and Mattelart 1990: 20–2).

In a similar manner, the Mexican government enabled Telesistema Mexicana to create Channel 2 as a national network with the provision of a national microwave system (Sinclair 1986: 92–4). In the 1980s domestic satellite development under state control became the new form in which public expenditure on infrastructure benefited the networks. In Mexico the government moved into this area with its Morelos satellite system to prevent Televisa from taking the initiative, but Televisa co-operated, much to its ultimate advantage (Mody and Borrego 1991). In Brazil Globo and the other networks now are carried on the domestic system Brasilsat 1 and 2, operated by Embratel (BIB 1992: B17).

At the broad level, the pattern which seems to emerge from this comparison is that Televisa has been formed out of conflict with the state, while Globo has emerged out of collaboration. However, this conclusion needs to be qualified with the understanding that Televisa is known to have close connections with the ruling party in Mexico and indeed is notorious for the favourable treatment it gives it in news and current affairs programmes (Marín 1986), while Globo's behaviour over the years of the dictatorship can be seen as the pursuit of its own interests, albeit working through those of the state. In both cases, it is crucial to recognize the 'relative autonomy' of the corporations from their respective national governments, as much in the pursuit of their business interests as in whatever political projects of their own they might pursue from time to time.

Horizontal and Vertical Integration

As was suggested in the previous section, the absence of cross-media ownership regulation in Mexico and Brazil has been important in allowing radio and press entrepreneurs to move into television, and so through a process of horizontal integration create Televisa and Globo as cross-owned media conglomerates. Thus, certain economies of scale in production and synergies in distribution can be achieved: record sales of the music from popular television programmes, for example. However, the dominance of these organizations within their domestic markets must also be explained by their vertical integration. Above all, there is the fact that they produce so much of what they broadcast and, as well, the manner in which they are organized to cultivate the audiences for their programmes as markets. This section will outline the structure and scale of both organizations within their respective countries, taking account of their predominance across the cultural industries, and the integration of production and distribution relative to their particular audiences.

Going Public

An unusual amount of detailed information about Televisa became available in 1991–2 when the corporation underwent a major restructuring, reducing it from 288 to 211 companies. This was in conjunction with the flotation of a portion of Televisa shares on the Mexican and international stock markets: for the first time Televisa became, at least in part, a 'public' company, raising a net $US800 million (Martínez Staines 1991: 33; Bear, Stearns 1992: 4). The Azcárraga family extended its control over Televisa shares, and at the same time, kept selected parts of the former conglomerate under their private control. Of the 77.7 per cent of Grupo Televisa shares which are still privately held, the Azcárraga family has 62 per cent (Warburg 1992: 3). They retain all of Televisa's former cable television operation, Cablevisión, and its former video and radio companies under the Grupo Videovisa and Radiópolis umbrellas (Martínez Staines 1991: 33).

Of course, both cable and video represent the profitable new age beyond broadcast television. Cablevisión leads its competitor in the cable market, Multivisión, and offers Televisa programmes as well as broadcast and cable channels from the USA, including HBO Ole, and Time-Warner movie channel in Spanish (Warburg 1992: 9). Grupo Videovisa is a group of four companies which lead the market in home video in Mexico, once again thanks to vertical integration; in this case, blank tape production; licensed reproduction and distribution of major films and games from the USA; and rentals through a range of franchised outlets (Gutiérrez Espíndola, 1992: 21). As of 1992, between a third and a half of all Mexican television homes had videos, compared to cable which was in only 3 per cent of television homes in Mexico City (Warburg 1992: 4). Thus, cable is a growing but élite niche market and video a booming mass market, both of which are domestic market segments which the Azcárragas dominate above and beyond the major interest they still maintain in broadcast television through Televisa.

However, it should be emphasized that in spite of Televisa's much-vaunted international activities and its ventures into new forms of signal distribution, television production for its domestic broadcast networks remains the basis of its economic strength. About 85 per cent of Televisa's total revenues are obtained from within Mexico, and 75–80 per cent of total revenues comes from television production and broadcasting. Domestic broadcasting is organized into three national networks and one Mexico City channel, as follows:

- Channel 2 is Televisa's national flagship channel and the largest Spanish-language channel in the world. Broadcast twenty-four hours per day, it reaches 96 per cent of Mexico's television homes. Almost all its programmes are aimed at a broad audience and produced by Televisa: *telenovelas*, comedies, music, variety, and news. It also forms the content of Galavisión, the international entertainment service transmitted direct to the USA, Spain, and elsewhere.
- Channel 4: in a significant move at the end of 1991, this was changed from a popular programme format to carry the ECO (Empresa de la Comunicación Orbital) news and information service which Televisa has been developing since 1986 as a kind of Spanish-language CNN, and which is also transmitted internationally with Galavisión. However, the domestic audience dropped as a result.
- Channel 5 carries foreign cartoons in the afternoons and foreign series in the evenings to young urban audiences throughout Mexico. Televisa has its own dubbing operation for the foreign material it broadcasts, as well as for re-export and external customers. Most of this material is from the USA.
- Channel 9 also has gone through a change of format, in this case from non-commercial cultural programmes to a commercial popular format of films, *telenovelas*, comedy, sport, and Channel 2 re-runs (Bear, Stearns 1992: 3–5; Warburg 1992: 4–5).

Given that TV Azteca's competing networks attract only 10 per cent of viewers (Paxman 1993), it is clear that Televisa has a virtual monopoly of the broadcast audience, and so can segment it by offering different types of programme to particular demographic target groups. These audiences in turn attract different types of advertisers. Channel 2 has the broadest appeal with a 'mass' audience attractive to (trans)-national advertisers; Channel 4 has a small but potential 'up-market' audience; Channel 5 attracts middle-class urban youth; and Channel 9 has a more 'popular' working-class appeal of interest to local advertisers. This capacity to deliver segmented audiences to advertisers is part of the traditional basis of Televisa's commercial success.

Another part of the formula is the vertical integration of broadcasting with production. As noted, Televisa produces nearly 80 per cent of what it broadcasts, and in terms of quantity it is not only the largest producer in the Spanish-speaking world, but produces more television programming than the four US networks and the major producers combined (Warner, Paramount, Disney, King World, Universal, and Columbia). With its dozens of studios and state-of-the-art equipment, 'the company is operated like a highly efficient factory in this regard', as one analyst comments (Warburg 1992: 1–5). Yet in spite of Televisa's reputation as a producer of *telenovelas*, it is worth noting that over 1988–91 this kind of programme represented only about 8 per cent of hours produced. At the same time there was much experimentation with new genres such as telemarketing and talk shows, sports programmes increased steadily, and the greatest number of hours were for ECO news and information material (Bear, Stearns 1992: 6). Since this service has the least appeal to domestic audiences, it seems that Televisa's international activities might have begun to influence programme production priorities, even though its greatest revenues are still derived from the domestic market. This contradiction might prove to be a source of difficulty for Televisa in the long term, particularly if TV Azteca becomes more competitive as a result of its collaboration with the US network NBC (Malkin 1994).

The 'pattern of quality'

Because Globo remains in the private hands of the Marinhos alone, rather less detailed and up-to-date information is available, but enough to establish certain structural similarities with Televisa. In the first place, it can be deduced that, like Televisa, the bulk of its revenues also come from domestic television production and broadcasting, given that television has attracted the majority of advertising expenditure for nearly two decades (Mattos 1992: 18), that Globo receives 'a steady 60%' of this (Besas 1992: 82), and that it produces up to 95 per cent of its own programmes (BIB 1992: A209). Furthermore, it is known that export profits are less than 3 per cent of total sales revenue (Marques de Melo 1992: 8). However, it is important to remember that although its audience share and profits are well ahead of its competitors, Globo does not have the same kind of market dominance in Brazil that Televisa enjoys in Mexico. Because Globo's number of stations and audience coverage are not significantly greater than those of SBT, its major competitor, there is constant competition for audience share. In recent years SBT has made some serious challenges to Globo's ratings dominance, most surprisingly with a badly dubbed Mexican *telenovela* in 1991 ('Carrossel mexicano' 1991).

To attract the more-affluent audiences, and with an eye also to international sales, Globo cultivates its 'pattern of quality': competitive programmes, high technical standards, and a professional look. Quality has not always characterized Globo's style, however. In the 1960s Globo first sought out the more 'popular' audiences, a reaction to the commercially unsuccessful élitism of Brazilian television's initial phase. In particular, programmes took on an 'aesthetic of the grotesque', a kind of folk populism, calculated to attract the 'archaic' marginalized sectors of society into 'modern' markets for consumer goods. Yet from the early 1970s, with the advice of its newly founded Department for Market Research and Analysis, Globo started the shift towards the quality aesthetic. In this process, live shows increasingly gave way to *telenovelas* in an ambiguous process of 'Brazilianization' of programming (Straubhaar 1984; Herold 1988: 44–5; Vink 1988: 26–7).

As to Globo's organization of the production of the *telenovelas* and other genres of programmes it produces, the same highly rationalized 'factory' model as for Televisa applies, although the higher cost structure in Brazil suggests there may be more attention to quality control (Marques de Melo 1992: 9–10). Also as in Mexico and other countries where formerly state-supported film industries have now withered, it is television production which attracts the best creative and technical personnel. The degree to which Globo and Televisa have been able to lock this talent into television production is another dimension of their vertical integration.

As to horizontal integration, Globo and Televisa are active across similar fields in other media, including radio, recording, and magazines, and show structural similarities. Print media are more important to Globo, both as businesses in their own right and because Globo faces major competition from Editora Abril in magazines as well now as in cable television. Abril is part-owner of TVA, a five-channel subscription satellite-to-cable service begun late in 1991. Globo launched its Globosat soon after (Besas and Hoineff 1992). Both Televisa and Globo have their educational and artistic enterprises, no doubt more for the sake of their corporate social standing and legitimacy in their respective societies, and each has some more profit-oriented promotional and other commercial activities related to their media interests, as well as a series of unrelated businesses.

Televisa-ion and Globo-ization

The programme-export activities and other moves to international expansion made by Televisa and Globo over recent decades are significant, but need to be kept in perspective. The challenge which they make to the traditional dominance of the USA in the world audiovisual trade is more conceptual than real: that is, it has more to do with our theoretical common wisdom about that dominance than with the actual degree of commercial threat. We have seen that the international growth has proceeded from the paradoxical exploitation of comparative advantages similar to those of the USA, but there are inherent disadvantages also in the dependent status of the respective home markets. Just as 'domestic opportunity advantage' has given rise to an export capacity, so do the limitations of the domestic market provide a spur to establish ventures in foreign markets, notably the richer and more stable ones of Europe and the USA. 'Growth in Brazil is little less than impossible in the 1980s', declared Roberto Irineu Marinho, heir apparent to the Globo founder (quoted in *Der Spiegel*, 12 Sept. 1986), while at the same time Miguel Alemán took the view that 'As the Mexican economy shrinks, it is a struggle for Televisa just to remain the same size' (quoted in Marín 1986: 7).

Yet because US producers are based in the world's richest

market, this problem does not arise, and in fact they are able to extend themselves beyond their home market to a much greater degree. Over the last three decades about half of the sales of the major US producers have been made to foreign markets (Wildman and Siwek 1988: 1). By contrast, Televisa and Globo each remain dependent on the domestic markets which are both their strength and their weakness. For Televisa, television revenues are about 80 per cent of total sales, and of this, 85–90 per cent is from advertising sales in Mexico, with the remainder divided between advertising sales on Galavisión (its international cable service) and all sales of programme licences outside of Mexico. Less than 10 per cent of Televisa's sales revenues derive from outside Mexico. These come from the US, Latin America, Europe, and elsewhere, in that order (Warburg 1992: 2 and 8). For Globo, it has been noted already that its export profits are less than 3 per cent of total sales revenue.

It is helpful to distinguish between the different forms of international activity. With both Televisa and Globo, programme exports were the first form of foreign incursion, going back to the 1950s in the first case, and the 1970s in the latter. Programme exports to the USA were backed up by direct investment from Televisa's corporate predecessor in the 1960s, while both Televisa and Globo have gone on to make direct investments in foreign stations in the 1980s and 1990s. In recent years Televisa has gone a stage further with the institution of direct international satellite transmission of its Galavisión programmes and ECO news and information service, as well as having struck agreements with US satellite services. Let us look in more detail at these activities for each corporation.

Televisa: A New Stage of Expansion

It was mentioned above how Emilio Azcárraga Vidaurreta from the earliest days instigated exports from Televisa's corporate ancestors, especially after 1960 with the adoption of videotape and the establishment of Teleprogramas de Acapulco as a production arm. The first direct move into a foreign market was made in 1960, when Azcárraga opened up stations in San Antonio, then Los Angeles and New York, in partnership with certain US citizens, notably René Anselmo. These and other stations acquired later formed the Spanish International Communication Corporation (SICC), while the Spanish International Network (SIN) was created to distribute the programmes and sell advertising. In time, the Spanish-speaking minorities of the USA were built into a national audience for Televisa programmes, delivered by satellite from Mexico. Apart from its geographical proximity, this audience had attracted Televisa's investment because it was the most affluent Spanish-speaking population in the world, as well as one of the largest. By 1986 the network claimed to reach 82 per cent of Hispanic households, that is, 15 million viewers, and the USA had become the centre for all Televisa's international activities.

However, when the SICC eventually was found to be in breach of the foreign ownership provisions of the US Communication Act, the courts obliged Emilio Azcárraga Milmo (the son who had taken over in 1972) to sell the stations. In fact by 1988 both the stations and the network, by then named Univisión, had been sold to Hallmark Cards, with Televisa retaining what was then only a minor cable service, Galavisión. The divestment was a serious setback for Televisa's international ambitions. However, it continued to supply programmes to Univisión, and as well, to Telemundo, the competing national network which had emerged in the latter 1980s. It also built up Galavisión as a commercial service. Furthermore, all of Televisa's international operations continued to be based in the USA, notably ECO and the programme-sales division, Protele, since the USA was its most profitable market (Sinclair 1990).

Televisa has since entered into a new stage of international expansion in the 1990s. It was noted earlier how the restructuring and public flotation consolidated the group under the Azcárragas' control: what it also did was to enable accumulated corporate debts to be paid out, and provide a reserve fund for expansion. 'Management considers its target audience to be the 350 million Spanish-speaking people around the world, not simply the 82 million at home' (Warburg 1992: 5–6). The restructuring and flotation needs to be seen not just as a solution to Televisa's immediate financial problems of the late 1980s, but also as the means by which Televisa has shored up a position from which it can defend and extend its interests in the face of two fundamental changes in its accustomed environment, one internal and one external: the advent of a private competitor in Mexico, and the threats and opportunities imminent in the North American Free Trade Agreement (NAFTA). Televisa's return to the USA and its investments in Latin American television stations should be understood as manœuvres in response to these changes.

Early in 1992 Televisa put forward a carefully structured bid for its former property in the USA, Univisión. This was in conjunction with the Cisneros family's Venevisión of Caracas, and a US majority partner, A. Jerrold (Jerry) Perenchio, a television producer and owner of independent Spanish-language stations in the USA. In order to observe the relevant foreign ownership limits, the bid proposed Perenchio as 75 per cent owner of the stations, giving Televisa and Venevisión each half of the remaining 25 per cent, while the network was to be owned half by Perenchio and half shared by the other partners. Univisión would have a twenty-five year contract with Televisa and Venevisión to supply programming, for which it would pay royalties of 15 per cent of advertising revenue (Moffett and Roberts 1992: A6). Televisa has thus made its return to the USA, this time on a firm legal basis.

In a separate but related development, it was announced later in 1992 that the president of Venevisión, Gustavo A. Cisneros, was to join the board of Televisa, thus consolidating Televisa's Venezuelan connection in both the USA and Latin America ('Venevisión Joins Entire South American Continent' 1992). Televisa has a joint venture arrangement with Venevisión for the distribution of their programmes outside of their respective countries, and the negotiation of licence rights for each others' programmes in their own countries (Morgan Stanley 1992: 10). In this way, Televisa has formed an alliance with a producer which was formerly one of their major competitors: this had been a proven Azcárraga strategy for dealing with competition in the domestic market.

Of the more than 29,000 hours of programming Televisa has been exporting around the world in recent years, 46 per cent goes to South America, 24 per cent to Central America, 10 per cent to the Caribbean, 9 per cent to the USA, 6 per cent to Europe, 4 per cent to Asia and Australia, and 1 per cent to Africa. Of all network hours produced, 40 per cent is for ECO, so it should not be thought that this is primarily a *telenovela* trade, although that was the case until 1986 when ECO began (Toussaint 1990: 53; Warburg 1992: 4–5). If the proportions going to each destination are compared with the geographic sources of sales revenue, an interesting anomaly arises: while 60 per cent of programme exports go to Latin America, only 3.5 per cent of sales come from that region. On the other hand, the 9 per cent of exports that go to the USA return 5 per cent of sales (Warburg 1992: 2).

This discrepancy underscores the profitability of the US market and its importance to Televisa, and suggests that Televisa engages in differential pricing for its various markets, just as the US distributors have long been known to do (Wildman and Siwek 1988: 3–7). Furthermore, it is an index of the degree to which barter arrangements for programme exchanges have been institutionalized in debt-laden countries where hard currency is scarce. During the 1980s Televisa and other exporters set up such a system under which their client stations, instead of paying for programmes, would barter advertising time which the exporter could then sell to transnational advertisers (Mattelart and Mattelart 1990: 12).

Programme exports to Latin America have long been at least a minor staple of Televisa and its predecessors: what is new in the 1990s has been the advent of select direct investments by Televisa in Latin American stations. This gives a wider dimension to the internationalization of television in the region, as Televisa proceeds to integrate countries of the Latin American continent into its sphere of operations. This process has been facilitated by the shift towards privatization in those few Latin American countries which were not private from the start. Such was the case with Televisa's first direct investment in Chile, of strategic significance because of Chile's free-trade agreement with Mexico signed shortly before the investment was made, and because Chile is expected to be the next nation to join the NAFTA.

In December of 1991 it was announced that Televisa had paid $US7 million to acquire 49 per cent of Megavisión, the first private channel to be licensed outside of the unique state and university ownership system in Chile. The arrangement with Televisa included 'technical and commercial advice in the fullest sense'; an agreement to co-produce programmes in both Chile and Mexico for export to third countries; the incorporation of Megavisión input into ECO; and a seat for Megavisión on the Televisa directorate in Mexico. Furthermore, it was planned that Televisa programming would make up almost a third of Megavisión's content within the first year (Ehrmann 1991: 72; 'Televisa compro 49 por ciento de Megavisión' 1991; Ehrmann 1992: 99).

It is worth noting that the deal also permitted Megavisión to be admitted to the OTI, the Organisación de Televisión Iberoamericana, created in 1971 for special event and other programme exchanges by international satellite between the countries of Latin America, Spain, and Portugal. It is controlled by Argentina, Brazil, Spain, and Mexico, with close ties to Televisa (Mejía Barquera 1987: 33–4).

In July 1992 Televisa announced that it had also acquired 76 per cent of the capital of Compañía Peruana de Radiodifusión, the licensee of Channel 4, the oldest but second-ranked television network in Peru, and an associated chain of radio stations. Like Megavisión, the company was known to be in serious financial difficulties. The price compared closely with what was paid for Megavisión, and the terms of the arrangement also were reported to be similar to the Chilean deal ('Televisa anunció oficialmente la compra de canal peruano' 1992: S33).

In the same year Televisa struck a deal in Argentina with the state-owned channel ATC (Argentina Televisora Color). No purchase was involved, but ATC was incorporated into Televisa's Latin American activities by means of a programming arrangement under which ATC shows six hours of Televisa programmes per day ('Televisa compro 49 por ciento de Megavisión' 1991). It also has been reported that

Televisa has supplied equipment to ATC as well as to Megavisión. This was used equipment, superseded by Televisa with the purchase of new equipment in Mexico, another example of the corporation's talent for vertical integration, this time at an international level ('Televisa enviar equipos usados a Megavisión' 1992).

As well as selective direct ownership, the establishment of programming arrangements seems to be an important objective in itself for Televisa, most notably with its ECO news venture. Together with popular Channel 2 programmes from Mexico, ECO forms the twenty-four-hour satellite feed which goes out as Galavisión to the USA and forty-five countries in Europe and North Africa as well as Latin America ('Este es el socio de Canal 9' 1991; 'Es mayor productor de programas en Español' 1992). This feed is central to Televisa's international strategies, and the incorporation of material from new participants such as Chile helps to create appeal for more national audiences as well as provide a further source of information input for the programme. ECO has been a medium-term investment which Televisa has made in its own internationalization: the service did not become profitable until the beginning of 1991 (Bear, Stearns 1992: 3).

Televisa has also been entering into various significant international ventures with media corporations based in the USA. Late in 1993 a programme production and exchange arrangement with Rupert Murdoch's News Corporation was announced (Amdur 1994: 120). Other initiatives have been participation in a Latin American version of the Discovery cable channel from the USA ('Regional roundup' 1994), and a deal to bring the teleshopping cable channel QVC to the Latin world—not just all of Latin America, but also Portugal and Spain (Warburg 1993).

It remains now to consider Televisa's operations in Spain, where it began transmitting its Galavisión/ECO service via international satellite at the end of 1988. Given Televisa's increased production of news and information over recent years and the evident priority given to ECO in its international expansion plans, it is not surprising that 68 per cent of the Galavisión programme day in Spain has been information programmes, compared to 9 per cent of *telenovelas*. Galavisión has already experimented with teleshopping, and since 1990 has included a local Spanish news programme. Audience studies commissioned in 1989–90 yielded implausibly wide variations in estimates of audience size, from 250,000 to over 2 million (Bustamante 1990: 11–13).

Since then, Televisa in Spain has engaged in a strategy of installing satellite dishes free in large apartment complexes, so all apartments can connect to the dish, the same means by which satellite/cable systems are now spreading so rapidly in Latin America. Televisa's return on this method of market penetration is that it generates demographic data which allows them to charge transnational advertisers for access to the Spanish audience. It has claimed that 2 million households, or 18 per cent of the Spanish population, now have access to Galavisión (Bear, Stearns 1992: 2). However, since Europe contributes only a third of 1 per cent of Televisa sales (Warburg 1992: 2), it seems that Televisa's presence in Spain is more for its symbolic than its economic value at this stage. Even in terms of potential prospects, Televisa faces both increased competition within Spain and EU content regulation which will make it difficult to maintain its present mode of operation (Bustamante 1990: 13–14). However, popular audiences in Spain have shown themselves receptive to *telenovelas* from Latin America (affectionately called *culebrones*, or serpents, either for their hypnotic appeal or serial length), and it may be that in the immediate term Televisa will do better with traditional programme sales than with its satellite service.

Globo: *Telenovela*-Driven Growth

Globo has been said to be more 'truly international' than Televisa because it exports to a wider range of countries outside of Latin America, and derives only 20 per cent of its 'offshore income' from the region (Mattelart and Mattelart 1990: 12). This is because although it has a 'domestic opportunity advantage' comparable to Televisa, the countries where Portuguese is spoken are far fewer and more dispersed than those that speak Spanish. As Brazil is the only Portuguese-speaking nation in Latin America, Globo therefore has not had the same chance as Televisa to cultivate the markets of the region, nor the geographic and demographic advantages which Televisa has with regard to the USA. Also in part for these reasons, an international orientation was much slower to develop with Globo.

Thus, it is no surprise that when Globo did enter the international market, it was with the export of a *telenovela* to Portugal in 1975. Whilst it had been TV Tupi and TV Excelsior which had pioneered the development of the *telenovela* as a programming genre within domestic Brazilian television during the 1960s, it was Globo which first 'appropriated' it to be built into an export product in the 1970s (Mattelart and Mattelart 1990: 14–17). The particular *telenovela* concerned was *Gabriela*, based on the popular novel by Jorge Amado, and distinctively Brazilian in its characters, plot, and setting. In spite of jokes in Lisbon about 'reverse colonization', the programme's fascination for the Portuguese audience was enough to encourage RTP (Rádio e Televisão Portuguesa: an advertising-funded state monopoly until 1992) to go on to acquire the rights to show a further fifteen Brazilian *telenovelas* over the next decade, most of which came from Globo (Marques de Melo 1988: 39–40).

For its part, Globo was encouraged also to pursue sales in the former Portuguese colonies of Africa, to the rather limited extent to which they could be developed as television markets. Rather more successful was the export of its *telenovela O Bem Amado*, first to Uruguay and then other Latin American countries, dubbed into Spanish. However, with the Latin American market there are costs not only for dubbing but also for transcodification from the unique Brazilian PAL-M television broadcast standard into the NTSC system used elsewhere in the Americas. Yet the absolute higher costs and consequent lower profit margins in the Latin American market are not the only reason why Globo has been more interested in Europe: there is also the barrier of the much lower relative prices for the products of the competing nations (notably Mexico, but also Argentina and Venezuela) and, furthermore, the fact that the Argentinian and Mexican markets are virtually closed to Brazil. By contrast, the rapid growth of European television markets has created a more open competitive environment (Marques de Melo 1988: 40–2). Globo entered the 1990s with offices in London and Paris as well as New York, while Latin America was dealt with through the head office in Rio de Janeiro.

After 1980, when Globo first set up its international division (the Department of International Marketing, corresponding to Televisa's Protele), the export effort had focused upon Italy, where the romantic historical *telenovela Escrava Isaura* had been shown with great ratings success, soon followed by another twenty-seven Brazilian programmes. This was a boom period for Latin American *telenovelas* in Europe in general, but for Brazil in particular, in spite of its higher cost structure. At a later stage a number of sales were made to France, once again following ratings successes in 1985, but Globo has been willing in this case to supply programmes on very narrow margins in the hope of opening up further French-speaking markets (Marques de Melo 1988: 42–3). Like Televisa, Globo engages in differential pricing for various markets: a *telenovela* chapter can vary from $US9,000 in Germany to $US150 in El Salvador (Marques de Melo 1992: 9).

It should be noted that Globo is not the only Brazilian network engaged in exporting programmes: both Manchete and Bandeirantes have sold programmes in Europe, the USA, and Latin America, where they are paying special attention to Brazil's partners in the new common market of the Southern Cone. However, as in the domestic market, Globo has a strong lead over its competitors, especially in distribution. SBT and Om Brasil are more notable as importers (Marques de Melo 1992: 7–10).

As for Italy, Globo sought to consolidate the early popular success there of its *telenovelas* as well as gain a toehold in European broadcasting by means of direct investment. In 1985 Globo bought TMC Telemontecarlo, a minor network which, although reaching 85 per cent of the Italian audience, had an audience share of only 4 per cent. This is in a country where television is dominated by the Italian government RAI and the Silvio Berlusconi RTI networks. In 1990 Globo sold 40 per cent of Telemontecarlo to a large Italian industrial finance group,

Ferruzi Finanziaria, and 'relaunched' the network, with plans to broadcast by satellite into the rest of Europe (McCarter 1990: 22). However, if Marinho intended to use Telemontecarlo as an outlet for Globo programmes, much as Televisa once used SICC in the USA, he seems to have been foiled by the peculiarities of the Italian market. In 1992 the programme director of Telemontecarlo advised: 'We have bought some Brasilian [*sic*] *telenovelas*, but they have not been successful' (Telemontecarlo 1992). By 1994 Globo had sold out its share to the partner ('News in brief' 1994).

Thus, as with Televisa's operations in Spain, it seems that Globo has found participation in European growth to be elusive. However, this has not stopped Globo from taking advantage of the recent privatization of television in Portugal. When RTP's monopoly ended in 1992 with the creation of two private channels, Globo secured 15 per cent of one of them, SIC. Interestingly, this move came after the first year ever in which Globo achieved greater levels of sales to Latin America than to Europe. Globo reported an overall increase of 10 per cent, especially of *telenovelas*, to a total of $US20 million. This figure may be compared with the $US16–18 million which Globo spends each year on programmes from the major suppliers in the USA (Besas 1992: 82).

The initial favourable reception of Globo's *telenovelas* from audiences in Italy and France, as well as their eventual success in Latin America, indicates that a 'cultural proximity' factor may be at work: 'the rediscovery of the symbolic ties to a "Latin community" seems to be looming' (Mattelart and Mattelart 1990: 4). However, it is also the case that Globo has found success with its *telenovelas* amongst audiences in quite alien cultures, notably the phenomenal reception given to *Escrava Isaura* in China, Poland, and the former Soviet Union (Marques de Melo 1988: 44–5), where the usual anecdotes circulated about how the streets emptied when the programme came on.

This success suggests there are more universal qualities which quite diverse audiences find in *telenovelas*, perhaps due to their intrinsic temporal rhythms or allegorical character, perhaps the result of Globo's experience in the cultivation of audience appeal across regional and other differences within Brazil, or perhaps some similarity in social desires generated in postsocialist and 'Third World' societies alike. A Polish newspaper had a simple explanation: 'in a situation of social disappointment, the public seek consolation in fairy tales' (quoted in Mattelart and Mattelart 1990: 13). A more complex analysis would need to take into account the melodramatic and narrative structures of the *telenovela* texts themselves; the seriality of their day-to-day scheduling; the domestic and other kinds of social circumstances in which they are consumed; and the expressed meanings which they have for individuals in different social positions. A great deal of research is in progress on all of these dimensions (Fadul 1993).

Crowding in the 'Latin audiovisual space'

The commercialization of international satellite capacity and the consequent growth in satellite-to-cable television services has ushered in a qualitatively new era, as terrestrial broadcasting learns to live with mushrooming markets for 'borderless television' channels from space. The Latin world has had a distinctive and leading role in this development, not just because of the rapid rate at which the new services have been taken up in countries such as Argentina and Spain, but because most of the new channels are carried by a private satellite service with longstanding connections to Televisa and its international operations. This is PanAmSat, the world's first private enterprise international satellite system, developed at different stages and now jointly owned by Televisa and René Anselmo, the same consortium as first brought Spanish-language television to the USA in the 1960s.

While PanAmSat has been strategic in the internationalization of Televisa's own services, it has also been instrumental in opening Latin markets up to the several US cable channels which produce versions of their service with Spanish and/or Portuguese soundtracks. First amongst these was HBO Ole, a Latin version of Time-Warner's US movie channel. This commenced in 1991, and is now operated in partnership with

Sony Pictures (Guider 1994). Others are CNN, TNT, and Cartoon Network from Turner Broadcasting; Tele-Uno and GEMS from Spelling; and Fox Latin America, ESPN, and MTV. Although drawing primarily on their own production and library resources in the USA, some of these are engaging in the production of Latin American material for these services (Amdur 1994). Clearly, US mainstream media corporations are interested in developing Latin markets, but in providing them with the means of distribution to do so on PanAmSat, Televisa has got itself into a bind. On one hand, it is successfully putting itself forward as a major world player in the provision of commercial satellite capacity. However, it is doing so at the expense of allowing strong competitors into a new growth medium in the very region where it has always held its comparative advantage.

We have seen how the international growth of Televisa and Globo has been driven by entrepreneurs seeking to capitalize upon their established capacity to create a large domestic market for their programmes, where those programmes are also tradeable exports by virtue of their linguistic or broader cultural similarities with other countries. These other countries may be close by in the region, but the use of satellite technology has made cultural similarity more of a determinant of international market formation than geographical proximity. At the same time, it has been recognized that the dependent character of the domestic markets within the global economic system produces instability and inherent constraints on growth, so that it is the weaknesses as well as the strengths of the domestic market which motivate the drive to internationalization. These observations should remind us that the economic, political, and cultural power attained by Televisa and Globo is historical and contingent, and in this most recent stage it appears that the 'Latin audiovisual space' which they have opened up across the globe is fast filling with new competitors who are not hindered by the same contradictions.

References

Amdur, Meredith (1994), 'Cable Network Heads South', *Broadcasting & Cable* (24 Jan.), 118–20.

Bear, Stearns and Co. (1992), *Grupo Televisa SA de CV: Company Report* (Thompson Financial Networks).

Besas, Peter (1992), 'Globo Grabs the TV Jackpot in Brazil', *Variety* (23 Mar.), 82.

—— and Hoineff, Nelson (1992), 'New Cable Venture May Break Even by End of Year', *Variety* (23 Mar.), 82–4.

BIB (1992, 1993), *BIB World Guide to Television and Programming* (North American Publishing Company, New York).

Bustamante, Enrique (1990), 'Galavisión en España y la CEE', paper presented to international colloquium, 'La televisión en Español: Una perspectiva global', University of California at Berkeley, June.

'Carrossel mexicano' (1991), *Veja* (12 June), 78–84.

Collins, Richard (1989), 'The Language of Advantage: Satellite Television in Western Europe', *Media, Culture and Society*, 11/3: 351:71.

de Lima, Venicio (1988), 'The State, Television and Political Power in Brazil', *Critical Studies in Mass Communication*, 5: 108–28.

Dunnett, Peter (1990), *The World Television Industry: An Economic Analysis* (Routledge, London).

Ehrmann, Hans (1991), 'Chile Ends Government Broadcast Monopoly', *Variety* (25 Mar.), 72.

—— (1992), 'Democracy Remakes Chilean Pubcaster', *Variety* (23 Mar.), 90.

'Es mayor productor de programas en Español' (1992), *La República* (15 July), 1992.

'Este es el socio de Canal 9' (1991), *El Mercurio* (22 Dec.).

Fadul, Anamaria (ed.) (1993), *Serial Fiction in TV: The Latin American Telenovelas* (School of Communication and Arts, University of São Paulo, São Paulo).

Fernández, Fátima (1987), 'Algo más sobre los origenes de la televisión latinoamericana', *DIA. Logos de la Comunicación*, 18 (Oct.), 32–45.

Ferraz Sampaio, Mario (1984), *História do Rádio e da Televisão no Brasil e no Mundo* (Achiamé, Rio de Janeiro).

Fox, Elizabeth (1991), 'Global Change and Mass Communication Policies: Latin America: Lessons of the Past', paper presented to the 15th Conference of the International Political Science Association, Buenos Aires, July.

Guider, Elizabeth (1994), 'Sony Buys into HBO's Latin America Cable', *Variety* (24 Jan.), 17.

Guimarães, Cesar, and Amaral, Roberto (1988), 'Brazilian Television: A Rapid Conversion to the New Order', in E. Fox (ed.), *Media and Politics in Latin America* (Sage, London), 125–37.

Gutiérrez Espíndola, José Luis (1992), 'Comunicación social en 1991: una retrospectiva crítica', *Revista Mexicana de Comunicación*, 4/21: 17–23.

HEROLD, CACILDA (1988), 'The "Brazilianization" of Brazilian Television: A Critical Review', *Studies in Latin American Popular Culture*, 7: 41–57.

HOSKINS, COLIN, and MCFADYEN, STUART (1991), 'The U.S. Comparative Advantage in the Global Television Market: Is it Sustainable in the New Broadcasting Environment?' *Canadian Journal of Communication*, 16/2: 207–24.

LITEVSKI, CHAIM (1982), 'Globo's *telenovelas*: A Brazilian Melodrama', in R. Paterson (ed.), *Brazilian Television in Context* (British Film Institute, London), 12–16.

MCCARTER, MICHELLE (1990), 'TV Net Grows in Italy', *Advertising Age* (17 Dec.).

MALKIN, ELIZABETH (1994), 'Will a *Yanqui* Partner Make TV Azteca a Player?', *Business Week* (30 May), 24.

MARÍN, CARLOS (1986), 'Alemán reconoce que la información Televisa se autocensura', *Proceso*, 515 (15 Sept.), 7.

MARQUES DE MELO, JOSÉ (1988), *As Telenovelas da Globo* (Summus Editorial, São Paulo).

—— (1992), 'Brazil's Role as a Television Exporter Within the Latin American Regional Market', paper presented to the 42nd Conference of the International Communication Association, Miami, May.

MARTÍNEZ STAINES, JAVIER (1991), 'Televisa: ¿Adios a la familia?', *Expansión* (1 May), 31–7.

MATTELART, ARMAND, DELCOURT, XAVIER, and MATTELART, MICHÈLE (1984), *International Image Markets* (Comedia, London).

MATTELART, ARMAND (1991), *Advertising International: The Privatisation of Public Space* (Routledge, London).

MATTELART, MICHÈLE, and MATTELART, ARMAND (1990), *The Carnival of Images: Brazilian Television Fiction* (Bergin and Garvey, New York).

MATTOS, SERGIO (1992), 'A Profile of Brazilian Television', paper presented to the 18th Conference of the International Association for Mass Communication Research, Guarujá, Aug.

MEJÍA BARQUERA, FERNANDO (1987), '50 años de televisión comercial en México (1934–1984)/cronología', in R. Trejo Delarbre (ed.), *Televisa: El Quinto Poder* (2nd edn., Claves Latinoamericanas, Mexico DF), 19–39.

MODY, BELLA, and BORREGO, JORGE (1991), 'Mexico's *Morelos* Satellite: Reaching for Autonomy?' in G. Sussman and J. Lent (eds.), *Transnational Communication: Wiring the Third World* (Sage, London), 15–64.

MOFFETT, MATT, and ROBERTS, JOHNNIE (1992), 'Mexican Media Empire, Grupo Televisa, Casts an Eye on US Market', *Wall Street Journal* (30 July), A1 and A6.

MORGAN STANLEY & CO. (1992), *Grupo Televisa: Company Report* (Thompson Financial Networks).

MURARO, HERIBERTO (1985), 'El "modelo" latinoamericano', *Telos*, 3: 78–82.

'News in brief' (1994), *TV International* (24 Jan.), 4.

PAXMAN, ANDREW (1993), 'The New TV Azteca', *Business Mexico* (Nov.), 39–41.

'Por baixo do pano' (1992), *Veja* (17 June), 96–9.

'Regiónal roundup' (1994), *TV International* (24 Jan.), 9.

ROGERS, EVERETT, and ANTOLA, LIVIA (1985), '*Telenovelas*: A Latin American Success Story', *Journal of Communication*, 35/4: 24–35.

SINCLAIR, JOHN (1986), 'Dependent Development and Broadcasting: "The Mexican Formula" ', *Media, Culture and Society*, 8/1: 81–101.

—— (1990), 'Spanish-Language Television in the United States: Televisa Surrenders its Domain', *Studies in Latin American Popular Culture*, 9: 39–63.

STRAUBHAAR, JOSEPH (1982), 'The Development of the *Telenovela* as the Pre-eminent Form of Popular Culture in Brazil', *Studies in Latin American Popular Culture*, 1: 138–50.

—— (1984), 'Brazilian Television: The Decline of American Influence', *Communication Research*, 11/2: 221–40.

—— (1991), 'Beyond Media Imperialism: Assymetrical Interdependence and Cultural Proximity', *Critical Studies in Mass Communication*, 8: 39–59.

Telemontecarlo (1992), Personal correspondence to author from Director of TV Programs.

'Televisa anunció oficialmente la compra de canal peruano' (1992), *La Época* (11 July).

'Televisa compro 49 por ciento de Megavisión' (1991), *El Mercurio* (22 Dec.).

'Televisa enviar equipos usados a Megavisión' (1992), *La Época* (2 Feb.).

TOUSSAINT, FLORENCE (1990), 'Mexico', in P. Larsen (ed.), *Import/Export: International Flow of Television Fiction* (UNESCO, Paris), 52–3.

'Venevisión Joins Entire South American Continent' (1992), Press Release, PR Newswire Association (12 May).

VINK, NICO (1988), *The Telenovela and Emancipation* (Royal Tropical Institute, Amsterdam).

WARBURG, S G & CO. (1992, 1993), *Grupo Televisa SA de CV: Company Report* (Thompson Financial Networks).

WILDMAN, STEVEN, and SIWEK, STEPHEN (1988), *International Trade in Films and Television Programs* (American Enterprise Institute/Ballinger Publications, Cambridge, Mass.).

World Almanac 1992 (1991) (Pharos Books, New York).

3

India

Part I: Indian Cinema Beyond National Borders

Manjunath Pendakur and Radha Subramanyam

In the 'Third World' the debate about the implications of the presence of Hollywood as a cultural 'Trojan horse' is growing with the spread of satellite delivery channels, many of which are parts of the vertical structures of transnational media giants. As the number of homes with television sets grows and the nation-state, once all powerful, is weakened in the age of globalization of the world economy, the debate about transnational media flows intensifies. Most chapters in this book deal with television exports from countries like Brazil and Mexico that seem to be going against this flow. The case of India, however, is vastly different because the export of made-for-television material is insignificant compared with film.

The most significant reason for this is that until the mid-1980s the government-owned and heavily controlled broadcasting organization, Doordarshan, exerted a complete monopoly on the television industry and under its auspices virtually no exportable entertainment programming was produced. It was not until privatization began in 1983–4 in the form of sponsored programming (Pendakur 1991) that a market for non-film television programming began to appear.

From the late 1980s onwards there were critical changes in the media landscape in India, leading to a boom in services outside of Doordarshan's former monopoly of television. Unregulated small-scale cable-television operations mushroomed in cities and towns to provide better-quality signals, as well as to supply popular movies to homes. In 1991 STAR TV, which is now owned by Rupert Murdoch, became available in

India, thereby for the first time bringing multinationals into play in a big way in Indian media. The first service with pan-Asian programming, STAR TV became also the first foreign-owned network in India with region-specific programming. At the same time Zee TV, an Indian-owned, private network, became the most popular satellite channel and by 1994 it was a fixture in over 7.3 million Indian homes (Aggarwal 1994). Zee TV formed a partnership with STAR in new areas like a pay-movie channel. Doordarshan, in turn, started five new channels to offset competition from private entrepreneurs. There were also developments at a global level, notably the growth in satellite/cable services and video sales to diasporic communities as a 'geolinguistic region'. Examples of this include Asia-Net in the UK and TV Asia in the USA.

The Indian content of these services is still very film-based and so far a large volume of specifically television programming has not yet resulted. This is true for Doordarshan's most popular new channels; for example, *Superhit Muqabla*, which is an Indian version of MTV's Top-20 countdown, is comprised of film song-dance sequences, and the hosts are often film personalities. Other popular shows that have to do with movies are *Cinema Cinema*, *Lizzat Masala Film Court*, *Jharokha*, *Sunehere Pal*, and *Ole Ole*. Moreover, both popular television serials that are not directly film-based and shows that achieve critical acclaim are often created by film people. For example, *Ramayana* and *Mahabharata*, two of the most popular programmes in Indian television history, were produced by two major Bombay film producers Ramanand Sagar and B. R. Chopra respectively. Sagar also made *Krishna*, which attracted huge audiences too. Similarly, Shyam Benegal, a well-known director of India's 'middle cinema', has done significant work with television. The audio music industry too revolves around film songs and personalities; Bappi Lahiri and Anu Malik are perhaps the most influential music personalities today at the national, Hindi-language level.

Both Zee TV, India's most popular satellite channel, as well as local cable channels are another frontier where the influence of the film world is omnipresent. Two other satellite delivery services grew rapidly between 1992 and 1994. The Madras-based Sun TV is available all over south India, and at the end of 1994 was to become available in northern and western states. It telecasts an abundance of Tamil movies of yesteryear. Jain TV (Joint American Indian Network), based in New Delhi, has a similar emphasis on cinema. Its staple of programming is old Hindi-language films from the Fifties and Sixties and inexpensively produced regional language film-song programmes (Pendakur 1994*a*).

Programming from India that is shown on television abroad is similarly dominated by films or film-based shows. For example, the Indian cable channel in Chicago shows Hindi-language films, *Chitrahaar*, or interviews with Indian movie stars who may be touring the USA. By the end of 1994 they had never televised a serial or game show that was made in India. The few exceptions to this include the televising of *Mahabharata* on BBC 2 twice a week in the UK. Some series that are made for television are available outside the country on videotape, such as *Nukkad* and *Tamas* in the late 1980s, but they remain few and far between, and none except *Ramayana* and *Mahabharata*, both based on the epics, were really successful with the diaspora audiences.

Thus, in its long history feature film has built up an enthusiastic following with diasporic audiences, and made-for-television programmes cannot compete with this. In addition, the role of stars, production values, and so on are important factors. Therefore, we construct our narrative around film exports. We have based our research on primary data from government (although this is not always completely reliable because of the haphazard nature of data collection in India), on industry sources in India, and on interviews with distributors of Indian cultural goods abroad.

Film Exports, Export Promotion Institutions, and their Problems

India, although an economically 'backward' country at the time, developed a large film production sector from the beginnings of cinema, and for many decades has been producing more films than any other nation. Indian films are widely viewed in many parts of Africa, Asia, the Middle East, Europe, and North America, by Indian diasporic and other audiences. By the beginning of the 1980s, Indian films were being shown in over 100 countries (Dharap 1983: 1). Despite a large output through these many decades, according to some scholars the Indian film industry has shown many of the signs of capitalist development under conditions of economic 'backwardness' and political servitude (Chakravorty 1993). Ongoing yet idiosyncratic censorship and high taxes contribute to this. While the output of films has increased consistently, market entry and profitability remain uncertain for producers. Similarly, while exports have risen steadily over the past few decades, the growth of exports has not been commensurate with the increased production of films.

Table 3.1 summarizes data for export of Indian films by decade. It shows that while a large number of films are exported, the revenues are small. The amount of all-India box-office collections in 1987 was 50,583 lakh (100,000) rupees (Ministry of Information and Broadcasting). In contrast, exports were only 718.42 lakh ($US239,4733), which is less than 2 per cent of box-office collections. The USA, on the other hand, in recent years, has produced less than a third of the films India has. But in 1993 its profits from exports were $US1,732,219,300 (Staly 1994). That amounts to

Table 3.1. Export earnings of Indian film industry, by year, 1947–1987

Year	*Number of companies*	*Number of films*	*Gross revenue (in lakh rupees)*
1947	40	na	25.00
1957	90	na	113.00
1967	100	na	389.00
1977	120	2,087	1,167.00
1987	125	413	718.42

Notes: na : not available.
1 Lakh = 100,000 rupees.

Source: *Report to the Ministry of Information and Broadcasting, Government of India* (1989).

approximately 750 times the revenue that India earns from film exports!

Most of the earnings have tended to be from countries in which people of Indian origin have settled. For example, in 1978–9 the traditional markets of the UK, Dubai, Fiji Islands, Singapore, Trinidad, Mauritius, and Sri Lanka accounted for about 58 per cent of export earnings (Working Group 1980). Truly 'foreign' markets have remained underexplored. And even in traditional territories, film exports suffered increasing setbacks from about 1980 with the rise of video technology.

Pendakur (forthcoming) has argued elsewhere that India was blessed with certain 'cultural screens' which offered a natural protection to the development of an indigenous film industry. Unlike countries like Canada and Australia where English-language audiences could be cultivated to consume American-made films, Indian film producers took advantage of the cultural differences. This was particularly obvious in the 'talkie' period when competition with local films from abroad was minimal. English was spoken only by a tiny minority of urban Indians, while the vast majority spoke region-specific languages.

D. G. Phalke's *Raja Harishchandra* (1913) was the first completely indigenous feature film. Phalke's films were mostly devotionals and mythologicals, genres that have remained popular over the years. These films were shown to Indian audiences in Burma, East Africa, and Singapore (Barnouw and Krishnaswamy 1980: 16). Phalke's endeavour to export Indian silent films had limited success because of the outbreak of the First World War, but by the 1920s film production had begun to increase steadily. Genres diversified to include the historical and the social. Between 1913 and 1934 India produced over 1,250 silent features (Chakravorty 1993). Towards the end of the 1920s Indian films of the silent period began to have a marginal overseas market in parts of Africa, the island of Mauritius, and other places with large diasporic communities.

The advent of sound with *Alam Ara* in 1931 established the dominion of indigenously made films because of the accessibility of the languages to the populace. Many powerful studios were in place by the mid-1930s. Production shot up and spread to various cities. Centres of production developed along linguistic lines in different parts of the country. Bombay became the centre for Hindi films, Calcutta for Bengali, Madras for Tamil, Bangalore for Kannada, and Hyderabad for Malayalam. The 'talkies' helped build up foreign markets, and from 1935 onwards organized attempts towards export were made by studios like Himanshu Rai's Bombay Talkies.

The Second World War brought further stability to film production while it resulted in the demise of the studio system. The larger domestic box-office returns of this period have been attributed to increased migration from rural to urban areas and to the increased purchasing power of the working classes. Investments of illegal war profits and the rise of the independent producer contributed to the decline of the studios. In the post-independence period, the industry has grown tremendously, despite obstacles that included certain forms of state intervention like censorship and high entertainment tax. Particularly in the realm of export, governmental policies have prevented the marketing of Indian films abroad from being as successful as it could be. For instance, in the late 1940s Indian producers sending their prints to East and West Pakistan had to pay import duties to their own government to get their prints back that far exceeded the value of those prints (Barnouw and Krishnaswamy 1980: 139).

From the 1950s on the industry grew steadily. Exports increased compared to previous years, but were nowhere near their potential. Raj Kapoor's films like *Awara* and *Sri 420*, with their proletarian themes, had a high degree of success in the former USSR, opening up another market in addition to others like Malaysia, Indonesia, Burma, Africa, and the Middle East. By this period the formulae for success of the films themselves were fairly well established and their influences persist even today. However, structural problems like those pertaining to the reimport of prints into the country after their exhibition in other countries continued.

In 1958 an Export Promotion Council was set up by the Government of India, comprising representatives of the Ministries of Information and Broadcasting, External Affairs, and Commerce and Industry, as well as the film industry. Its function was to give advice to exporters, research overseas markets, provide representation at international film festivals, lobby for export subsidies, and so on. Most producers at this time were not taking full advantage of markets abroad, as they often sold rights to overseas markets at prices dictated by urgent need for finance when the films were in the production process.

In 1963 the duties of export promotion were taken on by the Industry Motion Picture Export Corporation (IMPEC), which in 1977 was appointed by the Government of India as a full-fledged canalizing agency. By 1980 IMPEC had organized several international film markets as part of the international film festivals held in India and some sales efforts were also made towards regional language films. However, the 1980 *Report* of the Working Group on National Film Policy saw the IMPEC as a direct competitor to Indian commercial exporters as it concentrated on Hindi cinema (Working Group 1980: 58). Since the IMPEC had no films of its own and had to involve producers/rights holders who were often reluctant to co-operate, the need for the IMPEC to have its own stock of films became important. The IMPEC thus merged with the Film Finance Corporation (FFC) which had been established in 1960 to support 'serious cinema', and became known as the National Film Development Corporation (NFDC).

The aim of the NFDC was to spearhead and organize the gargantuan film industry of the country, discipline the commercial and high-risk financial stakes in the film business, promote the cause of 'good' cinema, and to control film exports and imports (Da Cunha 1984: 47–9). All exports were expected to go through the NFDC, which charged a 2.5 per cent fee on each transaction. The intention behind this policy was to achieve higher unit-value realization, discourage malpractices like underinvoicing and unauthorized exports, and to reduce costs of export marketing and monitoring markets abroad. The NFDC was to function not as a competitor, but as an adviser to Indian exporters.

By participating in film festivals in different parts of the world the NFDC embarked on a forceful policy to improve exports. It also explored new markets and television sales. This helped the cinema make some inroads into non-traditional markets like West Germany, France, Italy, China, Holland, Finland, Belgium, and Greece, according to Tambay-Vaidya (Sethna 1985: 571). Offices of the NFDC were opened in foreign cities like London and these kept an eye open for the latest market trends.

India did not have subtitling technology in the country, which meant that films for export were sent to Dubai for subtitling. To save the hard-currency outflow from such undertakings, the NFDC ventured into this field as well. It set up a laboratory that could subtitle films in English, Arabic, French, German, and Spanish, as well as a modern film-to-video transfer and duplicating unit, both of which provided further support for exports.

After the merger with the IMPEC, NFDC export figures touched an all-time high of 100.13 lakhs and Hindi cinema dominated the market. Table 3.2 shows the relative prominence of exports of films in the various major languages and the swing towards an even greater dominance by Hindi films over time.

Yet while the promotion by the NFDC may have made a substantial difference in the case of India's 'New Wave'

Table 3.2. Number of films (theatrical/TV rights) passed through the NFDC, by language (in lakh rupees)

Language	*1984–5*	*1987–8*	*1990–1*
Hindi	248	300	280
Tamil	129	74	118
Malayalam	72	67	45
Bengali	14	16	8
Telegu	49	5	4
English	2	3	2
Kannada	2	1	—
Punjabi	5	2	—
Gujarati	2	1	1
Marathi	2	3	—
Others	—	1	—

Source: National Film Development Corporation 1992.

cinema, given that the agency's impulse has been primarily towards encouraging and supporting this kind of cinema, popular film-makers have had little incentive towards developing ties with the NFDC. Following protests from the commercial industry at the end of the 1980s, there was a wider representation of members of that sector given on the board of the NFDC, but concerted attempts towards export promotion were not be found to any significant extent. In the 1990s, as part of the Indian government's general economic 'liberalization', the monopoly of the NFDC on the export trade began to be loosened. It is too early to tell exactly what the effects of this on export markets will be.

From the mid-1980s the growth of the home video industry began to produce a decline in overseas theatrical revenues. However, in spite of the serious effect that video piracy has had on export markets, combined overall revenues from theatrical and home video release have increased. For example, in 1980–1 833 film titles were exported, bringing total revenues to 15.0743 lakh rupees, whereas by 1990/1 this had fallen to 458 titles (and 252 titles on video) but overall revenue was 16.0290 lakh rupees (Ministry of Information and Broadcasting). Between 1984/5 and 1990/1 the export revenues from film increased by a little less than 50 per cent whereas those from video increased by approximately 400 per cent (NFDC).

Major Diasporic Markets

Table 3.3 provides a snapshot of the Indian diasporic populations in selected countries for 1981. Mauritius, Fiji, Bahrain, Kuwait, Oman, Qatar, Singapore, and Sri Lanka had sizeable percentages of their populations coming from the Indian subcontinent. In general, the presence of Indian people in these countries goes as far back as the late nineteenth century, when the British colonialists took Indians to labour as indentured workers in their plantations, forests, and factories abroad. The Middle East is another story. Large numbers of Indians of varying technical skill have been imported into the Middle East since the 1970s. If current data was available,

Table 3.3. Estimates of the number of persons born in India and of Indian origin residing in selected countries, 1981 (thousands)

Region	*Population born in India*	*Population of Indian origin*	*As % of total*
Australia	33	35	0.2
Bahrain	27–47	24–50	6.6–13.9
Burma	50	1,050	3.0
Canada	110	140	0.6
Fiji	na	325	50.0
Hong Kong	12	14	0.3
Kenya	20	100	0.6
Kuwait	65–115	67–120	4.6–16.3
Mauritius	na	649	69.0
Oman	50–94	53–97	5.8–10.7
Qatar	20–43	21–44	8.1–16.9
Saudi Arabia	66–180	68–184	0.7–1.9
Singapore	51	164	6.7
Sri Lanka	234	2,770	18.5
Tanzania	5	50	0.3
UAE	180–240	195–444	0.7–1.9
UK	380	500	0.9

Source: Serow *et al.* 1990.

percentages might be much higher in all the Middle Eastern countries included in the table. It is possible to argue that countries with large numbers of Indians born in India would import more films, as they still have strong family and cultural ties.

Since the mid-1980s revenues from newer territories like Australia, Canada, France, Germany, Hong Kong, Indonesia, Malaysia, Sir Lanka, the UAE, USA, and the former USSR have increased, related to the growth of diasporic populations in these markets. The third largest ethnic group in Singapore is of Indian descent and the revenues from that market increased considerably in the period 1980/1 to 1990/1. The UK, with a very large diasporic population, was the second-largest market for Indian films by 1983, with approximately Rs (rupees) 7.5 million worth of exports. By contrast, France, Morocco, and the former USSR, although without a sizeable Indian population, also had significant imports of Indian films. The United

Arab Emirates stayed atop the pyramid of importers of Indian features with revenues totalling Rs 36.4 million in 1983 which grew to Rs 48.9 million in 1991. The most remarkable increase occurred in revenues from the USA, from Rs 1.9 million to Rs 8 million in the years 1980/1 to 1990/1. We explore the reasons for this change below.

Table 3.4 identifies some key export markets for India and their relative worth in rupees from the sale of videotaped films and reflects the change that occurred between 1987/8 and 1991/2. There is growth in revenues from all countries, except the former USSR, in the years covered by the table. While this table does not tell us specifically which language cinemas produced these revenues, it is safe to assume that they are by and large Hindi-language tapes with possible exceptions in Fiji, Malaysia, Mauritius, and Singapore.

Of the international markets today, the UK, the Middle East, and the USA are the three largest in the world for Hindi films (in that order). The value of each market varies depending on the film. The Middle East has had fast-growing Indian immigration, but according to a Chicago-based

Table 3.4. Export of videotapes to selected countries (in rupees)

Country	*1987–8*	*1991–2*
Australia	—	479,594
Bahrain	5,359	272,905
Canada	469,782	2,119,192
France	—	25,850
Germany (West)	31,163	9,397
Hong Kong	927,767	11,791,130
Kenya	—	1,245,079
Malaysia	381,197	2,578,352
Mauritius	295,224	948,921
Nigeria	—	3,978,571
Singapore	369,208	15,276,088
UAE	4,515,795	10,334,904
UK	8,095,948	35,898,926
USA	915,066	4,990,632
USSR	4,585,000	128,431

Source: Reserve Bank of India.

distributor (Pendakur 1994*b*), the UK remains the largest market because of a good anti-piracy law and its strict enforcement. This law is a criminal statute in the UK, which enables the police to take strong action like the seizure of property to prevent piracy. If caught, the licence holders are permanently barred from getting another licence to sell or rent videos.

Western European territories are usually thrown in with the UK. Similarly, Canada gets coupled with the USA. There are five or six distributors in the UK, and the same number of exporters in India. The Indian exporters are Asrani of Neptune, Chandrakant of the CA corporation, Kishore of Eros Video, and Chabria of Spark. These exporting companies buy world rights from individual producers and operate as brokers between the producers and country or region-specific distributors abroad.

By 1994 the UK had an estimated 1 million households of Indian diasporic families and constituted over 50 per cent of the global market for Indian films (Pendakur 1994*c*). The UK market has taken over from the Middle East as the principal market abroad for Indian films, primarily because of the arrival of cable channels which have Indian programming. That has seriously affected the demand for films. The UK market grosses £100,000 on average every week in the 35 mm market, and around £15,000 per week in the video market. Vijay Soni of Om Video, Hounslow, UK, recently started Asia Net in partnership with Dr Vishwanath of ITV in the UK. This is based on a satellite dish system that is directly sold to households. It has entered 165,000 households in the UK and is slowly growing in the USA. Soni believes that the future of business is cable television, observing that satellite television killed the video market around the world, reducing it by at least 50 per cent. He sees the future not in video but in cable, which will bring entertainment from India to diasporic families (Pendakur 1994*c*).

The US market has retained its importance and in fact the theatrical market is growing in size. However, its piracy laws are civil statutes, making them much less effective than those of the UK. Atlantic Video and Video Sound are the two principal national distributors of Hindi-language films in the USA. Some video-rental outlets have joint ventures with one or the other of these companies, while other outlets are individually owned and operated. New York/New Jersey, California, and Chicago are the primary markets for theatrical release. Of these, the key cities are the first-run markets and then the film goes into smaller towns. Often the features are released by distributors on a 10 per cent basis, which means that 10 per cent of the grosses are paid to the Indian distributor by the US distributor. The maximum an Indian distributor can expect from the US market on average is around $US15,000. *1942, A Love Story* (1994) earned $US16,000 on a six-day run in Chicago for the Indian distributor. Typically, a film runs for a week in this metropolitan centre. A popular film, *Anjam* (1994), played one night in Chicago at the Gateway Theatre to full capacity in the 1,600-seat cinema. Another good example of a successful run of a recent film is *Ham Hain Aapke Kaun..!* (1994) which ran for nine weeks in the New York and New Jersey markets. The value of each market varies with the film. For instance, Atlantic Video bought the US theatrical, video, and cable rights of *Baazigar* (1994) for a total of $US50,000 and Video Sound paid $US200,000 for similar rights to *1942, A Love Story* (1994). However, the latter did not prove as successful as its distributor had hoped.

On the average, 90–100 titles are released annually by the Hindi film industry on the international market. If all languages are included, sixteen titles come on to the market every week. While Hindi-language films are able to extract some revenue out of the US market and while this is increasing, regional-language cinema produces absolutely nothing for the producers. There are different reasons for this pathetic state of affairs in regional-language cinema's distribution. The production and distribution sector in Bombay has finally got organized against piracy and recently succeeded in getting the Indian parliament to pass the Amended Copyright Act of 1994. This will provide more protection to the rights of producers than previous laws. For example, action could be taken against music companies which thrive on releasing 'cover versions' of film songs. However, while the law has been passed, the government is yet to proclaim it, which is typical of the disjuncture between law and its implementation in India.

Producers in the industry have recently imposed some conditions on the system of distribution. The recent decision to create a six-month gap between a film's theatrical and video release is a good instance of this. Individual producers have even taken out advertisements in newspapers and magazines to fight piracy. Signed by the stars, producers, director, and technical staff of the movie, they petitioned audiences not to patronize pirated videotapes of *Hum Hain Aapke Kaun..!* Such policies for the protection of the industry's interest have an effect on markets abroad, asserts Mr Gandhi of Movie King Inc. In the regional-language industries, however, such conditions do not exist. In fact some producers, like Raj Kumar in Kannada, who are strongly opposed to piracy, do not release any of the films on video at all. This is especially true of films in which Raj Kumar has an ownership stake.

In the USA, the Chicago area has a total of thirty-one video retail outlets which service the Indian diasporic market. The average price for each master copy sold to the store is $US30 (an exception to this rule in recent years was *1942, A Love Story*, which was sold at $US40 a master copy) and the retailers make (or promise to make) a certain number of copies from the master for rental purposes. Thus the total that a film producer can expect from video wholesale in the Chicago market is between $US680 and $US1,240 a year. Sell-through (outright purchase of videos by individuals) is very limited and brings in anywhere from $US5 a tape to a maximum of $US10 a tape. As small capitalists dominate the market, they do not have the necessary capital to invest more to provide high-quality videos in order to extract more revenue from sell-through and/or rental markets. A typical company in the area is Movie King Inc. Founded in 1978, it is a family-owned, private company and has only one outlet. Reportedly it has no joint ventures with any national distributors like Atlantic Video or Video Sound. Movie King has approximately 11,000 titles of Indian films on tape, 2,000 Pakistani television dramas, and 100 Pakistani film titles.

The cable/satellite television market in the USA is rapidly changing. In 1995 Direct TV, a new satellite channel will be available for Indian diasporic audiences there. In this system, a family would invest $US700–800 in an 18-inch satellite receive-only dish and other related equipment and would be able to receive many attractive channels for no monthly fee. The network would feature HBO, Cinemax, and other US channels but the only Indian channel available would be TV Asia. This company is owned principally by Amitabh Bachchan, the reigning male superstar of Hindi films in the 1970s and 1980s.

Direct television could well mean the end of the video business, but this is a matter of no regret to the video-store proprietors who see it as a very unprofitable business. There are too many stores, too many poor copies of films, and no understanding among the store owners as to how to work out a price that would sustain them in the business. Parag Ghandi (Pendakur 1994*b*) has asserted that this is partly due to ethnic divisions between the various proprietors, but we would argue that it is not ethnic divisions as much as the very nature of small capital. Risks are high and hours are long, and each entrepreneur has to try and make money as soon as possible.

This chapter has attempted a historical sketch of the patterns of film exports from India. It has also examined national policy toward film exports, the institutions that were created by the government, and their troubled history. The statistics that we have used to build our case provide one side of the story, but Indian cinema beyond national borders has another, perhaps more compelling, story to tell. What we find most interesting in the North American context is how different audiences relate to Indian films. Many African people and people from the Middle East are full of praise for the melodramatic elements of the feature film, the song numbers, the costumes and the 'beautiful' ladies as they call them. For people of Indian origin who are living abroad the cinematic experience connects them with a past that they left behind and allows their children, if encouraged, to enter into it. Some even think that elements of Indian culture could be taught by a smart selection of Indian films for their children. Others totally shun them, calling them unprofessional trash. The cultural signficance of Indian film in the various territories abroad needs to be explored in greater detail than we have been able to do here.

References

Aggarwal, Amit (1994), 'From Rice to Riches', *India Today* (15 Aug.).

Barnouw, Eric, and Krishnaswamy, S. (1980), *Indian Film* (Oxford University Press, New York, Oxford, and New Delhi).

Chakravorty, Sumita S. (1993), *National Identity in Indian Popular Cinema, 1947–1987* (University of Texas Press, Austin).

Da Cunha, Uma (ed.) (1984), *Indian Cinema, 83–84* (National Film Development Corporation, New Delhi).

Dharap, B. V. (1983), *Indian Films 1983* (National Film Archive of India, Pune).

National Film Development Corporation (1992). Value of shipping bills passed through NFDC—Language wise export of titles. Bombay.

Pendakur, Manjunath (1991), 'Political Economy of Television in India', in Gerald Sussman and John Lent (eds.), *Transnational Communications: Wiring the Third World* (Sage Publications, Newbury Park, London, and New Delhi), 234–62.

—— (1994*a*), fieldwork notes, Hospet, Karnataka, India, August.

—— (1994*b*), interview with Parag Gandhi, owner of Movie King Inc., Chicago, September.

—— (1994*c*), interview by phone with Vijay Soni, November.

—— (forthcoming), *Indian Cinema: Industry, Ideology, Consciousness* (Lakeview Press, Chicago).

Report to the Ministry of Information and Broadcasting (1989) Government of India, Ministry of Information and Broadcasting, New Delhi, October.

Serow, William, Nam, Charles, Sly, David, and Weller, Robert (1990), *Handbook on International Migration* (Greenwood Press, New York).

Sethna, Hilla (1985), 'National Film Development Corporation', in T. M. Ramachandran (ed.), *Seventy Years of Indian Cinema, 1913–1983* (Cinema-India International, Bombay), 564–77.

Staly, Leonard (1994), 'US B.O. report', *Variety* (13–19 June), 10.

Working Group (1980), *Report on National Film Policy*, Government of India, Ministry of Information and Broadcasting, New Delhi.

Part II: Indian Television: An Emerging Regional Force

Manas Ray and Elizabeth Jacka

As indicated in the first part of this chapter, in spite of its huge domestic market and its regional dominance, India has not yet produced a sizeable export market in made-for-television products. Its central position in a geolinguistic region that stretches from the USA to Europe, and from Africa to Fiji, is so far based almost entirely on film exports, which are numerically considerable, although not very significant economically. However, at the time of writing this situation is undergoing a profound transformation which will see India in the next few years become a significant producer and exporter of television as well as of film. At the end of 1994 India was very much in the midst of a television revolution, the emerging contours of which are far from clear. With the public broadcasting network, Doordarshan (also referred to here as DD) waking up to the changed reality of the 1990s and a host of private networks fighting it out for a part of the lucrative pie that the small screen offers, the scene is fierce, tense, and fluid.

Background

The television scene in India cannot be understood without appreciating the particular features of Indian society. It is a vast, geographically diverse, country of 900 million people with a great number of cultural and linguistic differences; it is composed of twenty-two states; there are sixteen regional languages and over 800 dialects. In addition there is a great disparity between levels of development, wealth, and education—as an Indian commentator expressed it: 'India lives simultaneously in two centuries—with bullock carts and satellites' (Abdi 1994). From the point of view of the disparities of wealth, there are three distinct audiences in India—the educated urban élite; the semi-urban market—both of these audiences are fluent in English; and the rural uneducated population. Of India's 40 million television sets, 77 per cent are owned by the first two groups even though they comprise only 27 per cent of the total population (Kak 1994).

As well as infrastructure problems, the cost of television ownership has meant that penetration in rural India has been slow. Nevertheless, television reaches 75 per cent of the country—67 per cent of the rural population and 90 per cent of the urban (Kishore 1994: 100). Although a large percentage of the country has access to a television signal, the cost of television sets, even black-and-white, is prohibitive for the working-class individual. In 1988 a colour television set cost the equivalent of six months' salary for a factory assembly worker (Singhal *et al.* 1988: 224). While the rural and working classes are devoid of basic information access, the middle classes have a range of information technologies available. As indicated above, the majority of viewers are middle-class urban dwellers. However, community viewing is popular in over 2,400 villages across the country.

Television made a comparatively late entry to India. It first began in September 1959 as a pilot UNESCO-sponsored educational project, and thus started as a medium of development communication and with a corresponding ethos. By 1962 it was securely established under the control of Doordarshan as a state-owned monopoly. Its technical infrastructure has always been a mixture of satellite and terrestrial transmission. In 1975 NASA loaned India a satellite to conduct the Satellite Instructional Television Experiment (SITE) in 2,400 villages (Singhal *et al.* 1988: 224). In the 1960s television policy in India was dominated by American media theories of functionalist persuasion on the one hand, and nationalist ideologies of various shades on the other. This left very little room for any consideration of the medium's potential as being other than strictly educational, although non-educational slots were mostly filled in then, as until very recently, by Hindi feature films. By the 1970s, however, as the food shortages of the previous decade disappeared, there were some indications of moves towards liberalization and diversification with debates about the wisdom of heavy state control being aired, although no change actually occurred until the 1980s.

On the programming side, talk shows, quiz, and current affairs programmes started featuring more regularly in the 1970s. At least in the urban centres, the age of community watching was left behind by the boom in private ownership of television receivers. It was also the decade when advertising stills began to be permitted, as was a small amount of sponsoring by private agencies (Mitra 1993*a*). Liberalization might have occurred at that point had it not been for the Emergency (1976–7) that imposed Draconian media censorship.

The Janata government (1977–9) was long on promises of reform but short on execution. It appointed a twelve-member commission to suggest policy formulations for the broadcast media. The result of their deliberations—the Prasar Bharati Bill, as it was called—recommended a balance between commercial and public service broadcasting, with a latter organized as an autonomous corporation along the lines of the BBC, with an independent board of directors with strong decision-making powers. The Janata government delayed over the recommendations and it was not until March 1980, when the Congress party had regained its majority, that the Bill was placed before the parliament and not unexpectedly voted down.

The New Delhi ASIAD Games of 1982 gave the technical development of television a further boost with the launch of a new satellite system and the change to colour (Singhal *et al.* 1988: 224). At the same time, the drive to bring the whole country under the television umbrella accelerated. The prime minister at the time, Rajiv Gandhi, placed enormous emphasis on the spread of the network, but it remained firmly in the hands of the government, which critics saw as a crude attempt to retain political control. The second major television event of the 1980s was the appearance of two sponsored megaserials based on ancient Indian epics, the *Ramayana* and *Mahabharata*.

Their popularity was absolutely unprecedented, firmly inscribing television on the national imaginary of the country. These serials even had an impact on the political process when the Bharatiya Janata Party (BJP), the political vehicle of the Hindu Right, soared to popularity after remaining dormant for decades.

Throughout the 1980s the question of government control of broadcasting remained an unresolved issue. The Prasar Bharati Bill was ultimately passed in the parliament but with as many as seventy amendments. This occurred during the regime of the National Front Government (NFG), the second non-Congress experiment, as part of its election platform. Both the NFG and subsequently the Congress party government of P. V. Narasimha Rao maintained a studied silence regarding the implementation of the Act, as well as on other similar policy matters. Thus in India, as elsewhere, broadcasting reform did not occur as a result of a conscious policy decision, but rather consisted of a set of *ad hoc* responses to the unstoppable advances of new television delivery mechanisms and of globalization.

The Dominance of Hinduism in Indian Television Culture

Up until the appearance of the new private broadcasters, as a government monopoly, Doordarshan tended to produce and circulate a 'Hindu-Hindi' image of Indian national identity. Its ability to do this was boosted considerably when it became nationally networked in 1982. Ananda Mitra (1993: 40) argues that: 'Doordarshan reproduces a selective set of language, religion, and regions in attempting to produce an unequivocal, homogeneous national image. This is achieved by a series of signifying strategies that make up the variety of texts on Doordarshan.' Productions like the *Mahabharata* and *Ramayana*, with their overtly religious themes, are examples of this. Although in fact Hindu rituals vary from region to region, they are presented in a standardized form within DD programmes, thus marginalizing other religious practices and producing a hegemonic national cultural identity and an imposed political consensus which erases regional and religious differences. The repeated use of the Hindu images on national television emphasizes the 'Hinduness of India and, consequently, the un-Indianness of the non-Hindus' (Mitra 1993*b*: 41).

As well as constructing national unity through religion, DD programming had also traditionally favoured the Hindi language. Hindi and English are the official languages of India but they are spoken by only 40 per cent of the population (Abdi 1994). Hindi speakers are concentrated more in the north of India and yet, even when not required by historical or religious context, the primary location of most of the programmes on DD is north India. Furthermore, the majority of programmes broadcast on DD are in Hindi, reinforcing the idea that Hindi is the national language. Programmes in other regional languages, such as Urdu, Bengali, Gujarati, and the Dravidian languages of south India (including Tamil, Malayalam, and Telegu), are identified to indicate the language of broadcast, although this is not done with those in Hindi. Languages other than Hindi are seen not as national but as regional (Mitra 1993*b*: 42). As Mitra (1990: 174) puts it: 'In some ways, television has drawn heavily from cinema, and somewhat from traditional mass media. It has also re-coded the literary texts, from various languages, constantly trying to create a cultural ensemble that will overcome the diversity of cultural practices that are found in India. Yet in doing this, it has often remained Hindi- and Delhi-centric.'

Hindus make up an estimated 82 per cent of the population, with 12 per cent Muslim and 2 per cent Sikhs (Schauble 1993: 240). Research conducted in the mid-1980s indicated that 90 per cent of Hindu viewers felt their customs and practices were adequately presented, but 90 per cent of the Muslims and 92 per cent of the Sikhs believed that Indian television did not adequately project their religions, customs, and practices (Singhal *et al.* 1988: 228). As will be outlined below, the breakdown of DD's monopoly and the introduction of new private services has begun to reverse this process of Hinduization.

The Transformation of Indian Television

Television broadcasting hours increased in 1984–5, and this meant that production, previously a monopoly of Doordarshan, became open to outside producers. This happened via a process of sponsorship whereby a number of hours were given to independent producers who financed programmes by selling advertising time (Abdi 1994). The development of this sector and the possibility of a programme-export industry was stunted by the fact that independent producers had to seek government approval for their access to the airwaves, and political expediency tended to dictate that access to this valuable source of revenue was spread around. Few producers were ever given permission to produce more than thirteen episodes of a programme, and this had the effect of preventing the growth of a core of highly skilled production houses with large volumes of programmes suitable for export (Kak 1994).

The percentage of the population who could receive television rose from 28 per cent at the beginning of 1984 to 62 per cent in 1987. The number of television sets multiplied by roughly three times between 1983 and 1987. Cable began unofficially in India in 1984, originally spreading through tourist hotels, then apartment blocks, and finally individual households. At first the cable networks were fed by videocassette players, linked centrally to the cable network. By May 1990 there were 3,450 cable TV networks. In the four metropolises, Delhi, Bombay, Madras, and Calcutta, over 3.3 lakh (1 lakh = 100,000) households had been cabled with an audience of 1.6 million. By 1991 cable networks had become equipped with satellite dishes and thus gained access to STAR TV/BBC and CNN channels (Rahim 1994: 15). The rapid spread of this unauthorized cable network with satellite access was the principal catalyst for the explosive changes that have occurred in the Indian television landscape in the 1990s.

As recently as 1990 Indian audiences had to be content with DD fare exclusively. But by 1994 a cabled household was receiving no fewer than twelve channels. The coming of Indian-owned private satellite channels in 1992 started what has been called 'the great television scramble'. On Independence Day (15 August) of that year, Zee TV beamed a half-hour capsule of Hindi songs into India through Asiasat satellite. Also, on the same day, the Bombay-based Asia Television Network (ATN) introduced a channel via a Soviet satellite. Zee TV was fully operational from 1 October 1992. Since then a host of other satellite channels have been introduced. But Zee is undoubtedly the most popular, winning a substantial portion of advertising revenue, prompting it to start another prime time service, EL TV.

Zee TV is a model of the future of India's television industry. It has an audience share of 50 per cent in prime time, and broadcasts seven of the top ten programmes on all channels in India. Its gross monthly advertising revenue of over $US2 million accounts for about 20 per cent of television advertising spending in India (Dziadul 1994: 17) and it is seen in 25 per cent of India's TV households. It broke even within six months of its launch. It provides a combination of programmes on politically sensitive issues and entertainment such as quizzes, game shows, and Donahue-style talk shows. It broadcasts seventy hours a week and has seventy serials in production and twenty-four feature films in development. Regional-language production began in 1994 when studios in Bombay and Delhi were opened, although the results were not broadcast in prime time (Lall 1994: 25).

Zee TV's programming is provided by a subsidiary of its major owner, Asia Today Limited, Zee Telefilms. Although the channel can be expected to remain principally Hindi, it aims to employ producers in Madras and Hyderabad to increase output of programmes in south Indian languages such as Tamil, Telegu, Kanarese, and (later) Malayalam. As of 1994 it was also looking at producing programmes in Bengali and accessing programmes in north-eastern Indian languages such as Assamese and Origo (Dziadul 1994: 16).

Towards the middle of 1992 Delhi-based PTI-TV launched a new network, Asianet. It hired a transponder on a Soviet satellite and from November 1992 began to beam programmes in Malayalam, targeted not only to the Malayalam-speaking people of India (Kerala being their home state) but also to the large number of Malayali expatriates in the Gulf. The menu consisted of Malayalam films, serials, regional news, and education programmes. Regional language programming is becoming increasingly popular on Indian satellite channels, drawing substantial advertising revenue. For instance, Zee has Bengali programmes on certain days of the week; Jain TV has slots for programmes in six different languages.

Rupert Murdoch's STAR TV also began beaming into India in 1992. The package has five channels: Plus, Prime Sports, Channel V (an Indianized imitation of MTV), the BBC World Service, and the recently launched Movie, India's first pay channel. On top of this, STAR had links with Subash Chandra Goel's Zee Telefilms Ltd. in which STAR's equity is 49.9 per cent, and STAR also has 50 per cent equity in Zee's second channel, EL TV, launched in December 1994. STAR has two beams—the northern and the southern. For the northern beam the primary focus is China (although satellite television is officially banned in China), while for the southern beam it is India, where viewership is the highest. STAR now has the capacity of putting up two different programmes on the southern beam, one for India and the other for the Middle East. But in both of these areas most of the programmes are targeted to the Indian audience. India is the primary focus of all advertising on this service.

Indian advertisers who wish to target the wealthy élite have found an ideal platform. However, since STAR is a niche channel and only broadcasts in English, its total advertising revenue and ratings are far below those of Zee TV. Although there is considerable publicity in the West about STAR's inroads into India, its impact is overemphasized. It is estimated that STAR only reaches 5 per cent of homes in India (Kak 1994) and in Bombay, for instance, which has 20 per cent of its households cabled (and thus able to receive satellite channels), the ratings of STAR TV are much lower than those of the movies that local cable operators show. It is Zee, more than any other major network, that has posed a challenge to the traditional monopoly of Doordarshan.

DD has made a number of responses to this challenge, the most important of which is the introduction of DD Metro in an attempt to halt the flow of revenue from DD to the satellite channels. At the end of 1994 DD Metro was enormously successful, its advertising revenues soaring. It is an entertainment channel with portions of current affairs and business programmes thrown in. It also features MTV programmes between 4.30 and 7.00 p.m. The production quality is mostly high, with sponsored programmes from such notable independent producers as Nimbus, Plus Channels, Fame TV, and Times TV. Programmes are in English as well as Hindi, with the two tending to amalgamate at times into a strange hybrid popularly known as 'Hinglish' (a phenomenon not restricted to DD alone). DD has also introduced regional language services (as many as ten, with the number to increase in 1995) on the national network. DD management are also working on DD1 (the channel that enjoys the highest reach and consequently viewership), trying to modernize it while maintaining a balance between social commitment (the putative guiding principle of DD) and entertainment to suit the changing realities.

Most of the state capitals have regional centres (kendras, as they are called) with relay stations in the surrounding areas, beyond which they are linked into the national network (DD1). Much of the material produced by regional kendras is 'simply primitive' (Ghose 1994). Ghose predicts that standards will be improved by the emerging competition from regional language broadcasting of the private networks.

In spite of the rapid growth of satellite and cable, DD is still the unquestioned major broadcaster in terms of reach and viewership. A study report in *The Times of India*, Bombay, in November 1994 indicated that only about 20 per cent of Bombay's population, and under 10 per cent of the population in other urban centres, watch satellite. By contrast, DD reaches more than 80 per cent of all households in the country. This dominance is in no small measure due to two peculiar legislative features of the television landscape: no other network in India is allowed either to transmit terrestrially or to provide satellite uplinks from within Indian territory. This severely limits the ability of other networks to offer a news service. DD's dominance is indicated in Table 3.5.

Table 3.5. Reach of DD Metro and Zee TV compared, by region (millions)

Region	*DD Metro*	*Zee TV*
Maharashtra	2.22	1.31
Delhi	2.31	0.46
West Bengal	2.15	0.20
Tamil Nadu	1.05	0.12
All India	10.40	6.10

Source: IMRB, Doordarshan, and industry estimates, reported in *Business Today* (22 Sept.–8 Oct. 1994).

While advertising revenues do not reflect DD's audience dominance, in 1994/5 they were still the biggest revenue earners, as is illustrated below (*Business Today* 1994).

Table 3.6. Projected advertising revenues for 1994/5

Service	*Revenue (millions of rupees)*
DD	4,500
Zee	1,000
STAR	400
Other satellite	500
Barter	1,050

Source: IMRB, Doordarshan, and industry estimates, reported in *Business Today* (22 Sept.–8 Oct. 1994).

Changes in Programming

The introduction of competition has had the result that programming generally, apart from DD's kendras and to some extent, DD1, became much more polished and production values have improved. Programmes are bolder and more frank, venturing into areas of personal relationships that previously were considered taboo by DD, and the urban Indian audience has apparently accepted the changes readily. Megaserials, of which there were previously only a few, not only multiplied in number but moved thematically from the mythological and historical to becoming family-oriented and dealing with contemporary issues. Other entertainment genres, new to Indian television, such as sitcoms and quiz shows were also introduced. The most significant implication of multiplying channels is that there is no longer any single programme which will draw a mass audience, meaning that the possibility of a repeat of the *Mahabharata* phenomenon is now quite remote. Be that as it may, with entertainment (and viewer preference) being the sole criterion, Indian television is now the site of commercial exploitation as never before and consumer sovereignty is the guiding ethos.

An overwhelming number of programmes are film based—film songs, stars, and feature films. At present the satellite channels have no daily news programmes because of the restrictions on uplinking. Instead, there are a host of weekly news programmes. Several business programmes have appeared, dealing with business news, views, analysis, and advice. This reflects the new tide of interest in business affairs which was evident after the economy was liberalized. There are also fitness and health shows, chat shows, game shows, horror shows, and raffles. Understandably, a good majority of these programmes are mere imitations of their Western counterparts, though experiments within permissible limits are not ruled out. For instance, in a programme called *Antaksari* on Zee, musicians play tunes from popular Hindi scores and competitors are asked to identify the song.

The channel boom has its multiplier effects, the prime beneficiaries of which are the music and hardware industries. The record companies' revenues have soared and the film industry's main earnings now come from its sale of music. A number of programmes deal with forthcoming films, which has given a fillip to the film industry. Doordarshan formerly charged producers of new and forthcoming films a fee for showing songs and clippings of those films. Now the system has reversed, with DD having to pay the producers. This indicates the popularity of these programmes as well as DD's lost monopoly.

The main barrier to further development of the television industry is a shortage of sufficient high-quality programming. The infrastructure does not yet exist to support the amount of production required, and there is a shortage of professionals highly skilled in television production as opposed to film. By 1994 this was beginning to change as investment in the industry began to increase, much of it coming from non-resident Indians (NRIs), as well as from the so-called Bombay–Dubai mafia.

DD's particular weakness in programming lies in the regional kendras, whereas the private networks were quick to identify the vast opportunity offered by regionally specific programming. Among the regional centres, the Madras kendra made some headway, but its success prompted the Madras-based Sun TV to greater efforts. Both have observed the low popularity of Hindi programmes in the south, and thus the very real potential for programmes in Tamil and other regional languages.

Jain TV (on air from 14 January 1994) was the first to launch a number of regional programmes from which it derives 50 per cent of its revenue. Jain TV presents an interesting case of the resistance to the strands of conservatism and religious chauvinism that presently characterize Indian politics. For example, it amply manifests the contradictions within the ranks of the BJP, since as a production house it both actively campaigned for BJP and has programmes like *India Awakening* and *Ved Vani* (Hindu scripture) which actively promote a Hindu national identity, but at the same time it has programmes about the Koran. In fact, the menu of Jain TV—which includes *Corporate News Watch*, *Force 10 Aerobics*, *Science and Technology*, *Videocon Top Parade*—can be read as one strategy for a profoundly religious society like India in coping with a technology-based corporate world order.

Sharply increasing regional advertising revenue is the reason why the satellite channels are surging ahead in regional programmes. Asianet and Jain TV are pioneers in this area, though Zee TV is not far behind. In fact, Zee TV has taken a step ahead by splitting its Bengali broadcast into Calcutta and Dhaka dialects, hoping to cash in on the Bangladesh market if and when cable operation takes off there. DD, on the other hand, is seeking to beat its private competitors at the regional game, by taking advantage of its superior resource capacity. It plans to extend its regional language services to eight or even ten hours a day on national network. This will be possible when DD begins to broadcast from PanAmSat 4 in 1995. The satellite channels, with their limited infrastructural resources, cannot hope to come anywhere near this.

India and its Regions: The Potential of Television Export

The export activity of Doordarshan has never been extensive because, since most of its programmes are sponsored (that is, financed by the independent producers selling advertising time within programmes), it does not hold rights to any of its programmes, save a few free repeats. However, there is a continuous exchange of its news, music, and dance programmes either through an organization called Asia Vision (an agency of the Asian Broadcasting Union) or through direct bilateral exchange between countries. In the case of the independent producers and private satellite networks, the export business is yet to take off, though the potential is enormous. As with film and videos, the primary target groups are expatriate Indian communities spread across the world. Serials form the main item of export and, as they gain in production quality, export to Indian diasporic communities can only increase.

The emerging export market can be divided into two zones. The primary market is what can be called 'Greater India'—that is, India, Pakistan, Bangladesh, Nepal, and Sri Lanka, countries that in spite of all the religious and other differences, share a cultural ethos and common attraction to Hindi films. In the future, as television in each of these areas liberalizes, and provided no regulatory barriers are erected, considerable cross-border trade in programmes within this area can be expected. However, at the moment, given the political impasse in which the two countries are caught, no official programme exchange takes place between India and Pakistan and there is unlikely to be any change in this in the near future. There is evidence, though, of regular cross-border pirating of both film (video) and television serials. STAR/Zee and Pakistan Television (PTV) are beamed from the same satellite (Asiasat 1) and have close frequencies. As a result, Indian audiences have access to PTV which regularly broadcasts anti-Indian views (the main thrust being the issue of Kashmir). However, according to both government and private sources, PTV does not win any sizeable audiences within India.

By the end of 1994 the move towards liberalization of television in Bangladesh was very slow. Private purchase of dish antennae is not altogether unknown in a big city like Dhaka, but so far there is almost no cabling. The reasons are both political and economic. There is really no substantial middle-income segment in Bangladesh, only the super-rich and very poor. In addition, both the present political regime, with tendencies towards Islamic law, and the Bangladeshi ruling class are very wary of the social fallout of the sort of programmes that private satellite channels like Zee broadcast in India.

Bombay films have had a conspicuous presence in rich urban Bangladeshi households via video for quite some time. The Bangladeshi advertising lobby is particularly keen on the importation of television serials and films and film-based programmes, since this is expected to boost television viewership considerably. However, the Indo-Bangladesh trade in television software is primarily a political issue and will depend on the political course of events of the two countries in the coming years. Media opinion in India is bullish. It hopes that, with cable operation picking up in Bangladesh, Indian exports will have an automatic viewership. Zee TV's move to produce its Bengali programmes in both Calcutta and Dhaka dialect, mentioned before, is an early indication of this.

In the secondary market there are four sectors. The first, and almost contiguous, market is West Asia, which has considerable cultural affinity with India and, most importantly, has a substantial population from the subcontinent. The next most important sector in the secondary market is the UK, which again has a large population of Asians and already has an Indian channel called TV Asia. BSkyB has also begun to carry

Zee TV programmes by teleporting beams from Asiasat 1 to Astra. The third sector in the secondary market is North America, where the subcontinental diaspora is extensive, and the fourth is South Africa. Given the latter's large Indian community, it holds tremendous prospects for Indian television software export.

Zee's plans extend beyond India. It already has sizeable audiences in Pakistan, Bangladesh, Nepal, Burma, and the Gulf. It has set up a company in Sharjah, Zee Arabia, which aims to produce at least two hours per day for the network. There is also the possibility of joint productions with Pakistan in Sharjah and Dubai. It is likely to take over the new Mauritian terrestrial channel TV 5, and in Africa it has held talks with South Africa's SABC and M-Net, as well as with broadcasters in Kenya and Tanzania (Dziadul 1994: 16).

A competitor to Zee TV in the export stakes is Jain (Joint American Indian Network) TV. It is currently distributed by satellite to fifty-six countries from the Gulf to the Pacific, and terrestrially in Sri Lanka and Nepal. It is a nine-strand package with religious, political, children's, sport, entertainment, business, health, and population, development, and environmental issues (Dziadul 1994: 16).

A number of Indian-based programme suppliers produce especially for networks abroad, including the BBC, Channel 4, ABN, and TV Asia. They are paid in foreign currency. As yet, this is very low-volume trade but it is the prestige end of the market and is expected to increase in quantity. The sorts of programme category included in this kind of trade are magazine and business programmes, star interviews, documentaries, chat shows, and 'Bollywood' (Bombay Hindi movies). Important among such production companies in India are New Delhi Television, owned by Pronnoy Roy, and TV 18, owned by Raghav Bhel, and also Sagar and Nimbus.

The greatest volume of exported material after films is in the category of serials, one-off telefilms, and sitcoms. This, the entertainment end of export, is expected to grow phenomenally in the next couple of years. Already, megaserials like *Ramayana* and *Mahabharata* and *The Sword of Tipu Sultan* are reaching the various networks that cater to Indian diaspora and parts of

South Asia. Since Hindi film's popularity extends beyond the South Asian community, subtitled or dubbed versions of these programmes are expected to have a large clientèle. Theoretically, English-language serials with high production values should find automatic entry to networks in UK and North America, targeted primarily at the immigrant communities, but to date there is no evidence to indicate whether or not this is happening. At the end of 1994, as the production and export industry began to take off, there was still very little infrastructure in existence for programme export. However, there is no doubt that programme export from India will soon grow. Global companies with Indian audiences will look to India for programme supply and the Indian industry itself will reach out. But, at the time of writing, the picture is far from clear, with precious little consolidated data available.

The private satellite industry in India has known from the start that the real source of money is in pay television. And now DD, hoping to attain global reach by the end of 1995, has similar strategies, though as a public broadcaster it has other dimensions to its broadcasting as well. With an estimated 300 transponders by end of 1995, and with digital compression, the number of channels will inevitably lead to more segmentation of programmes. Gradually the Indian diasporic market will take the form of a cluster of niche markets. For a start, the diaspora is divided into two segments—those over the age of 45 who have close ties with the subcontinent, and the young people who exist, in Salman Rushdie's memorable phrase, as a 'comma between East and West'. These two groups do not have the same cultural bearing, needs, or desires and hence in marketing terms they form two different zones. In the future this and many other such segmentations will be the way of life for Indian television.

The Future

The global reach of Indian television can only be expected to increase in the coming years. As free-to-air or ordinary broadcast television reaches its finite limits, expatriate Indians (usually wealthy) will become a crucial source of revenue. It is expected that in 1995 two more satellites will be launched over Asia: Apstar 2 and PanAmSat 4, the latter reaching from South East Asia to the UK and Europe. They will revolutionize the satellite broadcasting scene in Asia. Along with DD, a host of major international services have also leased transponders on these two satellites including Time-Warner, Home Box Video, CNN, MTV, NBC, Viacom, and ESPN. As far as India is concerned, this effectively signals two major changes: the loosening grip of Murdoch on global satellite broadcasting, and the entry of Doordarshan into global broadcasting to Indian diasporic audiences.

Government policy is having trouble keeping abreast of these rapid changes. In 1994 a bill was passed to regulate cable operations and various other measures were taken to try to control the explosion in the television scene, for example increased censorship of programme content. The government also appears to be trying to dampen the pace of expansion of private operators, notably by banning tobacco and alcohol advertisements. It is also conscious of needing to maintain the viability of DD in the face of political pressure in favour of a strengthened public service remit for it. Nevertheless, there can be no doubt that India will become an even stronger force in world television in the very near future.

References

ABDI, SABA ZAIDI (1994), 'The Global Village', presentation given (with Siddarth Kak) at the Indian Screen Event, Australian Film Television and Radio School, Sydney, October.

Business Today (1994), IMRB, Doordarshan, and industry estimates, reported in issue 22 Sept.–8 Oct.

DZIADUL, CHRIS (1994), 'The A–Zee of Indian TV', *Television Business International* (July/Aug. 1984), 16–22.

GHOSE, BHASKAR (1994), interview with Bhaskar Ghose, Secretary, Department of Information and Broadcasting, conducted by Manas Ray, New Delhi, December.

GUPTA, V. S. (1989), 'Case Study of Indian Rural Television', *Media Asia*, 16/4 (1989), 215–18.

KAK, SIDDARTH (1994), 'The Global Village', presentation given (with Saba Zaidi Abdi) at the Indian Screen Event, Australian Film Television and Radio School, Sydney, October.

KISHORE, KRISHNA (1994), 'The Advent of STAR TV in India: Emerging Policy Issues', *Media Asia*, 21/2: 96–103.

LALL, BHUVAN (1994), 'Developing Markets—India Hot Stuff', *TV World* (June), 22–5.

MITRA, ANANDA (1990), 'The Position of Television in the Cultural Map of India', *Media Asia*, 17/3: 166–76.

—— (1993*a*), *Television and Popular Culture in India* (Sage Publications, New Delhi).

—— (1993*b*), 'Television and the Nation: Doordarshan's India', *Media Asia*, 20/1: 39–44.

RAHIM, ABDUR (1994), 'Impact of Cable TV on Television and Video Viewing in Hyderabad', *Media Asia*, 21/1: 15.

SCHAUBLE, JOHN (ed.) (1993), *The SBS World Guide, 1993 Edition* (Text Publishing Company, Melbourne).

SINGHAL, ARVIND, DOSHI, J. K., ROGERS, EVERETT, and RAHMAN, S. (1988), 'The Diffusion of Television in India', *Media Asia*, 15/4: 222–9.

4

Egypt and the Arab World in the Satellite Age

Hussein Amin

Communication is no longer regarded merely as an incidental service and its development left to chance. The communication field has intensified with recent technological innovation and the identification of increasingly important social, cultural, economic, and political goals to be realized from it. Most countries have been willing, indeed eager, to participate in transborder communication in pursuit of such goals. Transborder transmission was led by developed countries and succeeded by developing countries wanting to join this new world of communication. International networks have been established for this purpose, and have opened the door to larger audiences, expanded the resources of information, and supported cultural and social change (Al Nick 1983).

In recent years the Arab world has witnessed the development of a large number of international television services. This wave began with the launching of the Egyptian Space Channel (ESC), soon followed by the creation of the Saudi Middle East Broadcasting Center (MBC), the Kuwaiti Space Channel (KSC), the Jordanian Arab Space Channel (JASC), the Space Network of Dubai, Tunisia TV7, Moroccan Satellite Channel, Oman TV, and United Arab Emirates TV. Other national television services, such as Saudi and Egyptian national television channels, were later put on ARABSAT for direct-to-home reception across the Arab world. The Arab region has also witnessed the birth of private specialized international television services, such as Arab Radio and Television, which carries four specialized television channels, and the Orbit television package to the Middle East that consists of sixteen television channels in Arabic and English (see Table 4.1).

The primary objective for the development of these services in each country is to project a favourable image to the rest of the Arab world. A secondary objective is to broadcast Arabic language programming to Arab nationals living abroad. It is estimated that there are over 5 million Arabs living in Europe and more than 2 million in the USA. This well-established diaspora has created new foreign markets for Arab broadcasting services.

Most programming originates in Egypt and is exported to these various broadcasting services. The Egyptian film and television industry has played a historically dominant role in Arab broadcast media. An average of 100 films are produced annually in Egypt and are distributed through Arab satellite services to the rest of the Arab world. Egyptian television sells an average of 300 television broadcast hours a year to each of the Arab television services (Amin 1990). Arab electronic media have been established on a weak economic base. Although some of the Gulf states enjoy state-of-the-art technological infrastructures, they lack trained personnel and creative cadres. Dependency on Egyptian programming, especially feature film and soap opera, has resulted in grudging but nevertheless significant *de facto* support of the Egyptian film and television industry.

It is a feature of Arab, and especially Egyptian, television that it is seen as an effective arm of government policy and national projection in the region. This politicized mission has its basis in the longstanding popularity of Egyptian film, as well as radio, throughout the region from the 1930s onwards. The Egyptian dialect is widely recognized and understood; becoming a kind of regional *lingua franca* of cultural and political communication. This situation has generated some political and cultural fallout, with concern over the spread of a relatively more liberal programming ethos being expressed by several Arab governments and their peoples.

Development of Television in the Arab World

The Arab 'world' is a huge geographical region, occupying 13,738,000 square kilometres. It extends from the shores of the Atlantic Ocean in the west to the Persian Gulf in the east. The population of this region was recently estimated at 200 million. Television broadcasting started in the 1950s. It was introduced first in Morocco in 1954, then in Algeria, Iraq, and Lebanon in 1956. Its introduction progressed to Egypt and Syria in 1960, Kuwait in 1961, Sudan in 1962, Democratic Yemen in 1964, and Saudi Arabia in 1965. Tunisia introduced a television service in 1966, and, after the Middle East war in 1967, Jordan established its television system. Libya started in 1968, followed by Qatar in 1970, Bahrain in 1973, Oman in 1974, and Yemen in 1975. In the United Arab Emirates, Abu Dhabi was the first to develop a television system, introducing its service in 1969, with Dubai following in 1972 (Labib *et al.* 1983: 15).

The official function of the media in the Arab world can be understood in terms of the following sequence of priorities: conveying news and information, interpreting and commenting on events, reinforcing social norms and cultural awareness, providing specialized data for commercial promotion, and, finally, entertainment (Rugh 1979). Most Arab television broadcast systems are under direct government control, with revenue derived much more from the state than from advertising (Amin 1995: 3).

However, there are significant differences among them. Arab television systems can be divided into two groups. The first operates under the 'mobilization' broadcast model, and includes Algeria, Egypt, Iraq, Syria, Saudi Arabia, Libya, Yemen, and the Sudan. Governments of these countries have exercised complete control over the broadcast media. The second group, including all other Arab states, with the exception of Morocco and Lebanon, exhibits a 'governmental' model, whereby governments exercise less control over the content of the airwaves. In many cases in the first group, television was promoted by revolutionary regimes. Learning

Table 4.1. Television systems in the Arab nations

Country	*Area (sq. km.)*[1]	*Population (est.)*[2]	*GNP per capita ($US) (1989)*[2]	*TV Networks*	*No. of Television Sets*[1]	*Terrestrial television*[3]	*Direct-to-home*[3]	*Cable*[3]
Algeria	2,381,741	25,010,000 (1990)	2,025	RTA-1	1,900,000	Two national channels	Permitted	None
Bahrain	369.6	503,022 (1990)	6,910	Bahrain TV	215,000	Two national channels	Permitted	MMDS system under consideration
Egypt	1,001,449	59,000,000 (1993)	620	ESC Nile TV	6,200,000	Two national and five local channels	Permitted	S.T.V. Cairo only
Iraq	438,317	17,250,000 (1988)	3,652	None	1,350,000	Two national and four local channels	None	None
Jordan	97,740	4,145,000 (1991)	1,242	JASC	330,000	Two national channels	Permitted	MMDS System under consideration
Kuwait	10,400	2,062,000 (1990)	11,224	KSC	590,000	Two national channels	Permitted	MMDS under consideration
Lebanon	2,505,813	2,740,000 (1991)	467	None	905,000	Forty private television channels	Permitted	None
Libya	1,759,540	3,770,000 (1988)	5,081	Libya TV	467,000	One national channel	None	None
Morocco	4,406,550	25,200,000 (1990)	915	Morocco TV	1,900,000	One national and one commercial channel	Permitted	n.a.

Oman	212,457	1,559,000 (1991)	5,131	Oman TV	150,000	One national channel	Liberal	n.a.
Qatar	11,000	369,079 (1990)	12,857	Qatar TV	198,000	One national channel	Banned	Qatar Cable launched MMDS service in 1993
Saudi Arabia	2,149,000	10,520,000 (1985)	7,070	Saudi TV 1 and 2 MBC, ART, ORBIT	4,100,000	Two national channels	Dishes banned	MMDS in process
Sudan	2,505,813	20,500,000 (1990)	320	None	2,000,000	One national network	n.a.	None
Syria	700,000	10,600,000 (1986)	1,110	None	770,000	Two national channels	Dishes not permitted	None
Tunisia	163,610	8,070,000 (1990)	1,319	TV7	650,000	Two national channels	Permitted	n.a.
UAE	83,600	1,612,000 (1985)	19,870	UAE TV	175,000	UAE TV in Abu Dhabi, Dubai	Permitted	Dubai Cablevision-operated MMDS service
Yemen	527,968	11,280,000 (1990)	761	None	330,000	One national television network	Permitted	None

Sources: [1] *Statistical Yearbook 1993* (UNESCO, Paris).
[2] *Europa World Yearbook 1993* (Europa Publications Ltd., England).
[3] Drost, Harry (1991), *The World's News Media* (Longman, New York).

from their experience of radio, they understood the potential of the electronic media for propaganda, for mobilizing popular support, and for placing the image of the revolutionary leader before the populace. In the second group, television was established to reach the widest locations and to communicate to populations with high levels of illiteracy.

Television is a very important medium in nearly all of the Arab world; the only countries where television is not used by large numbers of people are Yemen and the Sudan, as these countries are less developed economically. It was the desire of Arab governments, motivated mainly by political and social rather than economic factors, to support the development of a strong television industry. Since it is a domestic rather than a public medium, television has proven to be an efficient tool for communication, as most Arab households are closely knit and self-contained, and most entertaining is done in the home (Amin and Boyd 1993: 2–7).

The Development of ARABSAT

The Arab League was formed after the Second World War as a compromise between aspirations for Arab unity and sovereignty for each of the twenty-one Arab states. These competing aspirations continue to be a factor in television programme exchanges. The first Arab League mass-media co-operation began in 1951 with the establishment of the Administration for Information and Publication to promote the Arab perspectives internationally. The Permanent Committee for Arab Media was formed in 1960. In 1964 the Council of Arab Information Ministers first met. It was the forum with the highest Arab League media authority. The 1967 war precipitated communication changes among all Arab countries and especially prompted a re-examination of the role of the media. In this atmosphere emerged the 1969 establishment of the Arab States Broadcasting Union (ASBU), a specialized agency of the League to co-ordinate radio and television efforts and train personnel (Boyd 1982).

ARABSAT emerged at about the same time. Although

Arab countries participated in INTELSAT as early as its establishment in 1964, there was a desire to connect all Arab countries in a communication system to exchange cultural and educational television programmes. The ASBU Engineering Committee gave the ARABSAT movement one of it first boosts by recommending space telecommunication technology. However, the Arab Telecommunication Union was hesitant until 1974 when it formed a joint committee with ASBU (Al-Saadon 1990). The International Telecommunications Union (ITU) added momentum by predicting substantial growth in communications development among Arab countries and the profitability of ARABSAT. UNESCO advised the movement on three occasions and recommended community television services, among other proposals (Abu-Argoub 1988).

In 1976 an agreement was signed to create the independent entity called the Arab Satellite Communication Organization within the Arab League jurisdiction. The goal of ARABSAT was to form an Arab space segment for public service for all members of the League. INTELSAT allowed ARABSAT's formation because it was not going to cause INTELSAT economic harm and would complement or replace ground-based networks (Abu-Argoub 1988). ARABSAT members invested according to their means and interest. Today ARABSAT's twenty-two members are Algeria, Bahrain, Djibouti, Iraq, Jordan, Kuwait, Lebanon, Libya, Mauritania, Morocco, Oman, Qatar, Somalia, Sudan, Syria, Tunisia, the Palestine Liberation Organization, the United Arab Emirates, Yemen, South Yemen, Saudi Arabia, and Egypt.

The ARABSAT organization includes a General Assembly, a Board of Directors and an Executive Body. The Assembly, composed of Arab state ministers of telecommunications, is the highest authority. The nine-member board includes the five permanent members who have invested the most. The Executive Body administers the operation (Abu-Argoub, 1988). Television programme exchange essentially represents the policies of the information and telecommunications ministries. Services include exchange of news and other programmes, educational broadcasting, especially for remote areas, emergency communications, domestic telecommunications, and data transmission, including teleconferences, electronic mail, and newspaper publications (Al-Saadon 1990).

ARABSAT's capacity is impressive: it serves regional, national, and international needs with point-to-point telecommunications and with direct broadcasting (Abu-Argoub 1988). Each satellite has twenty-six transponders, 8,000 telephone circuits, seven television channels, and one large channel for community television. Yet the capacity was severely under-utilized for several years (Turkistani 1988). The development of community television, especially to remote areas, was hampered because governments had feared its use as a propaganda tool (Abu-Argoub 1988). A committee established in 1977 to co-ordinate the use of ARABSAT agreed in 1985 on programme guidelines. They were designed to encourage the quality of programme content, to maximize the use of ARABSAT, and to produce programming acceptable to all Arab states regardless of their political differences.

Nevertheless, Al-Saadon (1990) has found that the use of ARABSAT for television programme exchange has in fact reflected the political as well as social and economic differences among Arab states. Those countries with better diplomatic relations were more likely to exchange programmes, and the stronger the country's economy was, the more likely it was to exchange programmes using ARABSAT. However, Al-Saadon concluded that the introduction of the new satellite technology changed the attitude of media organizations toward more co-operation and programme exchange. Most Arab countries have established exchange departments or are currently in the process of establishing them. The second generation of ARABSAT satellites is expected to be launched from the beginning of 1996.

Egypt

Television pervades nearly all of Egyptian society, and the influence of Egyptian television reaches as well into other Arab and African states. Egypt's long history of film and television production began with the introduction of radio in the early

1920s, long before many of the current Arab nations had achieved statehood. The nation's well-developed film industry and theatre tradition provided the background to launch television that other Arab countries lacked. For over half-a-century the Egyptian cinema has been very popular throughout the Arab world, and the majority of the feature-length films produced in Arabic in the region are produced in Egypt. Most of these films are dramatized, fictional films, and docu-dramas designed mainly for entertainment purposes.

In general, the content of Egyptian films is mostly non-political and tends to be light comedy or serial drama. During the past decade few directors have made socially realistic movies, since these movies traditionally have not been box-office successes either in Egypt or in the rest of the Arab world. It is important to appreciate that Egypt is the only Arab country that has been producing feature films regularly since 1930, and is the only cinema industry in the region that has reached a reasonable level of production in terms of quality and quantity. Egyptian films are not only a significant entertainment force throughout the Arab world, but they are also recognized internationally. Egypt has been exhibiting films at international film festivals since 1936. Egyptian films have a strong impact on other Arab countries and have made Egyptian artists and the Egyptian dialect of Arabic familiar to viewers throughout the Arab world, in spite of a relatively hostile confrontation between cinema and traditional Islamic culture in some countries (Amin 1990).

The Egyptian film industry played a key role in the development of television in Egypt by supplying the new television service with a large supply of popular, well-known films. Because of its thriving film industry, Egypt had the talent to start a television industry without importing engineering or production staff from other countries. This comparative advantage also enabled Egypt to produce a relatively high percentage of its own programmes—something no other Arab country was able to do (Boyd 1982). Most Arab countries depend on Egyptian films for their television broadcast schedule since they are very popular and generally have high ratings (Amin and Boyd 1993). Egyptian Television currently

Country	Hours sold
Algeria	50
Bahrain	300
Iraq	200
Jordan	300
Kuwait	400
Morocco	60
Oman	120
Qatar	500
Saudi Arabia	300
Sudan	350
Syria	200
Tunisia	260
United Arab Emirates	500
Yemen	550

sells an average of about 300 television-broadcast hours a year to each of the Arab television services (Amin 1990).

In 1959 RCA was contracted to provide Egypt with its first television service. Transmissions began in 1960 with three channels and eventually evolved into a chain of transmitters linked by microwave along the Nile, where most of the population is concentrated. The president at the time, Gamal Abdel Nasser, and his advisers were unique among Middle Eastern leaders in the early days of television because of the role they envisioned for television and because of their commitment of financial resources and personnel to attain that vision (Boyd 1982).

Egyptian Television has one channel with popular, news, developmental, and educational themes. The second channel aims at urban, sophisticated viewers and offers programmes in French, English, and German as well as foreign programming. The third channel serves Cairo only and broadcasts locally oriented programmes. Egyptian serial dramas and variety or musical serials are the most popular television programmes in Egypt and in the Arab world. Televised football matches are also very popular. However, Egyptian television news and public affairs programmes are the most common programme type on the local broadcast schedule (Amin 1990).

The 1967 war was devastating to Egypt and led to both short- and long-range changes in its television broadcasting system. The third channel was closed due to breaks in relations with the USA and UK, and was not reopened until 1985. Programming became more oriented toward the Soviet Union and Eastern Europe with new incoming aid from the Soviets. Western programmes emerged again after the 1973 war when relations were re-established with the West after President Anwar Sadat expelled Soviet advisers following a coup attempt. Colour and the SECAM system were also introduced at this time. Revenue from advertising and programme sales abroad increased substantially. Competition for studio facilities, and the desire to avoid extra fees and taxes, prompted some independent producers to leave Egypt to produce elsewhere, such as in the UK, Germany, Greece, Jordan, or Bahrain. To counter the trend, the Egyptian Radio-Television Union (ERTU) established a production company more along private lines (Boyd 1982).

After the 1979 peace treaty with Israel, Egypt's relation with other Arab countries deteriorated. The Arab League moved its headquarters from Cairo to Tunisia, and Egypt was no longer part of ARABSAT. Some Arab nations boycotted programmes produced in Egypt, but not those produced by Egyptians outside Egypt (Boyd 1982). This situation remained unchanged for nearly a decade.

Egyptian International Services: Space Net and Nile TV

Although Egypt's economy has its weaknesses, its diplomatic contacts, rich television tradition, and long-term involvement in programme exchange set the stage for the development of the Egyptian Space Channel (Space Net) when Egypt returned to the Arab League in 1988. In December 1990 ERTU signed an agreement with ARABSAT to lease bulk capacity on the direct television broadcasting transponder on ARABSAT satellite 1-A for three years, with an option for extension. This was the start of the first international television broadcasting service to the Arab world. The Egyptian Space Net started transmission immediately, with a daily average of thirteen hours of programming, including news, sports, entertainment, and religious, educational, and cultural programmes to the region and to much of Africa, Europe, and Asia.

Space Net has continued to provide a wide variety of programmes, almost all of which are produced in Egypt. The most popular are serials and Egyptian movies. However, Space Net also provides news programmes (which comprise 12 per cent of the total weekly programming and include national and international bulletins and analysis), as well as children's puppet shows and cartoons (which account for 14 per cent of the total weekly broadcast schedule). Entertainment programmes account for about 42 per cent of the total weekly broadcast schedule and include different kinds of music shows and music programmes. Religious programmes, featuring religious leaders explaining the Koran and the Sunna, make up almost 3 per cent of the weekly programming.

Commencing during the Gulf crisis, Egyptian Space Net played a significant military and public information role during the war. It delivered information to the Egyptian and Arab military forces located in Hafre El-Baten, Saudi Arabia, Kuwait, and Shargha. Egyptian programmes on Space Net were received by the armed forces' VHF transmitters, which enabled Egyptian soldiers to watch home television from ordinary receivers. Space Net programming provided the armed forces with an alternative to the Iraqi media. Before its launch, the armed forces were exposed to propaganda from the Iraqi media designed to lower their morale. Space Net broadcasts redressed the balance of the situation (Amin 1992).

Space Net is transmitted by ERTU on an ARABSAT satellite whose footprint, the area over which its signal can be received, covers the following countries: Somalia, Sudan, Djibouti, Algeria, Tunisia, Mauritania, Morocco, Libya, Syria, Jordan, Egypt, Lebanon, Palestine, Iraq, Saudi Arabia, Bahrain, United Arab Emirates, Yemen, Kuwait, Qatar, and Oman. Because the UK is outside the main footprint, National Telecommunications Ltd. (NTL), a company that pioneered techniques in fringe satellite reception, was contracted to act as the agent for ERTU in establishing the service in London. The first service began in 1994 and was expected to spread through most areas of London in a short time. There are estimated to be nearly 200,000 Arabic speaking residents in London and 2 million Arabic visitors each year.

In 1995 ERTU is to move the Space Net transmission to INTELSAT to exploit the advantages of its more powerful transponders and better coverage. Space Net also plans to broadcast African programmes, including religious programmes, to African countries in their native languages. Also, English and French news services are planned for native Europeans. Some new Arabic programmes also might be designed for the Arab nations. Special development of education and information programmes might also emerge. As always, the official goals of this expansion are to project Egypt and its perspective on international issues, as well as promoting tourism.

Another Egyptian international satellite service, this time directed at Europe and North Africa, is Nile TV. It began broadcasting in October 1993 from the European satellite EUTELSAT II, and broadcasts mainly in English and French, with Russian added in 1995. Nile TV's main objectives are to promote the image of Egypt in Europe and to attract tourists. The content of the channel is mainly news and public affairs, tourist programmes, documentaries, and historical, cultural, and music programmes (ERTU 1994).

Saudi Arabia

Television broadcasting started in Saudi Arabia in 1965, but unofficial broadcast services were initiated in 1955. EGLTV went on the air in Dhahran, the eastern province of Saudi Arabia, and was operated by the US Air Force. A second station started in Dhahran in 1957, while another broadcast from the ARAMCO compound served the employees of American companies. Saudi Arabia initially operated two national television channels. Colour television made its entry to Saudi Arabia in 1976. Television programming is similar to radio in the sense that Saudi Arabia is the heart of the Islamic world;

therefore, religious programming has a special importance in Saudi television (Amin 1995: 15). Despite this, conservative religious groups such as Ulama have always been opposed to television. In the spring of 1994 pressure from religious groups finally led to the banning of satellite dishes in Saudi Arabia.

The Middle East Broadcasting Centre (MBC)

After two years of concentrated efforts, the Middle East Broadcasting Centre (MBC) launched the first privately owned Arabic-language satellite television station in September 1991. The aim of the service presented by MBC was to provide a communication channel linking Arabs who live, work, or visit in Europe with their homelands and cultures. However, the service was also extended to the Arabic-speaking countries from North Africa to the Arabian Gulf. MBC is a news-led service but also offers broadly based family entertainment and a wide range of life-style and informational programmes (Middle East Broadcasting Centre 1991). MBC has reflected a growing push by the Saudi regime to spread its views throughout the region. Abdullah El Masry, executive director of MBC's Board, stated 'Through MBC we hope to prepare the air for reconciliation in the Mideast, to be a bridge of understanding.' Reflecting the liberal, internationalist ethos of the channel, MBC deputy chief executive officer Robert D. Kennedy added: 'If our presenters covered their heads we'd be like everyone else. That's exactly how we don't want to be' (Waldman 1992).

MBC aspires to become an Arab version of the major American networks. MBC head of news Steven Maney has stated that MBC's owners directed him to produce 'CNN in Arabic' (Middle East Broadcasting Centre 1991). MBC also became the first Arab telecommunications company to open a correspondent office in Jerusalem: 'Israel is there, and we have to deal with it', said Walid Ibrahim, one of MBC's owners (Ibrahim 1992). MBC is owned by a range of Arab investors. Most of its capital comes from Salah Kamel, a prominent Saudi banker, and Walid Ibrahim, a brother-in-law of King Fahd of Saudi Arabia, through their company, World Space Corporation, based in Washington DC (Middle East Broadcasting Centre 1992). After investing in this company, they were granted permission by the US Federal Communications Commission to launch a satellite transmitting to the Middle East and Africa. MBC started with a working capital of $US300 million and a $US60 million annual budget (Marlow 1992).

MBC is also partially funded by advertising, which provides a valuable new means of communication for advertisers wishing to reach an Arabic audience in a number of markets. MBC has appointed Jeddah-based advertising representatives Tihama to sell advertising time. To support the launch, a major marketing and advertising campaign included press, television, and radio advertising, public relations and television materials in Arabic and English, and an extensive contract providing satellite feeds for apartment blocks.

MBC started broadcasting across Europe and North Africa via EUTELSAT II and across the Middle East through ARABSAT. MBC's transmissions are uplinked from its studios to EUTELSAT for European direct-to-home and cable coverage through British Telecommunication International's Docklands teleport. MBC studios are equipped with high-quality layout and production equipment. As a UK broadcaster, MBC is licensed by the Independent Television Commission (ITC). Coverage extends from Scandinavia to North Africa and from Ireland to Eastern Europe, reaching all major population centres of Europe as well as all of North Africa and the Middle East (Middle East Broadcasting Centre 1992).

The professional presentation of a broad mixture of programmes has very quickly earned MBC a large and loyal audience. In contrast to state-run television, production is high quality and meets high international standards. MBC provides family-oriented programming, including films, children's programmes, drama, and music as well as daily feature programmes, international news, sports, and current affairs. MBC transmission begins daily at 1400 GMT with a reading from the Koran followed by children's programmes. The latter are a mixture of cartoon adventure series and educational programmes. Adult programmes are broadcast in the late afternoon. These include documentaries with an emphasis on Islamic culture and art as well as sports and science programmes and a daily drama series.

The main thirty-minute news programme is transmitted at 1800 GMT followed by the evening feature film, usually from one of the major Middle Eastern studios or the West, mainly Hollywood. In the early evening magazine programmes from the London studios are shown, covering topics such as travel, pop music, fashion, business, and sport. A special medical programme reports on the latest developments in health-care, medicine, and the advances taking place internationally in the fields of medical technology and surgical practice. There is a daily programme that reviews the world press, highlighting the principal events of the day as seen by commentators around the globe, and a regular look at historical events and their relevance to today's world. Current affairs programming, including political debates and exclusive interviews with heads of Arabic states, are also featured. There is also a programme that reviews the latest cinema news weekly for both Arabic and non-Arabic productions, keeping viewers abreast of developments on the international film scene, a weekly fashion show reporting on the latest trends and collections worldwide, and a travel programme (Middle East Broadcasting Centre 1992). At 2100 GMT evening programming continues with more drama before the late-night segment, that includes variety shows, plays, interviews, and concerts by top Arab stars, followed by the late news and another reading from the Koran.

MBC's potential audience includes an estimated 5 million Arabic-speaking viewers across Europe and over 100 million viewers in the Arab countries. In the first month of transmission the station had in excess of 250,000 viewers able to receive the service. In addition, some of MBC's programmes are to re-broadcast on terrestrial transmitters in the Middle East, expanding the opportunity to view MBC's services (Middle East Broadcasting Centre 1992). MBC's plans for expansion include a movie channel, a family entertainment and educational channel, and a general entertainment channel; a sports channel and a news channel are also under consideration.

Other Saudi International Services: ART, Orbit, and Saudi National Television

In early 1994 the Arab region witnessed a new trend toward specialization in television broadcasting with the establishment of Arab Radio and Television (ART). ART is headed by entrepreneur and international businessman Sheikh Salah Kamel, a media tycoon who also was a key player in establishing MBC's network and later decided to develop his own satellite television service. The network is composed of channels for children, movies, sports, and variety. Each ART channel, except the children's channel, broadcasts twenty-four hours a day. ART's production headquarters is in Cairo, with subsidiary headquarters in Riyadh, Tunis, Kuwait, and Oman. Contacts are being made with other Arab countries, including Qatar. ART transmission covers all parts of the Arab world.

In May 1994 Orbit began its international satellite television service to the Middle East. Headed by Prince Khaled bin Abdel Rahman Al Saud, a well-known figure in the Saudi business world, Orbit's package consists of sixteen television channels and four radio networks. The television channels are Egyptian Television Channel 1, Egyptian Television Channel 2, an all-news network channel, Cable News Network International (CNNI), BBC Television's Arabic Service, the Fun Channel, ESPN-Orbit Channel, the Hollywood Channel, the Discovery Channel, America Plus C-Span, Music Now, the Super movies channel, Orbit 1 (Arabic movies), Orbit 2 (a variety channel), and Orbit news, which contains news and news programmes from ABC, NBC, CBS, and WSJ. Orbit is an encrypted pay satellite service on ARABSAT, and the price of the decoder is very high, at $US10,000. Saudi Arabia's national television channels are on ARABSAT as well. The first channel is primarily in Arabic and is the most conservative Arabic channel in terms of religion. The second channel has a programme broadcast mainly in English to serve foreign expatriates.

Kuwait

Television started in Kuwait informally at the end of the 1950s when RCA television started a low-power station in Kuwait City to promote the sale of television receivers. After Kuwait gained independence in 1961 the Kuwaiti Ministry of Information took control over the system and changed it to European standards. The Kuwaiti television system was advanced and developed strongly after the 1973 war because of the increase in oil revenues. Colour television began in 1974. Television in Kuwait consists of two channels and programming is a mixture of news and entertainment (Amin 1995: 16).

Kuwait's Space Network

In the wake of the Gulf War, Kuwait found it necessary to establish its own network despite the damage that had occurred to the Kuwaiti television studios. There were incentives that encouraged the Kuwaiti Ministry of Information to establish the Kuwaiti Space Network. After the invasion of Kuwait in August 1990, Kuwait realized the importance of communication and wanted to take its place in the new era of global communication. The Kuwaiti minister of information at that time, Badr Jassem El Yacoub, announced the inauguration of the Kuwait Space Network in July 1992. He stated that the network would transmit contemporary images of Kuwaiti life, its civilization, science, culture, and politics. In addition, it would provide the country with a means of projecting its perspectives to the world (KUNA 1992). The network is owned and operated by the Kuwaiti Emirate and affiliated with the Ministry of Information. The network is staffed by only fifteen persons, representing producers, anchors, engineers, technicians, and an executive director. All staff members are Kuwaiti citizens, as per the policy of the network.

Experimental transmissions by the Kuwaiti Space Network began in December 1991 in the wake of the war. Official transmission began in July 1992. Because it transmits solely on a low-power C band ARABSAT transponder, Kuwait's coverage area is limited to the Middle East, Southern Europe, and East Asia. Kuwait is trying to solve the problem of increasing the power and coverage area, so that its transmission can reach countries in Western Europe.

In the preliminary stage, the network is directing its transmission internationally. The local Kuwaiti audience will not be able to receive the transmission until a third channel is provided. The Ministry of Information has begun making contracts with hotels, shopping centres, and tourist locations to subscribe to the channel. The programmes presented through the network are targeted to convey uplifting images of Kuwait and to emphasize the plight of the Kuwaiti prisoners of war. This policy is different from the Egyptian Space Net, where programming is based on a fairly broad selection of programmes from domestic channels one and two.

Development of International Television in Other Arab States

Television started in Jordan in 1968 with a broadcast schedule of three hours on one channel. Another channel was introduced in 1970 carrying mainly foreign programmes, and colour television was introduced in 1974. Most programme formats are adapted from Western television (Amin 1995: 14). The Jordanian Radio and Television Corporation started broadcasting the Jordanian Arab Space Channel in February 1993 utilizing ARABSAT 1-C, covering most of the Arab world and parts of Europe. Future expansion of the Jordanian Arab Space Channel included transmitting its service to Europe, Canada, and the USA.

Programmes on the Jordanian Arab Space Channel cover a wide range. However, political programmes emphasizing the democratic process, confirming Arab human rights, calling for Arab unity, as well as stressing the effective role played by the Hashemite Jordanian kingdom in Arab political life are very much to the fore. Programmes on economics stress the recent developments in the fields of agriculture, trade, industry, and banking in both private and public sectors, as well as investment opportunities in Jordan. Other areas, such as children's, cultural, religious, and news and public affairs programmes, are included in the broadcast schedule.

In Morocco, RTM-TV, which made its entry in March 1962, is the main channel. In 1989 the first private television station, 2M International, was introduced. The national service was put on ARABSAT to transmit its programmes in 1992. Algerian television started in 1956. At first, Algeria relied heavily on transmissions from Europe, mainly from France. After the revolution the Algerian government started 'Arabizing' the television service. Radio and Television in Algiers (RTA) telecasts on one channel through microwave links and via satellite distribution through INTELSAT. Tunisia inaugurated its own international television network, TV7, in November 1992 on EUTELSAT. The coverage area includes all the European and west Asian countries as well as North Africa. The main objective for launching the service was to develop bridges and to improve communication between Tunisian expatriate labour in Europe and the Arab states and the home country.

Television transmission started in Abu Dhabi, one of the United Arab Emirates, in 1969. By the late 1980s the UAE added a second national television channel. The main channel, Abu Dhabi 5, also operates on ARABSAT 1-C with much of its broadcast dedicated to religious materials, such as a variety of programmes dealing with the Koran and the Prophet's sayings. Television broadcasting started in Dubai, the second of the United Arab Emirates, in August 1969 prior to the formation of the United Arab Emirates federation. After the formation of the UAE, Dubai's system became the national television channel owned and operated by the federal government. By the mid-1980s the UAE added a second national television channel heavily dependent on English programmes. Dubai has played a very important role in the UAE in terms of broadcasting services. The two colour television services that are a mix of Arabic and English are very popular (Amin 1995).

The Space Network of Dubai is part of the ARABSAT system. It began operation in October 1992 and covers all of the Arab region, southern Europe, Turkey, Pakistan, India,

Africa, and the Islamic republics of the Commonwealth of Independent States (CIS), nearly a third of the world. Its main programmes consist of news services (six news bulletins in Arabic, four news bulletins in English), cultural, documentary, and variety programmes, and drama (Arabic and English films and episodes), as well as social programmes. The Space Network of Dubai broadcasts around the clock, twenty-four hours a day. At the conclusion of the broadcast period of Dubai's general television channel, viewers are automatically connected to the space network, enabling them to access the network without a satellite dish (Space Network of Dubai 1992).

Lebanese television started in May 1959; a second commercial channel was introduced in 1962. Tele-Orient was the first television station and was jointly owned by a Lebanese interest group and by the American Broadcasting Company (ABC), which later sold its share to the British Thompson Corporation. Unofficial television broadcasting started during the Lebanese civil war. Since the war more than forty private television stations have begun operating in Lebanon. An owner of one of the most popular private stations, Mr Rafik El Hariri, Lebanese prime minister and a media entrepreneur, started an international television service called Future. The channel provided a mix of Western and foreign programming from the USA, Europe, and Egypt and was extremely popular in the region, especially in Saudi Arabia. This channel was eliminated by the Lebanese Cabinet in February 1994 during an effort to reorganize the radio and television industry (Amin 1995: 19). Finally, the small nations—the Sultanate of Oman, Bahrain, and Qatar—have each put their national services on ARABSAT, thus complementing the larger nations' offerings across the Arab world.

Issues for Arab International Television Services

Satellite channels are the newest media wave to hit Arab countries. The spread of channels and dishes does not mean that the development of 'global' television is proceeding smoothly in the Arab world. Many problems have developed in the area, including religious constraints, censorship, and the problems of cultural invasion and cultural imperialism.

Many voices, especially those of conservative religious groups, are opposed to international television and have put a great deal of pressure on different Arab countries to eliminate the spread of satellite dishes. Religious groups in Saudi Arabia and other areas of the Gulf have described satellite dishes as a means of cultural penetration and invasion. Most of the programming available from satellite services contains material that is not acceptable in Islamic societies. Sex, nudity, obscenity, and violence are considered offensive by Islamic leaders. In 1994 Saudi Arabia and Iran banned the importation of satellite dishes. In Egypt, the governor of Damietta and Dakhahlia banned public viewing of satellite channels in coffee shops. Resentment against satellite broadcasting from a religious point of view is spreading throughout Arab countries. Algeria is leading North African countries in a movement to control or ban the reception of satellite broadcasts.

Satellite services have made issues of globalization, privatization, democratization, access to information, and freedom of the press increasingly topics of concern throughout the world. The attractiveness and popularity of these services in the Arab world have created a major dilemma for Arab leaders as they struggle to balance media development with issues of culture, religion, politics, and their traditional desire to control the flow of information in their countries. Table 4.2 shows both the similarities and differences in the types of programmes carried by the international services discussed in this chapter.

The Arab world is divided into two camps in a debate on whether or not satellite services are instruments used to invade Arabic culture, traditions, and customs. The first camp is very sensitive about stereotyping and accuses satellite services of attempting to change the lifestyle of the Arab family and the education and manners of Arab children. This group also argues that the satellite services promote intracultural intrusion among the Arab states. Although it appears that Arabs share a common language, culture, religion, and geographical borders, there are many cultural differences and diverse political

Table 4.2. Programming on Arab international television networks (%)

Channels *Programs*	*Egyptian Network* %	*Dubai Network* %	*MBC Network* %	*Oman Network* %	*Moroccan Network* %	*Tunisian Network* %	*Jordanian Network* %	*Kuwaiti Network* %
Religious	2	3	6	8	3	5	3	13
Children's	10	3	7	11	12	10	7	5
Scientific	7	14	11	16	14	12	9	13
Economic	14	8	14	16	14	15	10	10
Art	3	1	3	—	5	6	1	2
Sports	1	14	4	6	8	11	2	4
Variety	18	10	11	7	12	13	15	20
Education	—	—	—	3	1	—	—	1
Arabic Soap Operas/ Movies	16	26	3	8	10	6	10	4
Foreign Soap Operas	—	6	3	8	8	2	—	4
Information	14	8	19	4	3	5	21	9
Social	5	—	—	1	4	8	5	5
Audience Request	1	—	3	8	—	—	2	4
Night Programmes	4	—	6	2	—	1	2	—
Others	5	7	10	2	6	6	13	6
Total	100	100	100	100	100	100	100	100

Source: *Satellite Guide*, No. 107, 23 September, 1995, 30–55

ideologies. The second camp claims that satellite services are essential to project Arab culture internationally, promote a sense of unity across the many nations of the region, and serve the widespread Arab diaspora.

Most governments in the Arab world are considering implementing a multichannel multipoint distribution system (MMDS) which will allow them to address many of these issues. MMDS systems will allow governments to offer access to what they think is acceptable to the Arab people and to filter out most of the material that is considered offensive to Arab citizens, as well as to censor programmes that are objectionable to Arab governments.

Conclusion

The use of satellite for direct broadcast television is very recent in the Arab world. The ARABSAT system was significantly under-subscribed until the beginning of the 1990s. Transborder television broadcasting creates a new situation in the Arab world. Many people living in the Middle East region have access to other Arab international television networks without any kind of control, censorship, and/or government approval of the content. Although it is still too early to assess the broad impact of direct-to-home satellite services, it seems that it already constitutes the third wave of television after the introduction of terrestrial television and the spread of home videocassette recorders. Inter-Arab conflicts and differences do not seem to have affected the flow of television programmes through international television networks. On the other hand, since most Arab television services are owned and operated by Arab governments, the misuse of the medium during times of conflict between Arab states may affect message content and create a form of communication war. On balance, however, international television networks offer great opportunities for political, economic, social, and cultural development in the Arab region.

Egypt and the Arab World

References

ABU-ARGOUB, I. A. (1988), 'Historical, Political and Technical Development of ARABSAT', unpublished doctoral dissertation, Northwestern University, Illinois.

AL NICK, JOHN J. (1983), *Communication Policy and the Political Process* (Greenwood Press, London).

AL-SAADON, H. T. (1990), 'The Role of ARABSAT in Television Program Exchange in the Arab World', unpublished doctoral dissertation, Ohio State University.

AMIN, HUSSEIN Y. (1990), 'Maximum Utilization of Egyptian Television Studios and its Impact on Sales', *Scientific Journal of Communication Research*, 3/6: 18–39.

—— (1992), 'The Development of Space Net and its Impact', in Ray E. Weisenborn (ed.), *Media in the Midst of War: The Gulf War from Cairo to the Global Village* (The Adham Center Press, Cairo).

—— (1995), 'Broadcasting in the Arab World and the Middle East', in Alan Wells (ed.), *World Broadcasting: A Comparative View* (Ablex, Norwood NJ).

—— and BOYD, DOUGLAS A. (1993), 'The Impact of Home Video Cassette Recorders on Egyptian Film and Television Consumption Patterns', *European Journal of Communication*, 18: 2–7.

BOYD, DOUGLAS (1982), *Broadcasting in the Arab World* (Temple University Press, Philadelphia).

ERTU (Egyptian Radio and Television Union) (1994), Document, Ministry of Information Files, Cairo.

IBRAHIM, YOUSSEF M. (1992), 'Arab World Tunes into Westernized TV Channels', New York Times Service, Office of the Washington Post, Cairo.

KUNA (Kuwaiti News Agency) (1992), interview with Jassem El Yacoub.

LABIB, SAAD, KANDIL, HAMDI, and BAKER, YEHIA ABU (1983), *Development of Communication in the Arab States: Needs and Priorities*, UNESCO Publication no. 95 (Paris).

MARLOW, LARA (1992), 'The New Saudi Press Barons', *Time* (22 June).

Middle East Broadcasting Centre (1991), document, London.

—— (1992), document, London.

Space Network of Dubai (1992), *The Collective Channel of the ARABSAT and its Uses* (Dubai).

RUGH, WILLIAM A. (1979), *The Arab Press: New Media and Political Process in the Arab World* (Syracuse University Press, Syracuse).

TURKISTANI, A. S. (1988), 'News Exchange via Arabsat and News Values of Arab Television People', unpublished doctoral dissertation, Indiana State University.

WALDMAN, PETER (1992), 'Anchorwomen Don't Cover Heads when Complaints Fly', *Wall Street Journal* (21 Feb.).

5

Television in Greater China: Structure, Exports, and Market Formation

Joseph Man Chan

The term 'Greater China' has been gaining currency in scholarship and popular publications in the 1990s. In spite of its growing popularity, there is a lack of consensus as to what it represents. Harding (1993) has identified three dimensions by which Greater China is conceptualized. First, it denotes the economic integration between China, Hong Kong, and Taiwan. Secondly, it refers to the cultural exchanges amongst people of Chinese descent around the world. Thirdly, it refers to the possible re-establishment of a single Chinese state, reuniting the now politically fragmented territories. Each of the three themes—economic integration, cultural interaction, and political reunification—has different boundaries, different capitals or centres of activity, and takes different institutional forms. This article regards Greater China as the economic, political, and cultural space defined by the interactions between its three primary constituent parts—Hong Kong, Taiwan, and the People's Republic or mainland China. The analysis of television in Greater China inevitably criss-crosses from one realm to another as television is dualistic in nature, possessing the properties of both commodity and culture, within a political context.

Each of the three Chinese societies represents a different approach to television development, ranging from cultural *laissez-faire* in Hong Kong, some cultural protectionism in Taiwan, to virtual antiforeignism in China until very recent years. Interactions between the television system of China and those in Hong Kong and Taiwan were non-existent before the mid-1980s. It is against this backdrop that this chapter seeks: (1) to examine the structural characteristics of these three television systems; (2) to focus on how each fares in exporting its programmes; (3) to analyse the primary factors of the emergent Greater China television market; and (4) to discuss the implications of the findings in light of the basic tenets of media imperialism.

Structure of Television Systems

The television system of the three constituent parts of Greater China is as different as their political configuration. Hong Kong is a British colony preparing to be returned to China in 1997. Taiwan is a new democracy, ruled by the Kuomingtang Party (KMT) which has been the political rival of the Chinese Communist Party (CCP) for the last seventy years. Mainland China is a socialist nation that is trying to modernize itself through economic reforms and an open-door policy. This diversity of political systems is mirrored in the regulation and structure of their television industries.

Hong Kong: Oligopoly and Cultural *Laissez-Faire*

Hong Kong, with a population of about 6 million, is a colonial administrative city state that has transformed itself from a fishing village into a metropolitan centre that boasts a per capita income of about $US18,500 in 1994 ('The Bottom Line' 1994). The increasing affluence in Hong Kong since the mid-1970s has sustained an average growth rate of about 25 per cent for the advertising industry, upon which the mass media thrive (Chan and Lee 1992). Television is the most important advertising medium, registering about 50 per cent of the total advertising revenue in the early 1990s.

Television in Hong Kong operates primarily within a market structure whose parameters are set by the government regulators. Hierarchically, the governor and his Executive Council make final decisions over the regulation and licensing of television and radio. They in turn are advised by a public statutory body formed in 1987, the Broadcasting Authority, which receives help and administrative support from the government's Economic Branch and the Culture and Recreation Branch.

Unlike regulatory regimes in many other parts of the world, the licensing conditions under which broadcast television was introduced to Hong Kong did not impose minimum requirements for the inclusion of local content. On the contrary, during the 1970s, Chinese language channels were required to carry a minimum of imported programming, in particular from Britain, the country which has long held sovereignty over Hong Kong (K. C. Chan 1990). This colonial practice was repealed in 1980.

While the government has set some limits on the publication of pornographic and politically sensitive materials, in practice its interference in media content is minimal. Without an explicit and elaborate cultural policy, Hong Kong is virtually a free port in information as there is no strict control over the flow of media in and out of Hong Kong. Consequently, Hong Kong television has to face competition from the world.

Internally, Hong Kong television is essentially a commercial system that has two private free-to-air terrestrial stations (TVB and ATV), a quasi-public channel that broadcasts its programmes over time slots on the commercial channels (RTHK), a pan-Asian satellite television broadcaster (STAR TV), and a subscription television service (Wharf Cable). At the time of writing (late 1994) what is socially significant are the Chinese channels of TVB and ATV, because they are watched by an overwhelming majority of the population. They also have English channels, but they are not popular, as less than 9 per cent of the population can effectively understand the language. Neither satellite television nor microwave subscription television is any match for terrestrial broadcast television in capturing audiences. STAR TV has a relatively weak position, due to the fact that it has only successfully penetrated a quarter of the households and that it is broadcast in English or Mandarin—languages alien to most of the Hong Kong population, who speak Cantonese. Local productions aired by broadcast television are more appealing to this audience. Wharf Cable, started in late 1993, still needs time to build itself up. Consequently, the television scene in Hong Kong remains dominated by the terrestrial broadcasters.

Broadcast television is an important institution in Hong Kong. In 1990 it took up 4.2 hours of people's daily activities on average (TELA 1990). From 1976 to 1992 the penetration rate of households with television grew to 98 per cent, with 26 per cent owning more than one set (K. C. Chan 1993). Closely related to television consumption has been the use of video-cassette recorders. The penetration rate of VCRs rapidly increased from 11 per cent in 1985 to 70 per cent in 1992. Many people use their VCR for viewing rented videotapes or for its time-shifting function (Chan and Lee 1992).

Like the USA, Hong Kong's television broadcasters have been suffering a gradual decline in weekday prime time ratings since the mid-1980s, registering a loss of a quarter of its audience for drama serials in the case of TVB (K. C. Chan 1990). This can be attributed to changes in the ways the population spend their leisure hours. Watching movies on video is generally regarded to be influential in this regard.

The free-to-air broadcasters have relied on in-house production for their Chinese programming. The licensing conditions require that they invest to make sure that they have enough studios and that they are well-equipped. Each station keeps its array of artists on regular as well as on contract bases. They run schemes to train artists and production personnel. The quasi-public channel RTHK uses much more in-house production than would the BBC. The English channels of TVB and ATV, on the contrary, base most of their programming on material imported from the West. So far, STAR TV has produced very few programmes on its own. What it carries are mostly programmes acquired internationally. For instance, its Mandarin channel features programmes from Hong Kong, Taiwan, China, Japan, and other places. Wharf Cable also acquires international programmes but it plans to depend on independent producers for local productions. Given the growing demand for programmes to feed the cable channels, the independent production industry is likely to flourish.

The free-to-air broadcasters have played an instrumental role in bringing about the development of popular music and movies. Thanks to effective promotion on broadcast television, Cantonese songs rose in tandem with television to dominate the local popular music scene. Television has had an impact on the revitalization of the local movie industry since the late 1970s, and stimulated export production to Taiwan, Japan, Korea, South-East Asia, and other parts of the world. This means that there is a rich stock of television programmes and movies which provide alternative choices to foreign productions in the video rental market in Hong Kong, and also compete elsewhere.

For decades Hong Kong has been known as a regional centre for film production. In the 1950s and 1960s, prior to the establishment of broadcast television, Hong Kong was an notable exporter of movies to Taiwan and South-East Asia (Leung 1992). The prior existence of the film-export trade served the emergent television industry in some important ways. First, it helped to maintain the cultural identity of overseas Chinese, and by cultivating their habit of watching movies from Hong Kong made them culturally more receptive to Hong Kong television programmes when they began to be exported in the 1970s. However, because of the essential difference between film and television distribution channels, television exports did not benefit in a direct manner from the distribution infrastructure developed by film. Secondly, the popularization of kung-fu movies with the rise of Bruce Lee and other stars in the 1970s paved the way for further commercialization of this traditional genre, and the subsequent proliferation of kung-fu television programmes throughout the world. Thirdly, the film industry also contributed by providing television with a large stock of movies with which to fill its airtime in the late hours.

On the other hand, when television was introduced to Hong Kong, it was a complete new medium fostered by younger entrepreneurs educated in the West, and inspired by their Western counterparts. Only a few were veterans of the film industry. In addition, the subsequent interaction between the film and television industries was marked by competition, with television drawing away audiences from the cinemas. A new equilibrium was reached only after an initial decline in the film industry, and a rejuvenation brought about by an input of television expertise. Television became a training ground for producers, directors, actors, and other creative and technical personnel, who characteristically would leave for film once they had gained experience and made a name for themselves.

Taiwan: Oligopoly and Limited Cultural Protectionism

Taiwan has a population of about 22 million, with a per capita income of $US10,215 in 1994 ('The Bottom Line' 1994). It has a long history of authoritarian rule which has become more liberalized since 1987. Even so, the ruling party, the KMT, still maintains heavy control in many realms, including broadcast television.

There are three terrestrial broadcasters in Taiwan, namely, Taiwan Television Enterprise (TTV), China Television Company (CTV), and Chinese Television Service (CTS) which began operation in 1962, 1969, and 1971 respectively. TTV is owned primarily by the provincial government of Taiwan, CTV by the KMT, and CTS by the Ministry of National Defence (Wang 1993). Control goes with ownership: the board directors and managers of each station have been dominated by people who are closely affiliated with the KMT, the government, and the military. Although these free-to-air broadcasters are owned and controlled by the state, they are run as profitable enterprises, resulting in a commercial model that appeared to have grown out of the government–business alliance and the reality of oligopolistic competition (Lee 1980).

Having no independent channel of its own and a very limited budget, public broadcasting in Taiwan has been insignificant in the past (Fang 1993*a*). Since 1974 each of the three broadcasters are required to carry programmes made by public television during certain time slots. The programmes are either imported or commissioned by the Public Television Production Group established by the Government Information Office (Ho 1990). It is planned to expand public television into a full-blown service in 1994.

In addition to the three channels mentioned above, there was a 'fourth channel', an illegal operation comprising numerous rudimentary cable networks (Weng 1993). In 1992 it was estimated that there were as many as 500 such cable operators, capturing 500,000 subscription households. While the programming for individual networks might vary, they carried mainly television programmes and movies that were pirated or acquired from suppliers and satellite television. According to one report, the majority of programmes on the fourth channel were foreign made (Wang and Chung 1988). In 1993 the fourth channel was transformed into formal cable networks with the passing of the Cable Television Ordinance. While cable television is also under the jurisdiction of the Executive Yuan's Government Information Office, it has set up a Cable Television Examination Committee, manned by officials, experts, and social celebrities to supervise licensing and assessment (Chung 1993).

Prior to 1976 Taiwanese television was controlled not by law but by the state's administrative rules (Wang 1993). The government unit that was responsible for managing television had shifted from department to department. With news, the control rested in the hands of the KMT's Cultural Work Association which implemented the policy made by the Party's Central Committee. The Government Information Office at the Executive Yuan has been the state organ that legally makes and implements the policy since 1973. The spirit of the aforementioned administrative controls were formalized in 1976 to make up the Statute for Radio and Television Broadcasting. This ordinance bestows upon television the obligation to publicize national policies and administrative orders and to perform other functions for the government (Lin and Liu 1993). It also empowers the government with the authority to decide when the media have violated the law, and to specify the penalty. With the exception of news, television programmes have to be censored by the Government Information Office if they are so required.

The Statute categorizes programmes into five major types. These are news, administrative orders, education and culture, public service, and entertainment. Each type is required to fill a specified proportion of broadcasting time (Lin and Liu 1993). News, administrative orders, and public service have to make up no less than 50 per cent. More than 70 per cent of the programmes have to be local productions. With cable television, the minimum proportion of local productions will be raised from 20 per cent to 25 per cent after the first three years of operation (Fang 1993*b*). There are further restrictions on programmes imported from Japan, Hong Kong, and mainland China. All imports and exports have to receive permits from the Government Information Office.

Foreign programmes usually make up less than 20 per cent of Taiwan's television programming (Cheng 1988). The local programmes are either self-produced or produced by production houses. For instance, the sources of TTV's programmes in 1989 were: 15 per cent foreign, 31 per cent self-produced, 6 per cent commissioned, and 48 per cent produced by independent production houses (Li 1984; Kuo 1992). The production houses are also responsible for soliciting advertising. In programme commissioning, the broadcasters have some control over programme quality, weak as it often is, whereas broadcasters are just paid for the airtime when the programmes are produced by production houses. That explains why there were more than a thousand operations that engaged in programme production and television advertising in the late 1970s (*Almanac of the Republic of China* 1980).

China: State Monopoly and Cultural Antiforeignism

Chinese television achieved its greatest growth since the reform years in the 1980s. By 1992 China had a total of 676 stations, forming a four-level network, with one national broadcaster, 30 provincial stations, 295 municipal, and 350 prefectural ('China Becomes a TV Giant' 1992). About 80 per cent of China's 1.3 billion population was covered by television broadcasting in the early 1990s (Ai 1991). In 1992 there was one television set for every five people, and a prime time audience of about 850 million people, or 75 per cent of the population. It is estimated that about one-third of the prime time audience are from the urban area and the rest from the rural community, but in a society where the ratio of urban to rural dwellers is 1 : 4, this means that about 90 per cent of city dwellers are in the prime time audience, but only half of the rural dwellers (Hong 1993). The fact that the majority of the audience is rural has an implication for television production. Television stations at the national and provincial level have to ensure that the rural population is not ignored in their news and regular programming. That explains why Chinese television quite often features drama serials with a rural setting.

Regarded as one of the most powerful means of educating and reaching the public, television is all state-owned and Party-controlled in China. Television is controlled by two agencies at the national level: the CCP's Propaganda Department and the Ministry of Film, Radio, and Television. The former is in turn subject to the heavy influence of the ideological group of the CCP's Politburo and is responsible for setting ideological and propaganda themes in programmes, whereas the latter deals with regulatory, technological, and administrative affairs (Hong 1993). These two agencies have their counterparts to take charge of television at the provincial, municipal, and sometimes county levels.

Communist China has a tendency towards cultural anti-foreignism which has only been tamed in the last decade (Liao 1990). Prior to the reforms, the only foreign programmes that were broadcast were imported from other socialist nations. Now stations are allowed to broadcast programmes originating from Hong Kong, Taiwan, the USA, and other parts of the world, provided that they get political clearance from the Ministry of Film, Radio, and Television (J. Chan 1994*a*).

As television stations are classified by the four administrative levels mentioned and virtually no two television stations are allowed to compete head-on at the same level and with the same target groups, competition has been reduced and brought under control. At the provincial level more than one station may exist. But then they would have to have a co-ordinated division of labour, obliging them to differentiate their programming to meet varying target audiences. In general, the higher the status of the station, the more heterogeneous is its target audience. China Central Television (CCTV), for instance, has to cater to the needs of the huge national audience. In contrast, cable television, regarded as a local medium, serves a much more homogeneous community.

Cable television in China ranges from community antenna networks and residential networks run by large factories or units, to formal networks. By mid-1993 China had a total of about 2,000 cable operators, the majority of which are unit-run, commanding a penetration of about 20 million households (Liu 1993). Required to carry the signals of national television (CCTV) and other local wireless broadcasters, Chinese cable television services are forbidden to relay foreign satellite programmes, including those from Hong Kong, Taiwan, and Macao. All foreign programmes have to be politically cleared by the Ministry of Film, Radio, and Television and imported through the Chinese International Television Service Company. To protect domestic production, cable operation has to limit its foreign programming to less than 30 per cent.

To a large extent, television production in China is planned by guidelines and quotas set by the relevant authority at the central, provincial, municipal, and county levels. First of all, television programmes have to fulfil their ideological functions which often vary with the CCP's specific policy in a given period. The television stations behave more like state institutions than enterprises, although commercial considerations are becoming more important and their autonomy is increasing.

Traditionally financed by the state, television stations have diversified their revenue sources to include advertising, programme sponsorship, and other non-broadcasting businesses during the reform period (J. Chan 1993). Commercialization has given some autonomy to the stations at the operational level, introduced some competition to the television system, and rendered the stations more responsive. Television programmes produced in recent years are more attractive to viewers. In fact China has produced some drama serials that can rival foreign programmes in appeal. Despite this change, it should be stressed that television in Chinese remains a political mouthpiece of the CCP.

Being state-owned, television stations are used to sharing

what they produce. Provincial stations form an exchange system which facilitates a barter trade among the stations. If a station does not have tradable programmes, it can buy programmes from other stations for minimal fees. CCTV, by virtue of its national coverage and high organizational status, can request shows from other stations for no cost. This was particularly true before the mid-1980s when profit-seeking was less widespread. But now that television stations are required to be more independent financially, there is growing pressure to turn the exchange system into a market-place where one station can charge another according to market price.

Chinese television derives its programming from in-house productions, commissioned productions, coproductions with Chinese or foreign partners, and programmes acquired domestically or internationally. In recent years major stations have been building studios and setting up production centres for turning out programmes on a large scale. Another trend is for the movie studios to exploit their underutilized facilities to produce for television. More than twenty movie studios in such centres as Beijing, Shanghai, Sian, and Pearl River have set up television departments (Ching 1992). While private or collectively owned audiovisual production houses have been formed to produce soap operas, coproductions among television stations are on the increase.

It would be wrong to assume that Communist China's antiforeign tradition and state monopoly have successfully blocked out the influence of foreign media culture. As borne out in the next section, China's cultural protectionism is cracking as foreign programmes proliferate through satellite transmission, signal spillover, piracy, and formal trade.

Programme Exports

Given the diverse broadcasting policies in the constituent parts of Greater China, it is interesting to examine how each fares in its programme exports. As will be seen in this section, Hong Kong turns out to be the television producer for the region, in line with its free-flow policy. By contrast, cultural antiforeignism in China has not enabled its television industry to compete effectively with its counterparts in Hong Kong and Taiwan.

In addition to the immediate region, Chinese people all over the world constitute a potential market for television programmes that are made in any of the constituent nations of Greater China. The total market can be subdivided as shown in Table 5.1. The regional and national markets need to be evaluated in terms of distribution, purchasing power, and access to television as well as size. Thus, the largest single market is mainland China, followed by Taiwan in terms of population size. Taiwan is also one of the more affluent markets, along with Hong Kong, Singapore, and the various

Table 5.1. World distribution of Chinese population

Location	*Population of Chinese descent (millions)*
Mainland China	1,200.0
Taiwan	22.0
Hong Kong	6.0
Greater China subtotal	1,228.0
Thailand	6.0
Burma	1.5
Singapore	2.1
Malaysia	5.3
Indonesia	7.3
Philippines	0.8
Vietnam, Laos, Cambodia	2.5
South-East Asia subtotal	25.5
Japan and Korea	0.2
USA, Canada, and Mexico	2.3
Latin America	0.8
Europe	0.6
Australia and New Zealand	0.5
Other countries subtotal	4.4
Total population outside Greater China	29.9
Total world Chinese population	1,257.9

Source: *Yearbook of the Overseas Chinese Economy* (Overseas Chinese Affairs Committee, Taipei, 1991).

Western countries. Where there are relatively large concentrations of overseas Chinese in South-East Asian countries, they also serve as national markets. Taking all the criteria into consideration, Greater China constitutes the most lucrative television market, followed by Singapore and North America.

Hong Kong: A Regional Broadcasting Centre

Hong Kong has the world's largest Chinese television programme library and is an important exporter of audiovisual products. It has come a long way since the inception of broadcast television in the late 1960s, when the prime time programming on the Chinese television channels was dominated by foreign programmes imported from Japan, Taiwan, and the USA. It is estimated that some 70 per cent of the programmes were dubbed foreign products and the rest locally produced (K. C. Chan 1993). However, when overall programming is considered, local production has never been dominated by foreign programmes (Chan and Lee 1992). For instance in 1969, two years after the inauguration of broadcast television, already 63 per cent of the programmes on TV8 Jade were being locally produced. By 1985 local production had increased to 80 per cent. The same pattern applies to ATV. Since the late 1970s, prime time also has been filled with local programming. As of 1989, as much as 90 per cent of all programmes on the two Chinese channels were locally produced (Lee and Yung 1990).

Hong Kong television productions have proved to be very popular in overseas Chinese markets too. The means of distribution include videos, cable and satellite television, and piracy. By 1987 TVB was marketing 1,000 hours of its 2,000–3,000 hours of annual production to twenty-five countries, while ATV was selling 520 hours overseas at that time (Pomery 1988). These exports are estimated to have increased in proportion to the general growth in output. TVB was producing more than 5,000 hours of programming a year by 1993. It now owns a library of more than 75,000 hours of Chinese programming that ranges from classic Cantonese films and soap operas to musicals and sports (To and Lau 1994). This is of particular value for its cable ventures.

With the advent of video cassette recorders in the late 1980s, the Hong Kong television stations have started exporting video programmes. They are particularly popular among overseas Chinese in South-East Asia and North America, where TVB operates its own rental shops. At times pirates compete with the television stations by making programmes available which have been duplicated right off the air.

Hong Kong television programmes are bought and broadcast by overseas television stations which, in some cases, are self-owned subsidiaries. The major markets include Taiwan, China, South-East Asian countries, and Chinese overseas communities in North America and Europe. The Asian buyers are mostly free-to-air broadcasters who regard Hong Kong programmes as a major programming source. The North American and European buyers are cable operators who specialize in ethnic programming. TVB itself has cable subsidiaries in cities that have sizeable Hong Kong immigrant and overseas Chinese communities, such as Los Angeles, San Francisco, New York, and Toronto.

Hong Kong television programmes had a breakthrough in Taiwan when CTV first introduced a dubbed martial-art serial from TVB in 1982. It proved to be immensely popular, so the two competitors followed suit (Ho 1990). It has been observed that Hong Kong productions owed their competitive edge to higher quality and a greater sense of realism (L. L. Chen 1993). The appeal of Hong Kong drama serials were perceived to be so threatening to the local television industry that all the terrestrial broadcasters in 1984 agreed not to broadcast any Hong Kong television drama. Instead, they began to employ Hong Kong artists as leading characters, a trend that has continued even up to the present.

Since the early 1990s satellites have gained in importance as a means for exporting Hong Kong programmes. Accessibility to STAR TV varies across nations, depending on regulatory regimes and other factors (J. Chan 1994*b*). As of late 1993 STAR TV could reach a total of more than 40 million people right across Asia, with the majority being concentrated in China, Taiwan, and India. The most popular STAR TV channel in China and Taiwan is its Chinese language channel that carries programmes from Hong Kong, Taiwan, Japan, and other places. In late 1993 about 30 million Chinese households were capable of receiving STAR TV, often through rudimentary cable networks or reception dishes. In Taiwan, STAR TV reaches a quarter of households.

In 1993 TVB joined with Taiwanese interests to form TVBS so as to broadcast its programmes to Taiwan, using the Indonesian satellite Palapa whose signals are redistributed through cable. By 1994 TVB's 'Super Channel' (TVBS) had already reached a penetration of more than half of Taiwan's households, or 90 per cent of all the cable audience (To and Lau 1994). TVB is planning to expand the system to China and other parts of Asia, while it has licensed the Chinese Channel to broadcast its programmes over Europe. As well as its satellite transmissions, TVB licences programmes and sells videos in China, Taiwan, South-East Asia, North America, Europe, and Australia. However, in some of these areas the potential audience is too scattered or too poor to constitute a viable market. The most important audiences are in Taiwan, North America, and South-East Asia, a total of over 45 million people. Another major satellite television service originating from Hong Kong is the Ming Pao newspaper group's Chinese Television Network (CTN), launched in 1994. Broadcast in Mandarin, CTN is a twenty-four-hour CNN-like news station that views Taiwan as the initial market and China as the final target.

Hong Kong's television broadcasters also export their programmes by spillover (J. Chan 1994*a*). TVB and ATV can reach a large part of the neighbouring Pearl River Delta in Guangdong, covering a mainland population of about 18 million. Surveys in 1993 in the Pearl River Delta showed that more than 97 per cent of the households in the major cities, with the exception of Guangdong's provincial capital Guangzhou, owned at least one television set, and all have access to Hong Kong television through cable networks (Hong Kong TVB 1992; Hong Kong ATV 1993). Some local stations were inserting their own advertisements (Lee 1993). After several failed attempts to stop it, the provincial government has acquiesced to this illegal but widespread practice.

In spite of the introduction of some copyright laws, media piracy is so common in China that it has become an extension of the spillover process (J. Chan 1994*a*). According to a video operator in southern China, foreign movies and television programmes accessible in Guangdong and Fujian are often reproduced illegally and shipped inland for a profit. These illicit goods can be rented, sold, or shown in small video shops. It is also through piracy that video-cassette tapes, laser discs, compact discs, and movie videos originating from Hong Kong and Taiwan have made inroads into China in recent years.

The television genres most popular in Hong Kong are, in descending order, news, comedies, and drama serials (Chan and Lee 1992). While news also appeals to Hong Kong emigrants in North America and elsewhere, the serials, which range from comedies to tragedies and from traditional martial-arts stories to modern police drama, have notable popularity at home. The drama serials often reflect the conflicts that are experienced in a metropolitan centre which is also a cultural confluence of the East and the West, as well as the traditional and the modern. This dramatizes what is being experienced in other parts of Asia where similar kinds of value conflicts are taking place. Born out of a competitive market with cultural *laissez-faire*, the serials are fast-paced, melodramatic, apolitical, and entertaining. To many audiences in Asia these provide alternative choices to their local productions, which are often more serious and ideological in approach.

Taiwan: Awakened to New Opportunities

Taiwanese television has not been keen on exporting for commercial purposes. It does it more as a kind of cultural service, as a method to promote the image of Taiwan among overseas Chinese and other nationalities (Ho 1990). Consequently, all three broadcasters traditionally charge very low prices for foreign stations to air their programmes. However, as videocassette recorders became more common in the 1980s Taiwanese broadcasters began to engage in the video trade, which now makes up the bulk of their revenue from exports. Thus, it is generally believed that Taiwanese television companies cannot match their Hong Kong colleagues in marketing aggressiveness and know-how. Still, with the gradual opening of the China market and the penetration of satellite television from Hong Kong, Taiwanese broadcasters are developing a more acute sense of international marketing.

News and television drama are the two genres from Taiwan that have the widest appeal. The attraction of its news, however, is restricted mainly to Taiwanese who live in North America, which was Taiwan's largest export market in the 1970s. In other cases, foreign television stations may use their news feed as a wire source. In the 1970s Taiwanese programmes were carried for a couple of hours a day by some UHF stations in American cities with relatively large Chinese populations, which include San Francisco, Los Angeles, Houston, Chicago, and New York (Chen 1993). At the beginning of the 1980s the three Taiwanese television services and the Government Information Office formed a company to distribute Taiwanese programmes to American television stations in the form of videos. At the same time another company was formed to broadcast programmes from the Taiwanese stations via satellite, mainly news and serials.

Taiwanese television dramas, including martial-arts stories, period, romance, and contemporary serials are very popular in China. They are made in tens rather than hundreds of episodes. Taiwanese dramas are characterized by their emphasis on traditional values and virtues such as fidelity, loyalty, thrift, and the like. In fact, this has been required by television ordinances (Lin and Liu 1993). Such treatment of traditional values appears to have aroused a strong resonance with the Chinese audience, who perhaps want to have reinforced some of the personal values that have been strained so much by their numerous political and ideological struggles. Among the more famous are *The Star Knows my Heart*, *Stars of Last Night*, and *Emperor Quan Long* (Cao 1993).

Taiwan started its first television export to Hong Kong in 1971, later expanding to the USA, Canada, South Africa, Europe, the Middle East, Singapore, the Philippines, Thailand, Japan, and other countries on a modest scale (*Television Yearbook of the Republic of China* 1976). From

1971 to 1975, TTV had exported over fifty programmes totalling more than 1,000 hours. In more recent years mainland China has become a more important market for Taiwan and, in 1993, Taiwanese programmes began to enjoy a revived interest in Hong Kong. In fact, the highest rating programme in Hong Kong in early 1994 was a Taiwanese historical drama in weekly self-contained mini-series format, *Judge Bao*. Its traditional, moralistic values struck an unexpected chord, while its production quality drew unfavourable attention to the stagnation of production quality in Hong Kong television.

Taiwan is well aware of the numerous satellite channels with which China is able to deliver its programmes into Taiwan (Li 1993). The government is trying to find ways to face up to this challenge, but the reception of foreign satellite television in Taiwan is in a state of 'illegal openness' (J. Chan 1994*b*). However, in retaliation Taiwanese consortiums are being formed to broadcast over China via satellite. There are at least two initiatives in process, which seek to launch such services by the middle of the decade (Fang 1993*b*). One is the Taiwan League of Satellite TV Operators' plan to rent five transponders from an American satellite (the Tracking and Data Relay Satellite System, USA) for delivering music videos, movie, shopping, and other services. The other is Boxin Yule Company, a KMT operation, which has rented four transponders from Asiapac 1.

China: Cultural Deficit

While regulations in China require cable networks to limit foreign programmes to no more than one-third of their total programming (Liu 1993), fixed quotas have not been strictly enforced among broadcast television stations in recent years. They can import as many foreign programmes as they can afford, provided they are politically cleared. Many, however, take care not to let foreign programmes exceed an informal quota of about 20 per cent, for fear of provoking interference from Beijing, and even television stations that exceed this proportion during prime time nevertheless abide by the ceiling for the overall broadcast period.

China's television stations can export their programmes

either individually or through China Television United (CTU), which was formed in 1992 to make one-stop shopping possible for foreign buyers. Dominating the CTU are CCTV in Beijing and the provincial or municipal stations in Shanghai, Guangdong, and Sichuan. In fact, each of these four centres organize various kinds of television festivals to promote the exchanges of television programmes between China and the rest of the world. Stations that have programmes to sell from all over China set up booths at these festivals to display their wares.

In general, Chinese television programmes are not popular in Hong Kong and Taiwan. While Chinese television productions are not allowed to be broadcast in Taiwan, Hong Kong stations seldom features Chinese drama serials, not even as a time filler, simply because they attract very small audiences. Hong Kong audiences find the Chinese programmes dull, and their ideological tone overbearing. Because Taiwan cannot openly exhibit Chinese television programmes, productions of distinction such as *The Silk Road* have to be repackaged as 'tourism' programmes before they can be shown on Taiwanese television. This is done through companies set up in Hong Kong. However, China has been exporting its drama serials to ethnic stations in North America and as videos to other overseas Chinese communities. Other export genres are documentaries showing Chinese folk culture and landscapes.

China has become more aware of the importance of exporting its programmes in the 1990s. CCTV established Channel 4 to broadcast programmes over satellite for audiences in Taiwan and Hong Kong (Ai 1993). While some illegal networks in Taiwan are known to carry its programmes, reception in Hong Kong is scattered. Some UHF television stations in the USA began carrying Chinese programmes in the 1980s, and in the 1990s CCTV began broadcasting its news and other programmes into the USA in conjunction with Oriental Satellite in Chicago (J. H. Hong 1993). CCTV satellite transmission greatly enlarges the distribution of Chinese television to overseas Chinese in South-East Asia as well.

As China increases its domestic production and upgrades the quality of its programmes, exports are expected to increase.

China has plans to reduce its cultural deficit by doubling its domestic production in the decade 1990–2000 (Ai 1991). For CCTV and the major provincial stations, the target is to be able to produce ten hours of their daily programming; for others, four hours. China also plans to boost the international sales of its media products and to launch satellite television services over more countries. The dedication of CCTV's fourth channel for overseas Chinese has been mentioned already, as has the daily satellite broadcast to the USA, which amounted to twelve hours in 1993 (Yiu 1993). There is also a satellite television service over Taiwan, Hong Kong, and South-East Asia scheduled to launch in 1996, based in Fujian, and a global Chinese channel planned to be established by the year 2000 (Lu 1993).

The Emergent Market of Greater China

Greater China is far from being an integrated television market. Severe trade barriers exist between China and each of the other two Chinese societies. Relatively free television trade exists only between Hong Kong and Taiwan, which are much smaller than China in audience size. If China does not further open up, the Greater China television market will remain potential rather than actual. But limited as it is now, interaction between the television industries in each of the three societies is increasing. In this section we shall analyse the constraints and favourable factors of the budding Greater China television market.

Barriers

The programme flow between the constituent parts of China has been more of a one-way flow from Hong Kong and Taiwan to China, and two-way flow between Hong Kong and Taiwan. The one-way flow is reflected in both journalism and entertainment. Between 1987 and 1993 Taiwanese journalists have paid about 3,000 visits to China in gathering news ('The Currents of Journalism Exchange Across the Strait' 1994). On the contrary, only tens of Chinese journalists have visited Taiwan.

The major obstacle to the development of a unified Greater China television market is the political boundary that prevents the free flow of capital, personnel, and programmes between China and the other two Chinese societies. China, fearful that the popular culture from Hong Kong and Taiwan forms part of the force that will change China through 'peaceful evolution', has taken measures to reduce its influence (J. Chan 1994*a*). Indeed, antiforeignism is the theme of ideological campaigns that the Chinese Communist Party has waged since the reform era. The people are barred from free reception of foreign satellite television. Programme imports have to be politically cleared by the Ministry of Film, Radio and Television, which also controls by setting quotas and balancing programme genres and origins. China formally forbids co-ownership or joint ventures in television. All these restrictions have prevented the television industry in Hong Kong and Taiwan from exploiting the full potential that China holds.

Taiwan's television ordinance is a legacy from its authoritarian rule. It is filled with bureaucratic controls that inhibit the free exchanges of television programmes between Taiwan and the outside world. It defines political roles for its broadcasters that are out of step with its political liberalization. Its censorship standards are so vague and loose that television can easily fall into legal traps (Lin and Liu 1993). The political distancing that Taiwan maintains against mainland China also restricts the imports of television programmes from China. No Chinese television programmes are allowed to be aired on Taiwanese television. Also banned are programmes or movies that are made with personnel chiefly from mainland China. Programmes made in China have to be censored before broadcast. Such programmes must take up no more than three hours per week and no more than an hour a day. Taiwan requires that journalists and television workers report to the Government Information Office before leaving for assignments in China (Ho 1990). In addition, no media organizations are allowed to set up branches or agencies on the mainland.

Taiwan and China are at a stalemate in trying to outsmart one another in their negotiations. In order to give the impression of speaking with one voice and to prevent one's rival from using one's own media, there is a tendency for each side not to let the other side have access to its media. This is particularly the case with China, which is used to mobilizing the mass media to serve its negotiation strategies. Taiwan maintains that its television stations cannot broadcast interviews with Chinese officials unless China is ready to reciprocate (Li 1993).

For China to expand its exports to Hong Kong and Taiwan, its programmes will have to match the taste of their audiences and to improve in quality. This is more easily said than done, because television in China is subject to political directives which tend to strip their products of entertainment value. Chinese television in general suffers from the lack of capital which tends to drive down its quality. There is no reason for Hong Kong and Taiwanese television to import programmes that are not competitive in the war for audiences.

Hong Kong has the greatest freedom in importing television programmes. It allows unlimited imports from all over the world and allows free flow of media capital and personnel in and out of the colony. Its television imports depend on the relative competitiveness of foreign programmes and domestic demand. The market is the regulator. At present, the administrative control of television in China has prevented Hong Kong from exploiting the potential of the Greater China market. Hong Kong's television industry will reap the benefits of this enlarged market only when China liberalizes its television system.

Communication Technology

The advent of new communication technology has helped to reduce the political resistance to communication among the constituent members of Greater China. This shattering force is a result of the proliferation of satellite television, videocassette recorders, spillover, and piracy. As attested by the wide penetration of STAR TV and TVBS in both China and Taiwan, foreign borderless television can have an immense impact on a nation's mediasphere. Now STAR TV can be received with a reception dish that measures about 3 metres and costs about $US300, which is within the affordable range of many Chinese collectives or even individuals. Satellite television from outside has also become a convenient way to meet the demand for programming on the cable systems that are rapidly developing in China and Taiwan. The extensive redistribution of STAR TV and TVBS signals through such networks was noted earlier.

It has become increasingly difficult for national governments to fend off direct broadcast satellite television as a result of technological breakthrough. When the reception dish is miniaturized to a size of about 1 foot in diameter, it will become virtually impossible to police the reception over a vast region. Indeed, it has been reported that a reception dish of about 18 inches in diameter has become available in the USA (Baig 1994). It will not take long before such a device becomes available and affordable in Asia. Compression and multiplexing technology, through increasing the number of channels available and multiple sound-tracking, will make satellite television more language- and culture-specific, thereby increasing its attractiveness across boundaries. At the same time, because audiences still prefer terrestrial television to foreign satellite services, at least where programmes are comparable in quality, terrestrial television will likely adapt to remain a fixture of national television for some time to come (J. Chan 1994*b*).

Comparative Advantage, Market Forces, and Networking

The development of television production in each of the three countries is based on their comparative advantages. China owes its advantage to the abundance of natural attractions, low personnel and production costs, and a huge domestic market. Hong Kong and Taiwan owe theirs to their early mastery of the television cultural form, capital abundance, creative freedom, and international connections. Hong Kong and Taiwanese television, therefore, have a great incentive to produce in China, while their Chinese counterparts would like to benefit from foreign capital, technology transfer, and marketing networks.

The greatest attraction of China is the huge audience that it harbours. China has a population of over 1.3 billion and its economy has been growing at an average rate of over 10 per cent per year since the 1980s. The overall population is poor by international standards, but people in the coastal region have achieved an income high enough to have drawn the attention of transnational advertisers. Hong Kong and Taiwanese television want to tap this potential by selling programmes to Chinese stations, and try to bypass state restrictions by transmitting the signals through satellite.

Hong Kong television is particularly aggressive in this regard. A common arrangement is to let Chinese television stations broadcast the programmes of ATV and TVB in exchange for the use of advertising time. The Hong Kong stations are responsible for the solicitation of advertisements and the resulting revenue is split in a pre-negotiated proportion. An instance of such an arrangement is the broadcast of a weekly magazine programme produced by TVB at Beijing TV and Shanghai TV since January 1993.

A very important change in media development in China in the last decade has been commercialization, which is marked by the proliferation of the profit motive among media which depend less and less on state subsidy but more and more on advertising, sponsorship, and other income sources (J. Chan 1993). This provides great incentives for Chinese television to broadcast programmes from Hong Kong, Taiwan, and elsewhere, because they are more appealing to the audience and transnational advertisers. Chinese television has become more receptive to co-productions and other forms of co-operation with foreign media that bring them foreign currency, technology transfer, and capital.

The force of the market should not be underestimated. It is universally recognized among television players in Hong Kong and China that they should try to make headway into China so that they are in a strategic position to exploit more fully the Chinese market when more liberal conditions eventuate. The lure of profit on both sides has motivated a constant search for innovations to exploit the leeway that is allowed within the Chinese system. Very often networking becomes an instrumental means to get around what may have seemed insurmountable restrictions. The City Television network formed in Guangzhou in 1993 is a notable example of how such a network may work. As allowed by law, it first established a video production joint venture with a Hong Kong partner, which then contracted with the television network to exchange prime time programmes for advertising (J. Chan 1994*a*). In effect, it is an indirect form of media ownership. This arrangement would not have been possible without the understanding between both sides and the intricate connections that the Chinese partner has with the television regulators and personnel in China. It is out of this web of social connections that China is opening itself up to Hong Kong and Taiwanese television in a evolutionary manner. Breakthroughs are not achieved in a day. But the forces of networking and profiteering will persist and prove to be subversive of policy control.

Cultural and Linguistic Affinity

It is oversimplified to assume too much cultural similarity between the three countries of Greater China. In fact, each has developed a variation of Chinese culture that has its own distinct characteristics. It is generally agreed that television culture in Hong Kong is very much a reflection of life in a cosmopolitan city which has blended the East with the West. The tempo of television drama is fast and is filled with conflicts, as is real life. While familial and other traditional values are still treasured, divorces, extramarital affairs, and individualistic values are becoming more commonplace. Taiwan is less westernized. Familial and traditional ethics are still cherished in television drama. In fact, television critics have observed that Taiwan seems to have preserved Confucian teachings better than China, which has a much shorter history of opening up to the world (P. F. Chen 1993). Although Chinese television has learned from Taiwanese and Hong Kong television in now stressing interpersonal relationships as the primary element in their serials, they still bear the imprints of a socialist culture that stresses collectivism, patriotism, and nationalism. If television culture is linked to the social context in which it is produced, Taiwanese and Hong Kong television programmes can be said to give a sense of modernity, whereas

Chinese television reflects more the aspirations of its diverse population.

At the same time, one should not overstress the differences and underestimate the cultural affinity that does still exist. All three societies value interpersonal relationships and social networking. They share the same cultural tradition that dates back thousands of years. Although Hong Kong speaks Cantonese, China and Taiwan speak the same language, Mandarin. Even in Hong Kong, people are picking up Mandarin in view of the growing need to interact with both mainland Chinese and Taiwan. Both the past and the future of these three countries are intertwined with each other, and such cultural affinity has served as a positive factor in the formation of a Greater China television market. The three countries are different enough to produce television products each with its distinct flavour, yet similar enough not to have created cultural barriers. Indeed, Greater China can be thought of as a 'geocultural' rather than a geolinguistic region, in that the common cultural context of its television output is more fundamental than the difference in language. The language difference is not a barrier to trade, in that low-cost dubbing into Mandarin is available in China for Hong Kong programmes, which are valued for their entertainment appeal and quality, even in Taiwan, over the Taiwanese programmes in Mandarin.

Table 5.2 summarizes the comparative analysis presented here in relating the broadcasting systems of Greater China to patterns of programme exports by its constituent countries.

Political Periphery as Cultural Centre

This concluding section will examine export patterns in the light of the theory of media imperialism, a major concern of which is the domination by Western media fare in developing countries that adopt an open cultural policy (Boyd-Barrett 1977; Lee 1980). Hong Kong readily stands out as a case that defies the basic tenets of media imperialism. This can be viewed from two angles. First, in spite of Hong Kong's open cultural policy and politico-economic dependence on the West, it has successfully

Table 5.2. Television systems and exports in Greater China

	China	*Taiwan*	*Hong Kong*
TV ownership and control	State monopoly, all Party-controlled; being commercialized.	Major stakes owned by KMT, the military, or government; run as commercial enterprises with ideological constraints.	Privately owned; minimal regulation.
Policy on foreign programmes	Moving from cultural anti-foreignism to a less severe form of cultural protectionism; censorship and quota control.	Restricting imports to no more than 30%; bans Chinese programmes.	Free flow.
Audience characteristics	Population about 1.2 billion, about 60% urban, very diverse.	Population about 24 million, about 75% urban, relatively homogeneous.	Population about 6 million, about 95% urban, homogeneous.
Exports	Very limited; programmes uncompetitive in Hong Kong and Taiwan; exports via satellite TV, videos, and programme sales.	Awakened to the importance of exports; popular in China, Hong Kong, and overseas Chinese communities; exports via videos and programme sales.	Exports are of growing importance; popular in China, Taiwan, and overseas Chinese communities; exports via satellite TV, videos, and programme sales.
Centre–periphery relationships	Political centre with a huge and rapidly developing economy; cultural periphery of Hong Kong and Taiwan.	Political and economic periphery of the West; political periphery of China; cultural centre of China; cultural sub-centre of the West.	Political and economic periphery of the West; political periphery of China; cultural centre of China; cultural sub-centre of the West.

spawned a vibrant television and popular culture of its own, contrary to what media imperialism theory would predict. Its popular culture does not only prevail at home, but also enjoys great popularity in China, Taiwan, and other parts of the world, rendering Hong Kong a regional centre of culture and communication.

Secondly, Hong Kong and China are incommensurate in economic and political might. While Hong Kong is more advanced economically than China, as measured by indices such as per capita income, China is greater in absolute size. Politically, China is the centre of Greater China, whereas Hong Kong belongs to the periphery. However, Hong Kong's popular culture, spearheaded by its television programmes, has an impact on China which is far beyond its economic and political status. Hong Kong has been able to set the cultural agenda for Beijing and exert great influence on China's media landscape, and in that respect Hong Kong is the centre and China is on the periphery (Tu 1991; Gold 1993). That is, China is very much like a political Goliath and Hong Kong a cultural David.

Similar observations apply to the relationship between Taiwan and mainland China. In fact, the popular cultures of both Hong Kong and Taiwan have been so influential in China that they have been collectively referred to as Guangtai culture (Guan and Tai are the respective abbreviation for Hong Kong and Taiwan in Chinese) (Gold 1993). The theory of media imperialism has to be revised in the light of two of these important deviant cases. By the same token, thue traditional widsom of prescribing cultural protectionism to safeguard indigenous culture should also be reconsidered. For instance, Schiller has stressed the increased vulnerability of developing countries to Western cultural domination with the rise of the market economy and the collapse of the Soviet bloc (1991). However, while the success of Taiwan in avoiding Western domination can be attributed mainly to geolinguistic and cultural differences (Lee 1980), the case of Hong Kong pointedly highlights the importance of market competition in a country developing its own television culture.

Hong Kong's television industry developed most rapidly in

the mid-1970s when competition was at its peak, with three television stations vying for domination in the nascent television market. When one of the stations was driven out, the two survivors, TVB and ATV, continued to compete fiercely. Competition as such has enabled Hong Kong to establish itself as the world leader in Chinese television since the mid-1970s. But for various historical and management reasons, TVB has been triumphing over ATV and securing about 80 per cent of the audience for the last two decades. This lopsided situation has lasted for so long that internal competition has been reduced considerably and is beginning to take its toll. TVB is now seen to have lost some of its impetus to be creative and responsive, resulting in standardized productions that are less in step with the beat of Hong Kong (K. C. Chan 1990). A clear sign of the weaker programming in Hong Kong has been the recent revival of Taiwanese imports discussed earlier. But it is too soon to declare the demise of Hong Kong's television industry. Rather, market considerations at the regional and international level are redirecting its efforts. For instance, TVB is now deriving 85 per cent of its profits from local broadcasting business, with the rest accruing from overseas sales of television programmes and video rentals (To and Lau 1994). Realizing that the profits for local programming have passed their peak, TVB has had to expand overseas to maintain its profit margin. That explains why it is positioning itself as the most resourceful international broadcaster in Chinese language programmes, and embarking upon satellite television and other overseas ventures. Inspired by the regional penetration of STAR TV and the quick success of TVBS in Taiwan, and with a plateau having been reached in overseas video rental, satellite distribution is an attractive means to reach both foreign and domestic audiences. This shift of internal competition to the international level will help preserve the vigour of Hong Kong's television industry.

As noted, the diffusion of Hong Kong and Taiwan media fare into China has its impact on the Chinese mediasphere. It puts pressure on China's television industry to learn from its competitors, resulting in a growing homogenization of television culture in Greater China. Internal competition within the television industries of Hong Kong, Taiwan, and China will increase, as will competition between them, although China is urgently in need of a policy that will encourage internal competition, without which its industry will not be able to face the challenge from its two small neighbours. As argued above, the free-flow policy has seemed to work for this region only when supplemented with intense internal competition.

Satellite television across national boundaries within Greater China has put increasing competitive pressure on terrestrial broadcasters by offering alternative programming choice and more balanced news reporting. The popularity of TVBS, a satellite television service based in Hong Kong, for instance, is already exerting pressure on the Taiwanese terrestrial broadcasters to relax their standards. Being a foreign broadcaster, TVBS is not subject to the same political and cultural restrictions as its domestic counterparts. It can broadcast news and commentary that is less favourable to the ruling KMT, ignore duration constraints on airing Chinese and Hong Kong programmes, and engage freely in co-productions with counterparts in China. For its domestic terrestrial broadcasters to survive in the long run, Taiwan can only relax the rules for them, or ban the reception of satellite television. Given the increasing capability of satellite television to evade national boundaries, it is reasonable to expect Taiwan to face up to the challenge by liberalizing its broadcasting policy.

Similar pressure exists for China. However, for political reasons it is less likely that China will open up immediately. It will resort to occasional crackdowns in order to root out or slow down the growth of unauthorized reception of foreign programmes through satellite and other channels. However, after each crackdown there will likely be a spurt of growth. This may repeat until reception goes beyond policing, putting China in a state of 'illegal openness' to foreign media (J. Chan, 1994*b*). STAR TV has been attempting to appease China, for example, by cancelling the BBC news channel in the northern footprint, but without success. The handover of Hong Kong's sovereignty in 1997 poses questions about the future for STAR TV and other satellite services. Prospective new services and the Hong Kong regulatory authority have adopted the strategy of gaining the consent of the Chinese authorities before licensing. As 1997 approaches, satellite services based in Hong Kong may want to set up back-up uplink facilities in Singapore or other Asian cities.

With the Greater China television market already in a state of flux, political and other changes in any of the three countries may have important implications for the others. Reforms in China are building pressure for further media commercialization and liberalization. However, this tendency is susceptible to policy swings as a result of power struggles. In fact, since late 1993 China appears to have been tightening its control over foreign media (J. Chan, 1994*b*). As for Taiwan, its broadcasting system is expected to become more liberal as democratization continues. Whether Taiwanese television can play a greater role in China largely depends on whether the political relationship between Taiwan and China relaxes further. The ongoing political transition in Hong Kong has and will have important influence over its television development. At present the news media are politically pluralistic, ranging from the left to the right. However, there are signs indicating that the news media have been organizationally and editorially accommodating themselves to the coming power shifts in Hong Kong (Chan and Lee 1991). It is expected that the pace and extent of accommodation as such will accelerate in the run-up to 1997. As noted in the case of satellite television, the influence of China, both actual and anticipated, will most likely leave its mark on communication policy making in Hong Kong as well. As long as China's suppressive press policies lasts, communications in Hong Kong will have to face quite an uncertain future as its sovereignty changes hands.

The political and ideological differences between China and its two small neighbours are the most important barriers to the development of a real Greater China market. But as economic integration between China, Hong Kong, and Taiwan increases there is a growing demand for advertising channels to reach the Greater China market. Being commercial or quasi-commercial enterprises, the television stations have every economic incentive to exploit each other's markets to their own competitive advantage. The cultural and language affinity between the three countries is a basic factor favouring the development of the Greater China market, and underscores the importance of a geolinguistic or geocultural similarity in international television market formation. The development of satellite and cable television is instrumental in catapulting programmes across political boundaries but, for Hong Kong and Taiwan fully to secure the potential of the China market, China will also have to be more effective in legislating and enforcing copyright laws.

Summing up: to Hong Kong and Taiwan, China is a market whose potential has yet to be realized. To China, Hong Kong and Taiwan are sources of capital, programmes, and production inspirations. Until the political and ideological barriers between China, Hong Kong, and Taiwan dissipate, Greater China will not function like a unified television market or producer. However, technological change and growing economic integration between China, Taiwan, and Hong Kong are conducive to the development of this geolinguistic region into a playing-field of television exchange. The television industry of Hong Kong and Taiwan will benefit from greater economies of scale and more efficient use of its factors of production when China opens up. Meanwhile, China's television industry will have to undergo drastic changes in order to survive and prosper. If China liberalizes its broadcasting system, programmes from Hong Kong, Taiwan, and elsewhere may prove to be overwhelming at an initial stage. But if internal competition is allowed to work, television programmes made in China will sooner or later measure up to the competitiveness of its neighbours. In fact, Chinese television programmes already have become less ideological, more entertaining, and thus more competitive since the mid-1980s. It follows that the television production of Greater China as a whole will be of higher quality and better able to compete with the West.

References

AI, Z. S. (1991), 'On the State of Films and Television', speech given at the National Party Academy, Beijing, 14 December.

AI, Z. S. (1993), 'Raise the Quality and Strive to Have a Quantum Change in Television Programs', *Television Research*, 2: 4–7.

Almanac of the Republic of China (1980), Almanac of the Republic of China Association, Taipei.

BAIG, E. (1994), 'The Incredible Shrinking Dish', *Business Week* (30 May), 143.

BOYD-BARRETT, O. (1977), 'Media Imperialism: Towards an International Framework for the Analysis of Media Systems', in J. Curran, M. Gurevitch, and J. Woollacott (eds.), *Mass Communication and Society* (Edward Arnold, London), 116–35.

CAO, JINAGYUAN (1993), 'The Chinese folks liberated by satellite TV', *Zhonggvo Daily* (2 Oct.), 29.

CHAN, J. (1993), 'Commercialization Without Independence: Trends and Tensions of Media Development in China', in J. Cheng and M. Brosseau (eds.), *China Review 1993* (The Chinese University Press, Hong Kong), 25: 1–21.

—— (1994*a*), 'Media Internationalization in China: Processes and Tensions', *Journal of Communication*, 44/3: 70–88.

—— (1994*b*), 'National Responses and Accessibility to STAR TV in Asia', *Journal of Communication*, 44/3: 112–31.

—— and LEE, C. C. (1991), *Mass Media and Political Transition: The Hong Kong Press in China's Orbit* (Guilford Press, New York).

—— and LEE, P. (1992), 'Communication Indicators in Hong Kong: Conceptual Issues and Findings', in S. K. Lau (ed.), *The Development of Social Indicators Research in Chinese Societies* (The Hong Kong Institute of Asia-Pacific Studies, Chinese University of Hong Kong, Hong Kong), 175–204.

CHAN, K. C. (1990), 'The Media and Telecommunications', in R. Wong and J. Cheng (eds.), *The Other Hong Kong Report* (The Chinese University Press, Hong Kong), 507–36.

—— (1993), 'Television and the Local Culture of Hong Kong', paper presented to the Conference on Chinese Television, Guangdong Televison, Guangzhou, August.

CHEN, L. L. (1993), 'Popularity of Hong Kong TV Drama Fading', *Dacheng Daily* (5 Dec.), 14.

CHEN, P. F. (1993), 'Taiwanese Television and Mainland Television', *China Television*, 8: 36–8.

CHENG J. C. (1988), *An Analysis of Media* (Tianxia Press, Taipei).

'China Becomes a TV Giant' (1992), *People's Daily* (Overseas) (20 Nov.), 3.

CHING, M. (1992), 'The Trends of the Chinese Cinema', *Wide Angle Monthly* (Aug.), 86–9.

CHUNG, W. W. (1993), 'Cable Television', in J. C. Cheng (ed.), *Deconstructing Radio and Television* (Cheng She, Taipei), 411–40.

FANG, C. S. (1993*a*), 'Public Television', in J. C. Cheng (ed.), *Deconstructing Radio and Television* (Cheng She, Taipei), 317–410.
—— (1993*b*), '"Opening-up" of Television Spectrums in Taiwan: A Political Economic Perspective', *Taiwan: A Radical Quarterly in Social Studies*, 16: 79–118.
GOLD, T. (1993), 'Go With Your Feelings: Hong Kong and Taiwan Popular Culture in Greater China', *China Quarterly*, 136: 907–25.
HARDING, H. (1993), 'The Concept of "Greater China": Themes, Variations and Reservations', *China Quarterly*, 136: 660–86.
HO, Y. M. (1990), 'Television', in *Annual Journalism Review of Republic of China 1990* (Taipei).
HONG, J. H. (1993), 'China's TV Program Import 1958–1988: Towards the Internationalization of Television', *Gazette*, 52/1: 1–23.
Hong Kong ATV (1993), *Viewership of Hong Kong television in China*, ATV, Hong Kong.
Hong Kong TVB (1992), *Audience survey in Guangzhou and Shenzhen* (2nd report), TVB, Hong Kong.
KUO, C. (1992), 'A Reconsideration of *Media Imperialism Reconsidered*', *Contemporary* (Taipei), 78: 98–120.
LEE, C. C. (1980), *Media Imperialism Reconsidered* (Sage, Beverly Hills).
LEE, F. Y. (1993), 'Mainland China's Television is Making a Profit Without Cost', *The Next Weekly* (26 Mar.), 90–4.
LEE. P., and YUNG, D. (1990), 'The Program Problem of Cable Television in Hong Kong and its Policy Implications', paper presented to the Twelfth Annual Conference of the Pacific Telecommunication Council, Honolulu, January.
LEUNG, L. K. GRACE (1992), 'The Evolution of Hong Kong as a Regional Movie Production and Export Center', unpublished M.Phil. thesis, Chinese University of Hong Kong.
LI, C. (1984), *Television* (Wenchen Press, Taipei).
LI, W. L. (1993), *The Politics of Television Communications* (Zhengzhong Press, Taipei).
LIAO, K. S. (1990), *Antiforeignism and Modernization in China* (The Chinese University Press, Hong Kong).
LIN, T. Y., and LIU, C. Y. (1993), 'Radio and Television Content: Norms and Performance', in J. C. Cheng (ed.), *Deconstructing Radio and Television* (Cheng She, Taipei), 129–216.
LIU, L. (1993), 'A Study of Mainland China's Cable Laws', paper presented to the International Conference on Chinese Communication Research and Education, National Chengchi University, Taipei, June.
LU, Y. (1993), 'Directions on Developing Television', paper presented to the Conference on Chinese Television, Guangdong Television, Guangzhou, August.

POMERY, CHRIS (1988), 'Hong Kong', in Manuel Alvarado (ed.), *Video Worldwide: An International Study* (UNESCO, London).

SCHILLER, H. (1991), 'Not Yet the Post-Imperialist Era', *Critical Studies in Mass Communication*, 8: 13–28.

TELA (Television and Entertainment Licensing Authority) (1990), *Survey on Television Broadcasting 1990* (Hong Kong Government, Hong Kong).

Television Yearbook of the Republic of China 1961–1975 (1976), The Academy of Arts and Sciences, Taipei.

'The Bottom Line' (1994), *Asiaweek* (1 June), 47.

'The Currents of Journalism Exchange Across the Strait' (1994), *Yazhou Zoukan* (30 Jan.).

TO, Y. M., and LAU, T. Y. (1994), 'The Sky is Not the Limit: Hong Kong as a Global Media Exporter', paper presented to the Annual Conference of the International Communication Association, Sydney, July.

TU, W. M. (1991), 'Cultural China: The Periphery as the Center', *Daedalus*, 120/2: 1–32.

WANG, C. H. (1993), 'The Control of Radio and Television', in J. C. Cheng (ed.), *Deconstructing Radio and Television* (Cheng She, Taipei), 75–129.

WANG, G., and CHUNG, W. W. (1988), *The Second Generation Media: Post Communication Revolution* (Tonghua, Taipei).

WENG, H. C. (1993), 'Taiwan's Underground Media', in J. C. Cheng (ed.), *Deconstructing Radio and Television* (Cheng She, Taipei), 441–518.

YIU, S. W. (1993), 'The Black Horse in the Chinese Satellite Television Market in North America', *China Times Weekly* (USA) (18 Dec.), 80–1.

6

Canadian Television Exports: Into the Mainstream

Paul Attallah

Canadian television was officially launched on 6 September 1952. That night, the Montreal station of the Canadian Broadcasting Corporation (CBC) transmitted the first Canadian TV pictures: the CBC logo printed over a map of Canada. Both appeared upside down. Two nights later the CBC's Toronto station also took to the airwaves. By then, logo and map had been turned right side up.

Approximately fifty years later Canadian television bears almost no resemblance to its origins, save perhaps for the CBC itself. Television exports during that period fall into two large blocs: before Telefilm (1952–82) and after Telefilm (1982 to the present). Before Telefilm, television exports were largely an ancillary activity of the broadcasting industry. With few exceptions, programmes were rarely designed with export in mind. International sales came as a pleasant surprise, not as the result of careful strategy.

Since Telefilm, however, everything has changed. Television exports now form an integral part of the broadcasting system and programmes are self-consciously designed as part of an export strategy. Consequently, the television production industry has exploded in the last decade. Never before has so much successful and high-quality television been produced in Canada. Indeed, 'Canada's TV programming industry has grown into a $300 million-a-year-plus business, and made

Canada the second-largest exporter of TV programmes in the world, after the United States' (Knelman 1994: 63).

Canada has a population of approximately 29 million, dispersed over an area of 9.59 million square kilometres. The overwhelming majority of the population resides within 200 kilometres of the Canada/US border. This gives most Canadians direct access to over-the-air US broadcasting and to all other American cultural production. The population is also divided into two main language groups: approximately 7 million French-speakers, 80 per cent of whom are concentrated in the province of Quebec, and approximately 22 million English-speakers, of whom slightly fewer than 1 million reside in Quebec. Both language groups include members whose first language is neither English nor French, though most of these 'allophones' have adopted English.

Naturally, both groups are largely ignorant of each other's media. Stars who are household names amongst French-speakers evince blank stares elsewhere, and English Canadian passions about free trade or national identity are greeted with gasps of disbelief by most Quebecois. Even on the CBC, which runs parallel English and French television and radio networks, barely 25 per cent of the news is the same on both. This is what novelist Hugh MacLennan once called the 'two solitudes'.

A Brief History of Canadian Television

Although television came to Canada in 1952, there were already, by 1951, some 146,000 television households. Clearly, Canadians were watching American (US) television. This was the spur that created Canadian television. Many cultural nationalists opposed television, fearing it would become yet another conduit for American popular culture. However, faced with the behaviour of their fellow citizens, they had little choice but to create a system which, while satisfying the craving for television, would also be significantly different from the American model. Consequently, Canadian television was born into a paternalistic environment, its role to provide not what the masses wanted—indeed, their love of American culture disqualified them from knowing what they wanted—but what was good for them. If American television was devoted to fun and gratification, then Canadian television could not be.

The original television plan called for the CBC to construct and operate television stations in the major cities where it would produce its own programming. It would also construct and operate whatever networking facilities were required to link the various stations and transmit its content. The cost would be covered not by an annual licence fee but by a yearly parliamentary grant combined with advertising revenue. Parliament also conferred upon the CBC a cultural and political mandate. The mandate, enshrined in successive broadcasting acts, states in its most recent incarnation (1991), that Canadian television must 'safeguard, enrich and strengthen the cultural, political, social and economic fabric of Canada'. The CBC in particular must 'contribute to shared national consciousness and identity'.

Private television was to be licensed only after the CBC had established a national television service. Indeed, it was foreseen that private broadcasters would act as outlets for CBC programming, with the CBC handling their networking. Private broadcasters would, therefore, not be allowed to form competing networks though they would be allowed to provide competing programming which, it was hoped, they would produce themselves. In virtually all of its particulars, reality failed to conform to this plan.

Television was extremely popular and receiver sales sky-rocketed. However, the cost of implementing the CBC plan proved immediately prohibitive. Consequently, the first private television licences were granted in 1953. By 1961 the private stations formed into two private networks, the national English-language CTV network and the Quebec-based French-language TVA network. In the 1970s the provinces of Quebec, Ontario, Alberta, and British Columbia all formed provincial educational networks. In 1974 the Ontario-based English-language Global network took to the air, and in 1986 the Quebec-based French-language Télévision Quatre-Saisons network was formed. Several cities even boasted independent stations unaffiliated to any network. Through the past decade informal networks formed by large station groups have also emerged.

Cable television was launched in the early 1960s and achieved rapid success. In 1982 cable operators were authorized to distribute 'discretionary' or pay services. These could be of Canadian or other origin and their number is constantly growing. One major constraint on the addition of new services is simply the capacity of the existing technological infrastructure, which cable companies are furiously upgrading in order to stave off competition from both telephone companies and satellite systems. In 1994 approximately 84 per cent of Canadian homes were connected to cable (CRTC *Database* 1994).

For a country its size, Canada enjoys a number of television services well in excess of its indigenous production capacity. For example, remote communities are guaranteed eight channels (four Canadian, four American) through Canadian Satellite Communications Inc. (Cancom). Cancom's remote monopoly is guaranteed by the Canadian Radio-Television and Telecommunications Commission (CRTC). It currently supplies 1,526 small cable systems and 31,000 households (Enchin 1994*b*). Many remote communities, however, also use their receivers to pull in signals other than Cancom's. In urban areas, forty to fifty channels are not uncommon. In 1993 parliament's grant to the CBC was slightly more than $C1 billion and its advertising revenue approximately $C300 million. From this, the CBC operated two over-the-air television networks, one all-news cable network, four radio networks, international broadcasting services, native language services, studio facilities, networking facilities, import/export services, and other administrative services. Its English-language service obtained an audience share of approximately 10–12 per cent. Individually, private English-language broadcasters generated less than half the CBC's revenue but maintained audience shares of between 17 and 20 per cent. The remainder of the English-language audience was split amongst US networks, independents, superstations, discretionary services, provincial broadcasters, and videocassettes.

The Société Radio-Canada (SRC), the French-language service of the CBC, reached about 35–40 per cent of French-speaking viewers, with French-language private broadcasters reaching between 40 and 45 per cent. The remainder of the French-language audience was split in much the same way as the English-language audience. Audience shares can vary dramatically according to content type. For example, Canadian news and sports draw very large audiences but American drama and sitcoms draw larger audiences still (Ellis 1992; Atherton 1994).

Market Factors

Two main factors condition television production: (a) the differential cost of Canadian and American production; and (b) the differential value of the Canadian and American dollars. The widespread availability and appeal of American television have made its production values the *de facto* standard for Canada. American networks support their expenditures because of the size of the US market. The Canadian market, however, is too small to sustain equivalent costs. None the less, if a Canadian broadcaster does not *attempt* to match American levels, its product will look self-evidently cheap, thereby subjecting it to unfavourable comparisons and ridicule, and driving away viewers.

A Canadian network can, however, acquire popular American content at a fraction of its cost. For example, a programme valued at $US1 million can be purchased for approximately $C50,000. The low-cost American programme can then be used to attract large audiences and generate a consistent profit on the Canadian market. Canadian television, therefore, has traditionally faced the following options: (a) produce less-expensive programming, (b) acquire international content at a fraction of its cost, or (c) obtain external financing through tax concessions, government subsidies, or international partnerships. It has pursued all three.

The Canadian dollar has also traditionally been valued at less than the American dollar, sometimes up to 40 per cent less.

This is a distinct disadvantage for Canadian buyers of US content. However, it has helped draw American producers *into* Canada. Not only does their dollar go further but they also find highly professional crews, intimately acquainted with the nuances of American television, who speak the same language. As a result, more and more US production has shifted into Canada, and American networks themselves have become increasingly interested in acquiring Canadian content. The result has been to give Canadian producers opportunities and experience they might not otherwise have acquired and to create an appetite for their work in the world's richest market, the USA.

Exports Before Telefilm: 1952–1982

Information concerning Canadian TV exports does not become regular or reliable until the 1980s. Prior to then it is sketchy and anecdotal. This is hardly remarkable, as the overwhelming preoccupation up to that point was to account for the amount of television flowing *into* Canada, not the amount flowing *out*.

The failure to interrogate television exports, however, also points to some deeper questions. In the first instance, it points to the inability of Canadian television to attract its own audience. For example, most Canadians have long held the view, now slowly changing, that Canadian TV is really not very good: it is slow, awkward, and earnest. Indeed, this view is so deeply entrenched that when the CBC produced one of its rare sitcoms in 1989, *Mosquito Lake*, it advertised it with the slogan: 'We're on the CBC . . . but watch us anyway!' To many Canadians who watch little of their own television, the notion that others might actually *pay* for it stretches the bounds of credulity. Under such conditions, why bother to track exports? Lack of interest in exports, the disbelief that they could even occur, matches the absence of interest in domestic consumption, the belief that the content is not worth watching.

More significantly, however, the inattention also signals, within the intellectual community likely to study television, the triumph of a cultural nationalist view. That view holds that television should train audiences to like what cultural nationalists say they should like. It holds that the audience is or should be unified around certain themes, patterns, and beliefs. However, attention to television exports, no matter how modest, immediately complicates the denunciations of American cultural imperialism. Can we expect them to import our television if we do not import theirs? Can we denounce the cultural effects of their television without also suspecting the effects of ours? Does the modest export success of Canadian as compared to American television not raise the question of *why* American television is so much more popular in Canada and abroad? In short, it is infinitely easier to claim that Canadians are merely distracted from their own television by American imports than to ask how Canadian television can be made more appealing. To question the nature of the appeal of Canadian television is a tacit admission that the audience is not unitary or unified, and therefore not easily satisfied with the image of itself proposed by cultural nationalism.

Canadian television exports in the pre-Telefilm era (1952–82) can be characterized against that backdrop. Television was overwhelmingly produced in-house by the CBC or other networks for domestic consumption in order to meet content quotas. Such quotas had been imposed since the late 1950s with extremely variable effect. None the less, much of the production was unexportable either because of its specificity or because of its production values. Canadian sporting events, politics, news, and public affairs, for example, had only limited foreign appeal. Additionally, international buyers were unlikely to acquire programming whose production values Canadians themselves described as slow, awkward, and earnest. The comparison with American television was damaging even in the eyes of Canadians. Indeed, the types of content most likely to sell abroad were consistently produced the least by Canadian networks throughout this period. Hence, they produced a tiny amount of drama, which is very expensive and must compete with American counterparts, and huge amounts of sports and news, which are considerably less expensive and have a guaranteed domestic market. As a result, they acquired expertise in the news and documentary genre but not in drama or entertainment genres. This further contributed to the perception of awkwardness.

None the less, some CBC content obviously did prove exportable. The *Financial Post* reported in June 1957 that a kinescope of a CBC drama, *Flight Into Danger*, had been very favourably reviewed by London critics. Although 1957 effectively marked the end of the kinescope era, with the large-scale introduction of videotape recording, unnamed CBC executives enthused about the possibility of exporting Canadian kinescopes around the world. One executive even opined: 'We may have hit the jackpot.' ('Export Success For Canadian TV' 1957).

Although there exists little subsequent evidence of a pent-up demand for Canadian drama, one of the most successful exports from this first period was a CBC science series, in production since 1956, *The Nature of Things*. This programme has always dealt with themes of a universal, non-controversial, and educational nature in a high public service idiom. Another successful Canadian genre was the nature/adventure drama of which *Danger Bay*, *The Beachcombers*, and *Spirit Bay* are the most recent examples. Earlier examples include *Tugboat Annie*, *The Forest Rangers*, *Adventures in Rainbow Country*, and *Ritter's Cove*. These shows invariably feature children or adolescents surrounded by caring adults in a nature or wilderness setting. On a weekly basis, moral dilemmas confront the cast which the young people solve through spontaneous ingenuity and the help of a favourite animal, a kindly native person, parents, or the local detachment of the Royal Canadian Mounted Police ('Mounties').

As well as being an exportable genre, the nature/adventure drama corresponded to the objectives of the Broadcasting Act within Canada. By decentralizing production to the wilderness regions (or at least outside of Toronto and Montreal), it actually showed Canada to Canadians and gave all the regions a sense of representation. Furthermore, it was gratefully received by parents as non-violent programming which they could watch with their children, while being vaguely educational and clearly non-American. The genre has always enjoyed steady, if unspectacular, success.

The international success of the genre rests upon several factors. Importantly, relatively little high-quality children's or family drama is produced internationally, and especially not in the USA. This created an obvious opportunity for Canadian producers. Furthermore, the generally lower cost of these shows coincided with the resources of Canadian producers. These shows, however, also possess other qualities which account for their appeal with young audiences: exotic Canadian locations and animals (much as *Skippy the Bush Kangaroo* had for Canadian children), production values acceptable to the usually tolerant child audience, a marked lack of violence, heavily emphasized 'pro-social' values, and child actors. Finally, as the child audience is constantly renewed, the same programmes can be reissued every five or six years, thereby allowing companies to build up profitable catalogues. The international demand for this genre, which Canadian producers have continued to make with ever-greater refinements and higher budgets, has come from virtually around the world, irrespective of language and culture: Israel as much as Norway, Ireland as much as New Zealand, Germany as much as the USA.

In the current period, then, Canada has gone on to consolidate its comparative advantage in this type of programming. In the late 1980s the CBC explicitly undertook to schedule a regular 'family hour' during which drama suitable for families would be show-cased. This time slot allowed the perpetuation of children's drama initiated by the nature/adventure genre. As a result, the family hour became the home of some of the most successful Canadian television productions ever. The made-for-TV mini-series *Anne of Green Gables* even earned the highest ratings of any television show in Canadian history (5.8 million viewers). It was subsequently turned into a weekly series, *Road to Avonlea*. Both, based on the Lucy Maud Montgomery novels, have been widely exported with great success. The CBC also produced or acquired several TV movies recounting the adventures of young people: *Lost in the Barrens*, about two brothers struggling to survive on the tundra; *Tom Alone*, a nineteenth-century story about an orphan; *Degrassi Junior High* and *Degrassi High*, which follow the lives of a group of high-school friends; and *Brothers By Choice*, about two brothers, one adopted, whose mutual contempt turns to respect. This last programme also topped the ratings in Norway when it was shown there.

The insistence on family drama has also mutated into several fairly ingenious programmes involving non-saccharine families. For example, *Mom P.I.* involves a mother who works as a waitress and moonlights as a detective; *Airwaves* involves a teenage girl at war with herself and her family; *My Secret Identity* involves a teenage boy endowed with super-powers; and *Max Glick* follows the early-1960s adventures of the young title character. All of these shows have taken from the nature/adventure genre the elements of young heroes, lack of violence, and pro-social values, jettisoned the requirement for wilderness settings and animals, and substituted urban and frequently highly ironic plot lines. Again, they enjoy steady but unspectacular success.

On the French-language side in the pre-Telefilm era, the SRC also became the largest production facility in North America, outstripping in sheer volume even the Hollywood TV factories. However, little of its content could be exported, for two reasons: in the first instance the international market for French-language television developed later than its English-language counterpart. When it was established it was soon dominated by France, which had interests in Europe and several former colonies, rather than by Quebec, which had neither. Secondly, Quebec television seemed distressingly 'American' to much of the French-speaking world, a fact merely reinforced by the Quebec dialect which marked Quebec TV as strongly local.

These facts alone, however, did not exhaust the resistance to French-language television exports. Quebec television also shares relatively few stylistic attributes with French production. Like US television, it tends to be fast-paced and topical, with an emphasis on episodic drama and soap opera. It also tolerates commercial interruptions, outrageous promotions, and the emergence of a fawning star system. Indeed, in its overall tone and feeling, Quebec television resembles systems in which the commercial element is either dominant, such as Australia, or in which the public element has attempted to meet the challenge of commercialism, such as Britain. The ironic result is that Quebec television not only fails to resemble the French, it also fails to resemble the rest of Canadian television.

While these factors may have helped secure the loyalty of Quebec viewers they also helped alienate others unfamiliar with the fan culture or the plethora of star references. The embeddedness of Quebec culture within North American life, along with its strong autonomous development, therefore, made exports of Quebec television to the French-speaking world more difficult. Finally, however, the sheer volume of production also resulted in low production values, due to the size of the internal market.

In this first period of Canadian television the independent production sector was virtually non-existent. If the CBC was considered awkward, independent productions were simply ghastly. Again, they suffered from unfavourable comparisons with American television. For example, in the early 1970s the Colgate-Palmolive Company produced in Toronto a police-medical drama syndicated to the USA and titled *Dr. Simon Locke* (or *Police Surgeon* depending on the production year), of which *Variety* said: 'Sub-sub par . . . No viewer would return for a second look . . . No way, no way!' (Brooks and Marsh 1992). However, not everything independently produced was irredeemable. Independent producers did syndicate to the USA several game shows, most notably *Jackpot*, *Beat the Clock*, and *Let's Make A Deal*. Furthermore, some independent documentaries, such as Douglass-Leiterman's *Here Come the Seventies*, did find international distribution. Interestingly, because it demonstrates once again the Canadian penchant for children's programming, one of the most successful independent exports was *You Can't Do That On Television*, a sketch comedy programme for and by young people specializing in 'gross' humour.

Canadian TV, therefore, exported relatively little noteworthy content. However, over both periods under discussion it did export a great deal of talent. Scriptwriters, actors, and producers have moved in large numbers out of Canada and into other television systems. The full list of departing talent would be tediously long, but a few names might be mentioned: Lorne Green, William Shatner, Norman Jewison, Bernard Braden, Michael J. Fox, Lorne Michaels, Ivan Reitman, Sydney Newman, Dan Aykroyd, Margot Kidder. This phenomenon has repeated itself in the entertainment industry ever since the turn of the century. It is a measure of the insufficiencies of the Canadian system that so many people felt their talents could only be appreciated elsewhere.

Robert Lantos, head of Alliance Corporation, Canada's most successful independent production company, accurately described the pre-Telefilm period when he said: 'Actually, there was no business in the first place. The business had to be invented from scratch. There were nothing but obstacles, both at home and internationally. We didn't exist' ('Getting Along With the Rest of the World' 1994).

Programmes were not conceived with export markets in mind, for which their domestic orientation often made them unsuitable. Additionally, their low production values conspired to make them undesirable. Finally, their stylistic components helped make some of them incomprehensible on international markets. The successfully exported programmes tended to fall into clearly definable categories: children's or family drama, classic public service content, and game shows. The first were successful because of their cost, the absence of competition, their lack of violence, and their pro-social values. The second found markets wherever the need to satisfy public service requirements made itself felt. The third were exported exclusively to the USA for which they had always been intended; they capitalized on the lower production costs of Canada in order to capitalize on the higher advertising revenues of the USA.

The affinities between producers and buyers which emerge in this period are not initially based on linguistic or cultural similarities but rather on the character of broadcasting markets and on the peculiarities of their demand. The success of Canadian exports seems to depend, therefore, on factors such as an international demand for programming perceived as non-violent and pro-social rather than on 'geolinguistic' trade areas.

After Telefilm: Exports Since 1982

The shifts of the 1980s can best be understood by examining five interlinked trends: (a) changes in the regulation of television; (b) the creation of a specialty and pay TV market; (c) the creation of Telefilm Canada and changes at the CBC; (d) the rise of co-productions; and (e) transformations in US broadcasting.

The Regulation of Television

Although questions of television administration pre-date the 1980s, regulations established in the 1960s and 1970s play an important role in the present. The Broadcasting Act is interpreted and administered by the CRTC which licenses networks, television stations, cable companies, and discretionary services (specialty and pay TV), usually for periods of five to seven years. The CRTC may set content quotas, create policy when new situations arise, and set conditions of licence. These can require any particular licensee to spend fixed sums of money on specific content categories, to alter hiring practices, to restructure affiliation agreements, and so on.

Over-the-air broadcasters are required to programme 60 per cent Canadian content, a target widely surpassed by the CBC (approximately 90 per cent) and by the SRC (approximately 80 per cent). Provincial broadcasters also exceed the quota, but by lesser margins, while private broadcasters exceed it by much more modest margins. For example, the CRTC instructed the largest private network, CTV, to accomplish the following between 1987 and 1994 (CRTC 1987): (a) spend \$C403 million on Canadian programming; (b) schedule 120 hours per year of Canadian dramatic features, mini-series, and limited series in prime time; (c) provide an annual twenty-four hours of Canadian musical programming; and (d) provide a minimum of one-and-a-half hours of regularly scheduled Canadian programming in prime time rising to three-and-a-half hours per week. CTV met the obligations by (a) spending \$C417 million; (b) scheduling 126 hours of dramatic features; (c) programming forty hours of musical content; and (d) requesting that the minimum number of regularly scheduled dramatic hours not exceed three per week (CTV 1993). Cable operators are required to carry more Canadian than non-Canadian services. Discretionary services are also required to meet content quotas (usually well below 30 per cent). The CRTC has never revoked a licence. Its decisions may be appealed to Cabinet, and the minister of communication may suspend a decision or direct the CRTC to (re)examine cases and situations.

The CRTC's content quotas, first adopted in 1969, essentially created a permanent demand for Canadian content within Canada. Before the 1980s, however, broadcasters frequently met that demand by programming the least expensive content categories (that is, game shows) or by scheduling Canadian content in off-peak hours where it would do the least damage. In the last decade, however, with the explosion of viewing choices, Canadian content has become a distinguishing factor and hence a definite advantage for many broadcasters, who now accord it higher production values and more favourable scheduling.

The CRTC, however, does not act alone. Although it sets the content quotas, it does not determine the nationality of programmes. That determination is made by the Canadian Audio-Visual Certification Office (CAVCO) which administers the 'point system' by examining budgetary documents. The point system serves a double purpose: (1) projects conforming to it are eligible for governmental assistance and/or tax concessions; (2) content certified as Canadian counts towards the content quota. Indeed, a CAVCO-certified production can count for more than 100 per cent Canadian content, thereby freeing up additional time for non-Canadian content.

The point system works as follows: (a) the material must be produced by a Canadian citizen or landed immigrant; (b) its copyright must be owned by a Canadian citizen; (c) 75 per cent of remuneration must be payable to Canadians; and (d) 75 per cent of aggregate costs for services must be payable to Canadians. Additionally, the content must obtain six points on the following scale: (a) two points each for director and screenwriter; (b) one point for highest-paid actor; (c) one point for second highest-paid actor; and (d) one point each for art director, music composer, picture editor, and director of photography.

Government assistance is of two types: loans from Telefilm Canada and tax concessions. Telefilm funding can cover pre- and post-production as well as distribution, dubbing, international marketing, and so on. Telefilm, however, does not automatically invest in all projects conforming to the point system. It also evaluates the nature and quality of proposed screenplays, the track records of applicants, and so on. In this sense Telefilm resembles a Hollywood studio, assessing not only objective financial criteria but also more imponderable qualitative criteria. Private investors participating in certified projects may receive tax concessions. Provincial governments have instituted parallel structures to attract production to their territory.

The need of broadcasters to meet Canadian content quotas, CAVCO's certification procedure, and the funds made available by Telefilm in conjunction with tax concessions, combine to direct investment towards Canadian television production. However, the small size of the Canadian market continues to require Canadian producers to seek international partners. Fortunately, it is becoming increasingly easy to find international partners as they are increasingly eager to co-produce with Canada. Indeed, the number of outlets in which Canadian content can be placed, and which actively demand Canadian content, is expanding.

Specialty and Pay TV

Specialty and pay TV are separate entities known collectively as discretionary services. Both types of service are licensed by the CRTC but are offered differently to subscribers. Specialty services are bundled by cable operators as a package. Subscribers may not choose to receive only one specialty service; they must subscribe to the entire package. This boosts subscribership to weak services thereby guaranteeing their viability. Individual cable operators decide how to package them for their area. Pay TV is offered as a series of single channels which subscribers may receive if they wish. Specialty packages cost considerably less than single pay TV channels: $C2–3 per month as against $C18–25 per month. Specialty packages typically mix a few American services with the Canadian. Likewise, subscribing to Canadian pay TV channels gives one access to additional American channels. The American services are universally used as inducements to subscribe to Canadian services.

The immediate effect of these services has been to create a new market for independent producers. The most outstanding example is provided by CITY-TV, controlled by Moses Znaimer. CITY-TV began as a Toronto independent broadcaster in 1972. It had other interests, notably in radio. In 1984 Znaimer won the licence for a music video channel (MuchMusic), financed by both subscriber fees and advertising revenue. It was an instant success and the Znaimer empire has continued to grow. Indeed, MuchMusic is now exported to the USA where it is a more upscale alternative to MTV. From his success Znaimer also exports such programmes as *Fashion Television*, *Movie Television*, and *The New Music*. Znaimer, who is Canada's most innovative broadcaster, also controls the French-language music video channel (MusiquePlus) and is pursuing international broadcast investments. Znaimer's success, however, is only the most obvious. Other discretionary services have also spawned markets for independent producers who then resell their content internationally. For example, YTV, the Youth Channel, spawned both *Maniac Mansion* and *Adventures of the Black Stallion*, which have been widely exported.

Telefilm Canada and Changes at the CBC

Telefilm Canada was originally created in 1967 as the Canadian Film Development Corporation (CFDC). As its name implies, the CFDC attempted to stimulate the production of feature films. By the 1980s it was obvious that the only distribution system controlled by Canadians was television. The government, therefore, shifted its priority from film financing to film *and television* financing. The shift took two forms. In the first, the CBC, which had traditionally been the centrepiece of

Canadian cultural policy, began to be defunded. The yearly rate of budget increase was decelerated, production was scaled down, jobs were eliminated, stations were closed, and so on. In its second form, the CBC was required to obtain 50 per cent of its entertainment programming from independent producers. Hence, former CBC money was transferred to Telefilm which disbursed it to independent production companies, while the CBC was transformed from a producer to a purchaser of content, thereby creating an even wider, and more solid, market for independent productions.

Telefilm administers two funds, the Feature Film Fund and the Canadian Broadcast Program Development Fund. Each fund runs to approximately $C60 million per year and Telefilm invests in all phases of production, including scriptwriting, as well as dubbing, marketing, and distribution. The creation of a discretionary television market and the transformation of the CBC into a programme purchaser have given Canadian production companies two things they never before possessed: a track record and a backlog of marketable product. The need to market remains, for whereas US networks pay licence fees covering 80 per cent of production costs, Canadian networks rarely pay licence fees covering more than 20 per cent of production costs (Ellis 1992). Indeed, discretionary services and independent broadcasters often pay considerably less. Additionally, Telefilm funds rarely cover more than 33 per cent of production costs. Hence, Canadian production companies must either confine themselves to inexpensive genres—a practice adopted by some Quebec-based companies because of the loyalty of French-language audiences—or seek out international partners and outlets. The government has instituted a system of 'treaties' precisely for the purpose of international co-productions. Developments in American television, similar to those in Canada but on a much larger scale, have also created unanticipated outlets.

The Rise of Co-productions

Co-productions involve partners from Canada and another country contributing to the manufacture of a single film or television programme. They occur within the framework of treaties signed between the governments of Canada and the other country. The specifics of the treaties vary from case to case but generally cover financial participation, mutual tax concessions, national treatment, creative control, and copyright ownership (Bolduc 1991). Canada has over thirty co-production treaties with several countries, including France, Australia, the UK, Mexico, China, Israel, Germany, and New Zealand. Most co-productions, however, occur with European partners, with France accounting for over 50 per cent of all activity. Some of the treaties have merely languished.

The advantage of co-productions for Canadian partners are straightforward: (a) higher production values, which raise the value of Canadian content; (b) access to foreign markets which might otherwise be closed; and (c) opportunities for ongoing business relations. The second point is especially important, as France has agreed to count Canadian co-productions within the European television quota. The disadvantages are that they also create opportunities for conflict over financial and creative control, they can be nightmares to administer, and they can result in the dreaded 'Euro-pudding', a programme so culturally unspecific as to be of interest to no one.

For international partners, the advantages and disadvantages are much the same, which leads one to conclude that many countries are in a situation similar to Canada's. 'Natural affinities', based primarily upon language, therefore might be expected to arise between Canada and its international partners. However, while there is certainly no doubt that linguistic commonality can be a factor, it is hardly a rule.

One need only consider the following. Although France and Canada are the world's leading co-producers, much of their collaboration concerns English-language rather than French-language projects. Bolduc (1991) suggests that this 'unnatural' affinity can be explained by two factors: (a) the Quebec audience's love of its own television which makes television co-productions less desirable, and (b) the shared love of English-speaking Canadian and French viewers for American television. Whatever the case, the fact remains that, as an emergent market or 'geolinguistic region', France and English-speaking Canada constitute an unexpected union. Their collaboration is not based on language but on audience preference and perceived economic advantage.

Indeed, Quebec and French partners collaborate more on feature films than on television, whereas French and Canadian partners collaborate much more on television than on feature films. For example, the Quebec/France film *Jesus of Montreal* received extremely favourable reviews everywhere and went on to win the Cannes Jury Prize in 1991. However, the Quebec/France television series *Lance et Compte*, about the life and loves of a hockey player with an inexplicably French mother, played to predictably weak audiences in France and was soon cancelled. The same series also performed poorly in the rest of Canada. None the less, the Nelvana production of *Les Aventures de Tintin*, based on the popular Belgian comic-book character, did well in France, as did the SRC series *Les Filles de Caleb* (marketed internationally as *Emilie*), which reached as much as 19 per cent of the French audience.

The major French-language export initiative is an international television consortium known as TV5. This consortium, governed by international agreements, makes available a selection of French-language news and entertainment programming from around the world. In Canada the selection consists mostly of programmes from Europe (France, Belgium, Switzerland) with a smattering of material from Africa and Canada itself. In Europe the proportions are composed so as to give more prominence to material from Canada, and so on. Obviously, this service is of greatest interest to other French-language broadcasters, though in principle nothing prevents any broadcaster from obtaining it. The ratings for TV5, however, tend to be very low. Consequently, although French-language programming produced in Canada may be widely available, there is some question as to how much of it is actually consumed. In Canada TV5 usually gets less than 1 per cent of the viewing audience. It seems to be another example of how programming suited to one audience works poorly for another. Ultimately, the motivation behind TV5 may be as much political, to counter the perceived hegemony of English-language broadcasting, as cultural, to create *un espace audiovisuel francophone*.

The number of English-language television co-productions is much more impressive. These include *Katts and Dog*, about a police officer attached to the canine division; *BorderTown*, about a town on the border between Canada and the USA; and *Adventures of the Black Stallion*, about a boy and his horse. All three represent a very specific type of co-production because all three received funding from Telefilm, Canadian specialty services and/or networks, French networks, and American paycable channels. As such, that part of the production involving France and Canada fell under the official co-production treaty whereas that part involving both Canada and France as well as the USA was negotiated separately by the partners as a *non*-treaty co-production or 'co-venture'.

The need to target three separate audiences—Canada, France, and the USA—leads to some typical plot devices. For example, in *Katts and Dog* the city inhabited by the police officer Katts and his dog is sufficiently indeterminate to be either Canadian or American. However, his occasional partner is a French policewoman detached from the Paris police, thereby requiring that a certain number of episodes be set every season in Paris. Likewise, the town in *BorderTown* is both Canadian *and* American. Naturally, both the Canadian Mountie and the US sheriff fall in love with the same woman, who happens to be a French doctor. Finally, in *Adventures of the Black Stallion* one of the horse-fanciers who befriends the boy and his horse as they travel around Canada and the USA, proves to be another French woman. Whether these 'compromises' damage the integrity of the shows is a moot point. Like most television, they are easier to judge on the basis of their ability to hold one's interest than as canonical expressions of a national culture. None the less, all three shows also have strong family appeal.

As regards 'natural affinities', one might also expect Canada and the UK to co-produce extensively. In fact, they co-produce relatively little and usually in the form of 'twinning'. Twinning refers to a deal which allows a totally Canadian or totally British project to be produced without intervention from the other partner but to receive national treatment on the partner's territory. Every twinning deal, therefore, involves at least two projects. Twinning certainly avoids the potential cultural confusion of some co-productions, but it hardly smacks of a 'natural affinity' or synergy. It is fundamentally a means whereby domestic producers increase their budgets against a promise of national treatment for a foreign project.

Bolduc (1991) suggests that the frequency of co-production may depend less upon the existence of a geolinguistic region within which countries of similar language and culture produce and trade content, than upon similar regulatory environments. Hence, Canada and France may co-produce so extensively because both have centrally regulated television systems which make it easy to recognize structures such as co-productions. The UK, however, has no UK content quotas, thereby making the bureaucratic rationale of co-productions more difficult to grasp. However, many Canadian co-productions speak strongly to no obvious geolinguistic ties: *Destiny Ridge* (Germany), *Bethune* (China), *Buster's Bedroom* (Germany and Portugal), *Counterstrike* (Mexico and Israel), *Millenium: Tribal Wisdom and The Modern World* (Yugoslavia). In many cases, economic advantage appears to be as great a factor as cultural affinity.

Finally, it is worth noting that most of Canada's production companies produce in both English and French, making them linguistically unspecific. It would seem, then, in the case of Canada at least, that market and financial requirements, the regulatory climate of the respective countries, the flexibility of the production partners, and differential relationships to American television are as important in determining co-production partnerships as linguistic or other cultural affinities.

Transformations in US Broadcasting

Although co-production treaties are important, the real market which Canadian producers want to crack is the USA. Fortunately, the US market has undergone significant transformations in the past ten years which have created unprecedented opportunities. The transformations have involved two steps: the introduction of discretionary American services, and the need for the networks to rethink their strategies.

In Canada the introduction of cable preceded the arrival of

specialty and pay TV. Indeed, Canadians originally subscribed to cable in order to enjoy unimpeded access to American television. Only once that had been achieved were discretionary services introduced. The situation was very different in the USA, since American viewers suffered no longing for Canadian television. On the contrary, American cable was introduced in order to make available additional American services. For that reason, American cable is frequently called 'paycable' as the new services were introduced on a discretionary basis. The same logic drives DBS (direct broadcast by satellite) in the USA.

The first American pay service was Home Box Office (HBO), launched in 1975. Since then approximately 150 cable networks have been launched. The largest of these—ESPN, CNN, USA Network, TBS, and Discovery Channel—all reach over 50 million subscribers, dwarfing even the most successful Canadian operation, with approximately 7.5 million subscribers. Their outstanding characteristic, however, from the perspective of Canadian production, is their insatiable appetite. And Canadian suppliers have so successfully met the appetite that 'Canadian fare accounts for about 30% of original programming on American cable networks', making Canada the 'largest foreign supplier of original programming on U.S. cable' (Murray 1992). Furthermore, the cable networks' constant competition drives up licence fees for Canadian producers.

Success, however, did not come overnight. It required, first, that a track-record be established, that is, that Canadian producers demonstrate their ability to manufacture content with proven audience appeal and recognized production values. In this respect, two films of the late 1970s/early 1980s were particularly important, *Meatballs* (1979) and *Porky's* (1981). Although these films were denounced on cultural, national, and aesthetic grounds, both did extremely well at the box-office. They also demonstrated the emergence of a production infrastructure within Canada, that is, the constitution of technical and managerial crews able to produce for the market. At roughly the same time, for financial reasons, Hollywood began to make increasing use of Canadian companies for line-production. In both these instances American companies looked to Canada to provide market-ready content at reduced cost.

Indeed, some American production companies do not simply seek to acquire Canadian content, they seek to take up Canadian residence. This is most notably the case of Stephen J. Cannell Studios (*21 Jump Street*, *The Commish*) and Spelling Entertainment (*Beverly Hills 90210*, *Melrose Place*). Both have established important production facilities in Vancouver, where they produce some of the most popular programmes on US television. Paradoxically, their location and the sums of money spent in Canada can occasionally qualify them as Canadian content. This is notably the case of *Top Cops* (Global/CBS), a 'reality' show about US police exploits shot entirely in Canada, and is a particularly sore point with cultural nationalists. Of course, if all Canadian productions were merely 'fake' US shows, independent producers would be unable to justify the use of public money. Fortunately, they constitute a minority of cases. Ultimately, though, the 'threat' of these shows is not to the identity of Canadians but to the pride of nationalists, who fear not that Canadians will fail to recognize them for what they are, but that Americans will not know they are Canadian.

None the less, once the track record was established, it became necessary to break into television with original programming. This occurred initially via the cable networks. With smaller budgets than the major networks, the cable networks were forced to find suppliers who could deliver a market-ready product at reduced costs. They found them in Canadian production companies who suddenly found themselves with a paradoxical advantage. Obviously, many small American companies were also formed to supply the cable networks. The American companies, however, could not tap into co-production treaties, Telefilm funding, tax concession, or a lower dollar. Canadian producers, therefore, had a competitive advantage. Additionally, even if they failed to make the US sale, they could still produce for the guaranteed Canadian market, as well as its international partners, content to syndicate their shows later (Knelman

1994). The Canadian content quotas which had at one time seemed a disincentive now proved to be an economic cushion.

Hence, by the mid-1980s Canadian-produced programming began to make its way onto US cable networks. The CBC's venerable *Tommy Hunter Show*, a country music variety hour in production since 1965, found itself on The Nashville Network. The Disney Channel picked up *The Raccoons* (animation) and *Danger Bay* (nature/adventure). The USA Network proved particularly helpful by acquiring *The Ray Bradbury Theatre* (drama), the game shows *Bumper Stumpers* and *Jackpot*, and *Alfred Hitchock Presents* (drama).

Other shows began to be acquired by other outlets. The US public network PBS purchased both *Ramona* (children) and *Degrassi Junior High* (children). As well, syndicators such as Paramount and Tribune Entertainment variously acquired *Captain Power* (children), *Friday the 13th: The Series* (drama), *TNT* (drama), *Seeing Things* (drama), and *Hangin' In* (sitcom). The major networks did not fail to notice the success of these programmes and, in 1985, CBS, then near the bottom of the ratings, began to make room in its late-night schedule for numerous Canadian dramas: *Night Heat*, *Urban Angel*, *Diamonds*, *The Twilight Zone*, *Forever Knight*, *Sweating Bullets*, and *Adderly*. Meanwhile, US cable networks, syndicators, and the public network continued to acquire more Canadian content.

An extremely telling incident occurred in 1991. The CBC had been co-producing with Broadway Video, a New York-based company headed by expatriate Lorne Michaels, the original producer of NBC's *Saturday Night Live*, a sketch comedy series starring five young comedians known as *The Kids in the Hall*. Their humour was considered quite risqué but the CBC showed it in prime time. This is one of the great legacies of the public service ethos: the CBC has always felt that its audience should be exposed to difficult material, including sometimes vulgar and shocking humour. *The Kids in the Hall* was considered far too outrageous for the major networks, so HBO acquired it and it immediately gained a cult following. American viewers had never seen anything like it. The enthusiasm was such that in 1991 CBS outbid HBO in order to add the show to its own schedule. Slowly, Canadian content was gaining a foothold on US television.

In July 1990 the CBC mini-series *Love and Hate*, about a Saskatchewan cabinet minister convicted of murdering his wife, appeared on NBC. It received the week's highest ratings. It was also the first time a non-American programme had ever been aired in prime time on a US network. In August 1992 the CBC mini-series Conspiracy of Silence, about the murder of a Manitoba native girl, gained the highest ratings of any programme aired by CBS against the Summer Olympics. Other Canadian-produced TV movies did equally well. As a result, in September 1992 Jeff Sagansky, then head of CBS programming, invited Canadian producers to enter into agreements with him. He even committed CBS to several development deals with Canadian producers with an eye to airing Canadian content in prime time.

Through many small steps, therefore, we have now arrived at a situation in which, in September 1994, CBS did what no US network had done before, that is, air a Canadian-produced regular series in prime time. The series, *Due South*, is produced by Alliance Corporation and concerns a Mountie who, through some misadventures, finds himself posted to the Canadian consulate in Chicago where he teams up with a streetwise American cop. The two-hour pilot was very warmly received. *Variety* said: 'If ever a TV film begged for its own series it is this fish-out-of-water/buddy cop tale: Although it is formulaic, the action drama scores points in every other department . . . *Due South* . . . remains thoroughly entertaining fare' (Griffin 1994: 32). *People Magazine* gave the show an 'A-minus rating'. The Canadian *Globe and Mail*'s mercurial John Haslett Cuff (1994), however, reviewed the programme in words which seem to betray the insecurities and resentments of cultural nationalism:

> Yes, I *know* this is supposed to be funny and we're not supposed to be self-conscious about seeing ourselves as ludicrously polite hicks in ceremonial RCMP dress. But I thought we were finally growing up a little, that Canada and Canadians had become something more than snow-capped vistas, Dudley Do-Rights named Fraser and husky dogs called Diefenbaker. But here we are doing it to ourselves—taking

money and pats on the head from Americans and performing stupid human TV tricks . . . God help us all.

There was actually a friendly competition amongst production companies as to which would land the first continuing series. Although Alliance won the first round, several other projects are currently in development and it is likely that in the near future all the US networks will be airing Canadian series in prime time. The nationalist fear of US domination will have come full circle.

Although access to the American market is clearly desirable, exclusive dependence upon it can have negative outcomes. For example, in 1993 Skyvision Entertainment of Toronto began production on the television series *RoboCop*, based on the 1987 film of the same name. *RoboCop* was noteworthy for two reasons: it was the most expensive television series ever undertaken in Canada (its first season was budgeted at $C35.6 million), and it was an entirely Canadian project financed without public money. It was syndicated to 170 stations in the USA and to 120 other countries, and involved cross-media tie-ins (such as figurines and posters). However, United Chris Craft, a station group accounting for six of the 170 US syndication client stations, decided to drop it in September 1994. As some of the United Chris Craft stations were located in New York and Los Angeles, their withdrawal forced the cancellation of the entire series. They weighed more than all the other markets. Nothing better illustrates the importance, and the danger, of the US market as compared to all others.

Dependence on US markets also awakens other fears. There is the fear that Canadian producers will disguise their shows as American in order to please the market. That, however, appears to be a problem of the past. There was a time when Canadian street-signs, licence-plates, and mail-boxes were painted over to make the settings look American. However, emphatic references to Canadian cities, landmarks, cultural events, customs, laws, and so on, are fairly characteristic of the shows purchased since the late 1980s. Indeed, the humour of *Due South* comes precisely from the differences between Canada and the USA. It is just as likely that these markers of Canadianness are part of the appeal of Canadian shows.

Indeed, as viewer choice expands and as all channels tend to an inexorable sameness, the specificity of Canadian, or any other, production may well emerge as a market advantage, as an element of sufficient distinction to attract and hold audiences.

There remains the further possibility that Canadian shows, while maintaining their sense of place, will somehow become more American in theme and style. That fear presupposes the existence of an antecedent Canadian style or theme against which new products can be judged. However, the only antecedent style—slow, awkward, and earnest—has been soundly rejected. There is no reason that the new style should not be equally 'Canadian'.

Canadian Production Companies

The opportunities of the 1980s and 1990s have caused rapid growth amongst independent production companies. The largest are Astral Communications Inc. of Montreal, and Alliance Communications Corporation of Toronto. Other major players include Paragon, Atlantis, Nelvana, and Cinar. An examination of some of the leading companies reveals strategic differences and similarities.

Astral was founded in 1962 as a photographic store but incorporated under its current name in 1974. It currently owns 112 photographic outlets, distributes film, television, and video, and has a library of 2,000 titles. It provides video duplication, post-production, and dubbing services, and is building a motion picture laboratory in downtown Montreal. It also participates in production and has long-standing relationships with Disney, Warner Brothers, Columbia, Universal, Hearst, and other US companies. Astral also controls seven specialty channels: The Movie Network, Viewer's Choice, Family Channel, SuperEcran, Canal Famille, Moviepix, and Arts et Divertissement. Finally, it manufactures up to 32 million CDs per year for music, education, and video (Enchin 1994*a*). Its strength, therefore, lies not in the content which it produces but in the distribution networks which it controls and in its ability to market across media.

Alliance was formed in 1985 and directs its energies heavily towards film and television production and co-production. Although Astral is Canada's largest entertainment enterprise, Alliance is definitely its most successful. It has broken itself down into separate operating units controlling production, investment, and distribution. It co-produced (with Australia) one of the most successful Canadian films ever made, *Black Robe*, it has been increasingly successful at obtaining the distribution rights to big-budget films in Canada, and its television shows appear all over North America and Europe. It landed the first regular prime time Canadian series on a US network (*Due South*), and is currently developing several other projects. Alliance's strength lies in its use of the co-production treaty system to its fullest extent. However, it should be noted that public involvement in Alliance projects has been steadily dropping over the last ten years.

Paragon Entertainment Corporation, though based in Toronto, has located its chairman in Los Angeles. Paragon's strategy is not to rely on the Canadian market: 'Unlike our competitors, we feel it is important to do some shows that have no Canadian content, because there may come a time when Canadian financing is reduced or eliminated . . . Our goal is to be perceived as suppliers of programming that doesn't need Canadian financing' (Knelman 1994).

Astral has been a publicly traded company since 1974; however, Alliance, Paragon, Atlantis, and Cinar all went public in 1993. This is thought to prove 'that the TV business in Canada has matured to the point where it is possible . . . to raise money in the public marketplace' (Knelman 1994). Another factor which most of these companies have in common is their effort to acquire existing film libraries to feed their distribution channels. Finally, virtually all of them have major deals under way with US networks and all of them maintain offices around the world.

Canadian production companies are, therefore, increasingly integrated enterprises attempting to control as much of their production, financing, and distribution as possible. Control of distribution takes the form of exclusive distribution rights for content produced by third parties, acquisition of film libraries, and outright ownership of television channels. Production occurs in both film and television and typically involves international partners. Investment has long relied upon tax concessions and government assistance but is gaining increasing independence from these sources. Typically, then, Canadian production companies seek international markets as much as international producers seek Canadian partners.

Concluding Remarks

Canada has shifted from being a television importer to being a television exporter. The shift was dependent upon several factors: (a) the creation of a domestic market for Canadian content, (b) the transfer of public funding from film to television production, (c) the institution of co-production treaties, (d) the willingness to abandon an old television style by letting new independent players into the scene, and (e) the demand of international markets, especially the USA.

If there is a natural or spontaneous geolinguistic region within which Canada preferentially trades, it lies between Canada and the USA rather than between Canada and France, the UK, or Australia. The similarities of language and culture are sufficiently powerful, and obvious to even the most casual observer, to account for this situation.

Canadian producers, however, occupy a different position *vis-à-vis* the US than American producers occupy *vis-à-vis* Canada. American producers have always counted upon the simple facts of market dominance and economic advantage to ensure their success in Canada. Canadian producers, however, must ensure their success from the inside, from an intimate knowledge of the tastes of the American marketplace itself. There is no question of a Canadian production company simply imposing itself upon the US networks because of its size. Rather, Canadian production companies must seek to exploit opportunities as they arise by being as clever about the American market as American producers themselves must be.

The current conjuncture which favours Canadian producers

has not always existed and will most likely not continue forever. Canadian companies would, therefore, be well advised to plan for that eventuality. Their surest hedge against the future appears to be the creation of a reputation for quality and the constitution of a library of desirable product. Of course, the television landscape is unlikely to return to what it was before cable, DBS, and the VCR. Channel abundance appears to be a permanent feature of the future. In that respect, Canadian productions may well stand out against the fray. Such is certainly the hope of Canadian networks who are increasingly 'branding' their signals (superimposing logos) in order to orient viewers amidst the abundance and attempt to create loyalty. Certainly, as audiences fragment, smaller players will find the field equalized with larger players, and this will benefit all Canadian television.

Some of this also applies to French-language television in Canada. It too is unavoidably impelled to find export markets and naturally favoured by channel abundance. Its overall dynamics, however, are quite different. Its obvious natural market lies in the French-speaking world, but also seems to involve film more than television. The French-language television market, despite the restructuring of the audiovisual landscape in France, has not undergone the same shifts as the US market and, for cultural reasons, is unlikely to respond to them in the same way.

Right now, though, Canadian television has never been better, or luckier.

References

ATHERTON, TONY (1994), 'Mon pays, c'est le téléroman', *Ottawa Citizen* (23 July), F1.

BOLDUC, MARIO (1991), 'Co-production: Culture of Finance', *Playback* (Aug./Nov.).

BROOKS, TIM, and MARSH, EARLE (1992), *The Complete Directory To Prime Time Network TV Shows 1946–Present* (5th edn., Ballantine Books, New York).

CRTC (Canadian Radio-Television and Telecommunications Commission), *Annual Reports*.

—— (1994), *Database* (May).

—— (1987), *Public Notice CRTC 1987–200*.

CTV Television Network Ltd. (1993), *Application to the Canadian Radio-Television and Telecommunications Commission for the renewal of its network licence expiring August 31, 1994* (May).

CUFF, JOHN HASLETT (1994), '"Due South" Makes Hay Out of the True North', *The Globe and Mail* (23 Apr.), C8.

ELLIS, DAVID (1992), *Split Screen, Home Entertainment and the New Technologies* (Friends of Canadian Broadcasting, Toronto).

ENCHIN, HARVEY (1994*a*), 'Astral Focuses on Broader Picture', *The Globe and Mail* (8 Aug.), B1.

—— (1994*b*), 'Cancom Fights to Save Captive Cable-TV Market', *The Globe and Mail* (6 Oct.), B7.

'Export Success For Canadian TV' (1957), *Financial Post* (29 June), 15.

'Getting Along With The Rest of the World' (1994), *Television Business International* (June), 19–26.

GRIFFIN, DOMINIC (1994), '"Due South"', *Variety* (18–24 Apr.), 32.

KNELMAN, MARTIN (1994), 'Made-for-TV Movies', *Report on Business Magazine* (May), 63–70.

MURRAY, KAREN (1992), 'Local Fare Finds Hungrier Palates South of the Border', *Variety* (16 Nov.).

Telefilm Canada, *Annual Reports*.

7

Australian Television in World Markets

Stuart Cunningham and Elizabeth Jacka

Australian television programmes have begun to be a quite visible presence on the stage of world television. The success of *Neighbours* and *Home and Away* in Britain are the most dramatic sign of the export successes of Australian television, but there are few territories in the world now that do not contain Australian material as part of their programme mix. Following the initial acceptance of Australian cinema as an art house favourite in the 1970s, the next decade saw a large number of prestige Australian mini-series on screens in continental Europe, Britain, and New Zealand and, to a much lesser extent, North America. Since the mid-1980s Australian serials and series have become standard fare in many of these territories as well, and Australia is well represented world-wide in genres like children's drama, documentary, science and technology, comedy, and nature programmes.

The general elements outlined in Chapter 1 that have fostered increased globalization and peripheral nations' television export have specific inflections in the case of Australia. Indeed, Australia may be understood as a limit case in so far as it shares some characteristics which have produced the metropolitan (US and UK) dominance of television trade—the English language and high levels of commercialization—while also sharing characteristics of other peripheral nations, such as being a substantial net importer of film and television. This 'in-between' status arises from its Anglo-Celt white settler-dominion history which places it between 'core' and 'peripheral' countries in the world system.

Australian production costs are relatively low compared with other English-language production markets, particularly the USA. Because Australia's population (and therefore production) base is small, the industry has to be efficient to survive. Its relative efficiency is largely a function of sophisticated technical and creative resources. However, its domestic market is small relative to the amount of television material produced and this, combined with the rising cost of all forms of television, but particularly high-end quality drama, necessitates the search for external financing and markets. The subsidy, investment, and regulation infrastructure in Australia for film and television has contributed over the years to the diverse portfolio of formats and genres produced domestically, allowing the production industry and the viewing public to retain their own voice despite the small population base. Australia's high level of commercialization from the inception of its television system (which has meant the development of one of the largest advertising bases per capita in the world), in tension with its small market, has also meant that the production industry had to develop relatively cheap production protocols for a variety of long form series and one-shot drama.

It is significant that this predominantly anglophone country is an English-language production centre. This is becoming increasingly important because the more internationalized television becomes, the more crucial the language of production becomes. An English-language production centre automatically lowers its product cost and potentially increases its markets. Australia is not limited to export within its geolinguistic community or region—its biggest aggregate market is Europe (including Britain, it totals 40 per cent of total export trade), while the anglophone North American market is resistant to Australian (as well as most other foreign) imports—language is neither the major enhancer nor inhibitor of export success in these territories. While it is probably a support for the 'geolinguistic hypothesis' that Australia clearly enjoys a certain comparative advantage by producing in English and being primarily an anglophone culture, several factors parallel to the geolinguistic hypothesis are relevant to Australia—opportunities for export to rapidly expanding and commercializing territories (Europe in 1980s and early 1990s; Asia in the 1990s) and export to cultural as much as linguistic 'common markets' (the UK and New Zealand). A further point concerns the hybridity or recombinant nature of the Australian television system (Cunningham 1992: 28–32; O'Regan 1993). Having been largely modelled on and influenced by high levels of imports from the two premier television centres, the USA and the UK, it has internalized best practice in both commercial and public service practices.

The International Face of Australian Television

It is possible to argue that '[w]hen Australia became modern, it ceased to be interesting'—interesting, that is, to an international cultural intelligensia and anthropological audience (Miller 1994: 206). Equally, it is arguable that the country has attracted international interest again at present, due in no small part to its audiovisual output. What made the country interesting in the nineteenth century was the radically premodern cultural difference of its indigenous peoples set against a transplanted white settler colonial culture. What has produced interest again is its emerging profile as a postcolonial and multicultural society—a postmodern 'recombinant' culture—well suited to playing a role in global cultural exchange.

This view is put strongly by Andrew Milner, who argues that social and cultural modernity was only ever partially realized in Australia:

> Thus Australia has been catapulted towards post-industrialism at a speed possible only in a society that had never fully industrialized; towards consumerism in a fashion barely imaginable in historically less affluent societies; towards an aesthetic populism unresisted by any indigenous experience of a seriously adversarial high culture; towards an integration into multinational late capitalism easily facilitated by longstanding pre-existing patterns of economic dependence, towards a sense of 'being after', and of being post-European, entirely apposite to a colony of European settlement suddenly set adrift, in intellectually and imaginatively uncharted

Asian waters, but the precipitous decline of a distant Empire. (Milner 1991: 116)

Although it underlines reasons why Australian popular culture has a certain dynamism within globalizing and postmodern cultural exchange, this view is a partial and rhetorical account. There remain strong modernist institutions and structures, of which the public broadcasting sector is a major contributor, as well as a strong, if constantly deprecated, reliance on a central state, along with as a ramified series of local and regional structures which arose out of the prototypically modernist project of nation-building. John Caughie's comments on the way postmodernist trends overlay rather than eclipse modernist traditions in British broadcasting are even more appropriate for Australia, because it has had an embedded commercial ethos for longer than Britain, so the 'overlay' process has been a less traumatic one:

> British television, and much European television, is still rooted in modernity, the concept and practice of public-service broadcasting, part of an unbroken tradition of 'good works' dating from the administration of capitalism in the latter part of the nineteenth century. While that tradition is clearly under threat from the readministration of capitalism and the redistribution of power in global markets, nevertheless the scenario of magical transformation—the marvellous vanishing act of deregulation: now you see 'quality', now you don't—in both its optimistic and its pessimistic variants seems naive. (Caughie 1990: 48)

Australia's central public broadcaster, the Australian Broadcasting Corporation (ABC), exemplifies this combination in its performance of its charter functions as a modernist nation-building instrument, while also enthusiastically exploiting commercial and corporate opportunities in new markets (its satellite venture in Asia, ATV—Australian Television) and new media (pay TV). Australian historical mini-series of the 1980s (some of them exported widely, as we have noted) are also prime examples of this combination. Extremely popular commercial successes, screening almost exclusively on commercial networks in Australia, they were nevertheless imbued with the modernist educational public service ethos of reconstructing popular memory about major defining moments of the nation's history.

International exposure of Australian television product and representative figures span the modernist/postmodernist spectrum. Those stellar few who enjoy mogul status in world television include pre-eminently Rupert Murdoch, since 1985 an American citizen, but whose Australian patrimony and business roots are the subject of considerable review as commentators and antagonists alike seek to chart the causes and effects of his success as 'ringmaster of the information circus' (Shawcross 1992). Supposedly 'Australian' traditions of sharp practice and derring-do, anti-establishment commitments and brash populist beliefs, are held to contribute to his interventions in British television and press, the establishment and hard-won success of BSkyB and the continuation of that success with the take-over of Star TV, and his lead in the major expansion and commercialization of television in Asia, eastern Europe, and India. His mastery of populist press traditions are credited with underscoring the invention of tabloid television: 'Tabloid television, as the term is generally understood, was born in the United States . . . But before anyone cries Yankee cultural imperialism, they should consider this: if the Americans nurtured the genre, Australians fathered it' (Lumby and O'Neil 1994: 152).

The Australian system seems to have bred a talent for successful low-budget commercial television and has attracted a reputation, for better or worse, throughout the world for it. Australian producers, like some Latin American companies covered in this book, have churned out a considerable body of soap-opera hours which occupy considerable space in terrestrial and satellite schedules. In many situations, this means being able to substitute for and possibly even compete with US programme offers. This attracts criticism from countries which perceive themselves to be threatened by the Trojan horses of US culture. In New Zealand the view is put that 'Australian programmes are merely American programmes once-removed . . . as a consequence of the internationalisation of television, Australian television networks had readily adopted formats and styles "born in the U.S.A." . . . Such formats and styles have now been passed on to New Zealand; in the form of Australian-made programmes or as local adaptations of Grundy productions' (Lealand 1990: 102). It is ironic that Grundys was sold in early 1995 to the UK Pearson Group. While this acquisition dilutes the Australianness of the company, it is nevertheless an index of its high international profile. When a recent study showed Australia to be a significant supplier of light entertainment into Europe, this was seen as setting an unfortunate precedent for the further development of a local production industry: 'The question is whether the European programme industry has to follow the Australian recipe: imitation of American TV formulas, thus stimulating the globalisation and homogenisation of the international TV market' (de Bens *et al.* 1992: 94).

At the other end of the spectrum, producers of quality drama in the British tradition have enjoyed a royal road to the BBC and the ITV, and have established long-term co-production and co-venture arrangements with such central public services based on the highest quality values of television practice. Australian producers can 'play at being American'—the two-edged sword of the postcolonial condition, playing a game of reverse imperialism, but within the rules of subordination (Caughie 1990: 44)—without reserve. They can equally strongly eschew that path. The first model is exemplified by the advocates of increased off-shore production in Australia, or by those productions, like *Paradise Beach*, made primarily for the US market. The second finds no better exemplar than the Kennedy Miller company, whose outstanding historical mini-series of the 1980s were found too 'parochial' by many international buyers, who expressed bewilderment that a company with a world reputation for feature film successes (such as the *Mad Max* films) should evince no interest in 'modifying' their television output for the international market. In some cases, as with Village Roadshow/Warner Roadshow group, these two traditions can even exist under the same corporate umbrella (for example, with Village Roadshow producing *Paradise Beach* and Roadshow Coote and Carroll *Brides of Christ*).

The Australian system has neither the depth of public service ethos and product of the UK system, nor the universalist appeal and range of talent of the US system, but its recombination of both systems affords it certain strengths beyond that seen in similarly medium or small sized, peripherally placed industries. This does not guarantee export success, but it does suggest the variety of models available to Australian producers.

The Television System

Australia is a country of 17.6 million people; as such it must be considered a small nation as far as television goes. It compares with The Netherlands with 15 million, Canada with 29 million, is significantly smaller than the UK (56 million), France (56 million), and united Germany (87 million), and is dwarfed by the USA (256 million). This has implications for the television system; advertiser-supported television must struggle with a small population base and therefore a small pool from which to derive revenue to provide programmes; the operations of the public broadcasters (Australia has two) impose higher tax burdens per capita than many other countries. Australians spend less time watching television than people in comparable countries; far less than Americans and Japanese, and slightly less than Britons and Canadians (Molloy and Burgan 1993: 35).

In 1992/3 the three commercial networks made a profit overall of $A266.6 million before interest and tax. Revenues climbed by 9.5 per cent to $A2,035.8 million while expenditures increased 14 per cent to $A1,923.2 million, reflecting the continuation of the industry's recovery from the financial mismanagement and recession of the late 1980s and early 1990s (ABA 1994). Programme expenditure was divided between Australian and imported programming as shown in Table 7.1.

In 1990 television advertising revenue was $A1,738.1 million ($US1,332 million) (BTCE 1991: 35). This is high in per capita terms because Australia has a mature commercial industry compared with other much larger countries, especially in Europe, and because it allows more advertising time per hour than any other country except Canada (Molloy and Burgan 1993: 13). In per capita terms Australia has the second highest advertising expenditure in the world (after the USA). However, it is low in absolute terms if we compare it with the US television ad spend of $US27,970 million and with that in Japan at $US10,602 million. Canada, with a bigger population, spends considerably less than Australia—$US1,139 million. The volume of advertising revenue places a direct limit on funds available to commission and purchase programmes on commercial television. Given the differential cost of local versus imported programmes, economic rationality would favour imports, even at the expense of losing audience.

Australia's particular model of a broadcasting 'mixed economy' has begun to look increasingly attractive in the 1990s. Australia has had four television networks since 1963, three commercial and one public, the ABC. From 1980 the specialist multicultural SBS network was added; by 1994 its service reach has been extended to include most of the population. Until the so-called aggregation and equalization programme from 1988 to 1992 gave most of regional eastern Australia three commercial stations, commercial television networking extended only to the capitals. Even though Australia allowed a relatively high number of commercial services for such a small nation, the three networks were well insulated from competition. No new commercial services will be contemplated until a review in 1997, and the main public broadcaster, unlike in other countries such as Germany, South Africa, and New Zealand, does not accept advertising. Prior to cross-media ownership rules introduced in 1987, a powerful newspaper oligopoly dominated the television industry, ensuring healthy profit-making.

In return for this regulatory protection the networks were subject to a series of 'community service obligations', the most

Table 7.1. Expenditure on Australian and imported programming, 1992/3 ($ Australian)

	Seven Network	*Nine Network*	*Ten Network*
Australian programming	204.7	158.2	78.1
Imported programming	49.8	80.6	27.5

notable of which were Australian content requirements. Other obligations included requirements to broadcast regulator-approved children's programming and to provide a so-called 'adequate and comprehensive service' (which meant a broad-based service that covered all programme genres and was intended to offer programmes relevant to the particular nature of the community it served). The protected environment of Australian television was further ensured by Australia's geographical distance from the major television centres in Europe and the USA, so that Australia was never subject to cross-border spills of signals, though this will be an issue in the next few years as satellite services in the Asian region proliferate.

The ABC has never been subject to specific Australian content provisions, but its charter (in the ABC Act of 1973) required it to 'provide within Australia innovative and comprehensive broadcasting and television services of a high standard' which includes 'programmes . . . that contribute to a sense of national identity and inform and entertain, and reflect the cultural diversity of the Australian community' (section 6(1)a). The ABC was the first service to produce Australian-made drama and continued that tradition, despite a downturn in the late 1970s to the mid-1980s. In the current period it has aimed for and mostly attained the target of 100 hours a year of television drama (Jacka 1991: 28 ff.). Since 1988, when generous tax concessions for audiovisual productions (embodied in section 10BA of the tax legislation) were wound back and the commercial networks entered a period of financial crisis, the ABC has been dominant in drama production other than serials.

State Intervention

The state has intervened to ensure diversity and depth in Australian audiovisual production. Apart from significant, long-term, direct appropriations that provide the core finance for the public broadcasters, it has regulated and provided subsidy and investment funding. The most significant regulatory stimulus to the development of an Australian production industry with export potential has been the Australian quotas imposed on commercial stations by law and regulation since the early 1960s. Some commentators (Moran 1985; Papandrea 1994) have argued that they were not the most important factor in the development of indigenous drama programming; rather, it was audience demand for local programming that stimulated a drama production industry. However, regulation consistently reflected this community demand, and set benchmarks that acted as a 'safety net', that is, a mechanism for preventing attained levels being eroded in times of economic downturn in the industry (Molloy and Burgan 1993: 112). It seems reasonable to say that regulation has been a necessary but not sufficient factor; this has been acknowledged by the chief executive of the Seven Network, Bob Campbell, when he noted: 'We should say thanks in part to the regulators and their foresight in forcing us to make Australian content because I think that will be the driver for our ongoing success in the new broadcast environment' (*Sydney Morning Herald* (20 July 1994), 41).

Australian content regulation has been of signal importance in the country's 'mixed economy' of broadcasting, lending to that term another central meaning. The general objective that there should be about 50 per cent Australian content on television means that the system remains identifiably indigenous, while enjoying a structured, controlled access to a mix of American, British, and a wide range of other material on the SBS. Compared to the direct access US television services have to most of Canada's population, Australia enjoys a screening or filtering process embodied in the programming decisions made by the Australian networks in their development of their foreign portfolios. Changes to the structure of Australian content regulation will be driven by the growing transparency of the industry to international trends and pressures. While the aftermath of the conclusion of the GATT Uruguay Round has seen Australia taken off the US priority watch-list of countries maintaining restraints on free trade in services (such as its content regulation and production subsidies), this is an uneasy truce liable to change. The currently strong cultural rationale for an Australian look on the country's television screens will have to be reconciled with the need to find overseas finance through co-production. Australia also may have to modify its regulation to accord with its 'Closer Economic Relations' (CER) free trade agreement with New Zealand which would accord New Zealand programmes enhanced entry into the larger market.

State subsidy and investment financing started early in the film revival period when the government established the Australian Film Development Corporation in 1970, which became the Australian Film Commission (AFC) in 1975 (Dermody and Jacka 1987). Direct government assistance was supplemented in 1980 by changes to the taxation regime which allowed generous write-offs for private sector investment in film and higher-budget television drama and documentary (the so-called 10BA rules). These in turn were wound down in 1988 when a new state investment bank, the Film Finance Corporation (FFC), was established (Dermody and Jacka 1988*b*).

The AFC's brief was to provide loans and investments to films which qualified as Australian under the Act (Dermody and Jacka 1987: 137). Until the tax concessions were introduced in 1980 virtually every Australian film and high-budget television drama made was funded mainly through the AFC. The limits to direct government funding by this route put a lid on the production potential of the industry. Until *Water Under the Bridge* (1980) and *A Town like Alice* (1981) virtually no high-budget one-off television drama was produced by the commercial networks. This was exclusively the province of the ABC which, sometimes in co-production arrangements with the BBC and sometimes alone, produced ground-breaking titles like *Rush* (1973), *Power Without Glory* (1976), *Patrol Boat* (1979), the anthology *Spring and Fall* (1980–1), *The Timeless Land* (1980), and *1915* (1982).

The lack of sufficient funds to develop the industry to its full potential was what led the government to introduce the generous 10BA concessions, the reasoning being that the system would thus be market- rather than bureaucrat-driven. The 10BA concessions certainly produced a boom; the number of features produced doubled within a year, and the mini-series boom of the 1980s, and the 'golden age' of Australian television, began (Dermody and Jacka 1988*b*). The mini-series produced under the stimulus of 10BA are some of the finest Australian productions, including *The Dismissal*, *Bodyline*, *Vietnam*, *Return to Eden*, *All the Rivers Run*, *The Dunera Boys*, *Anzacs*, *A Fortunate Life*, *Harp in the South*, and *The Shiralee*.

Investment by the FFC effectively replaced the profligate 10BA scheme; while having a cultural mission—the restriction to *Australian* films—the FFC was to make decisions on a commercial basis. Its guidelines state that to receive investment from the FFC a project must have 'market attachment' as indicated by a pre-sale or other investment from a broadcaster or distributor—in practice, often a foreign entity. All three vehicles for direct government support—the AFC, the FFC, and 10BA—apply only to 'one-off' projects, that is, feature films, telemovies, mini-series, and documentaries. Thus, this funding is not available to serials or series or any non-drama forms other than documentaries.

Export-Oriented Production

As a consequence of Australia's long-established 'mixed system' of commercial and public service broadcasting, it has exhibited both a 'Fordist' and a 'post-Fordist' industry structure. Except for news and current affairs, there has always been a separation between broadcasting and programme production in commercial television since the 1960s, while the ABC mirrored the structure of the BBC and only began to disaggregate during the 1980s. Apart from the ABC, Australia's industry structure has been 'post-Fordist' since its inception. In the commercial sector drama, quiz and game shows, documentary, and children's programming were contracted out to independent producers. They in turn were lean organizations who by and large did not maintain permanent studios, equipment, or post-production facilities, except for the bigger-scale producers, such as Grundys and Crawfords. This encouraged the growth of a large number of small firms providing industry infrastructure. The creative personnel are also by and large freelance contractors, although the technicians, musicians, and actors are covered by industrial awards which include minimum rates of pay.

The basis of the present Australian television production and export industry lies in the period 1964–75 when commercial television began to produce significant quantities of indigenous programming. The advent of a third commercial network in 1963 created keen competition for and a shortage of available imported programmes with the result that a stimulus to local production was created (Moran 1985: 15). Two of the companies which are amongst the most prominent today, Crawfords and Grundys, had their beginnings then—Crawfords making cheap, popular, and social-realist cop shows and Grundys repackaging quiz and game shows like *Wheel of Fortune*. Grundys did not begin drama production until 1974 with their *Class of 74*, which began a cycle of long-running Grundy soaps which have enjoyed long export careers. Another drama packager in this period was Fauna Productions, responsible for *Skippy* (the 'Bush Kangaroo'), a ninety-one-episode package sold in over 100 countries and still playing today on various channels around the world.

The next period, 1976–86, saw a consolidation of the Australian film and television industry under the impact of the twin measures of content regulation and production support. Rupert Murdoch's takeover of the TEN network produced an invigoration of and capital injection into that network which led to the string of expensive and innovative Kennedy Miller mini-series (Cunningham 1988), and 10BA produced a boom in television drama production. Serial production also flourished, with Grundys and Crawfords continuing to dominate. Grundys produced a camp version of *General Hospital*, *The Young Doctors* (1976–81), which is still running in the UK; the show which became a cult hit in the UK and, for a short time, in the US west coast, *Prisoner* (1977–86); *Sons and Daughters* (1982–7); and its most successful export, *Neighbours*, which began in 1985 and continues to the present. Crawfords produced *The Sullivans* (1976–82), which started the vogue for period drama on television, and its most successful serial export, *The Flying Doctors*, which began in 1985 and ran until 1992. Only one other producer of long-running serial drama appeared during this period, JNP, with *A Country Practice* (1981 to the present), which also exported widely.

Most other television producers of this period were concentrating on mini-series production under 10BA stimulus as outlined above. Producers who have been developed during the 1970s by the new support mechanisms administered by the AFC and state film corporations began to move into mini-series production. The mini-series cycle commenced with two which created a huge sense of occasion and got very high ratings—*Against the Wind* (1978) a colonial story set in eighteenth-century New South Wales, and *A Town Like Alice* (1981), both commissioned by the Seven Network. The most notable examples of producers who moved from film to mini-series production were Kennedy Miller (*Vietnam*, *Bodyline*, etc.), Roadshow Coote and Carroll (*Barlow and Chambers*, *The Paper Man*, etc.), the McElroy brothers (*A Dangerous Life*), Tony Buckley (*Harp in the South*, *Poor Man's Orange*, *Heroes*), and Bob Weis (*The Dunera Boys*, *Cassidy*).

Between 1980 and 1991 Australia produced 334 feature films, 172 mini-series of between four and ten hours, and 148 telemovies (AFC 1992: 34). The vast majority of these were assisted by government funding through one of the AFC, 10BA, or the FFC or a combination of these. As well as this, as indicated above, thousands of hours of series and serial drama were produced, not directly assisted by government production-support measures but undoubtedly stimulated by the Australian television quota. In the latter part of the 1980s overseas finance began to play a more important part in the Australian film industry. This was necessitated by increases in production costs and the impossibility of fully financing them from either government sources or advances on expected returns in Australia.

From the mid-1970s the ABC had been financing some of its high-budget drama through co-production sometimes with the BBC, for example, *Ben Hall*, and also with Portman/Global and Channel 4 (*Tusitala* and *Boy in the Bush*) and the French company Revcom (*Captain James Cook*) (Jacka 1991: 37–40).

After the commercial television crisis of 1987/8 the ABC was left as virtually the only producer of high-budget 'prestige' drama. From 1990 to 1993 it produced *The Magistrate*, *Come in Spinner*, *The Paper Man*, *Brides of Christ*, *Children of the Dragon*, *The Leaving of Liverpool*, and *Frankie's House*, all of which were co-produced with ITV companies or the BBC except *Come in Spinner*, which was financed entirely by the ABC, although it was sold to the BBC.

In the 1990s the major players in export-oriented production continue to be the ABC, Grundys, and Village Roadshow. The latter is unique in Australia. It is the only completely integrated audiovisual entertainment company, having involvement in studio management, production of both film and television, film distribution and exhibition, television distribution, video distribution, and movie theme-park management. Within the Village Roadshow Organization we see two very different internationalization strategies. One side of Village Roadshow's activities (Roadshow Coote and Carroll, producers of *GP* and *Brides of Christ*) emphasizes modest budgets and indigenous flavour and recognizes the necessity of overseas financial input, particularly from the UK, while retaining a high level of local control and local specificity. The other strategy is to attract mainly US overseas or 'offshore' productions to its Warner Roadshow studios at the Gold Coast in south-east Queensland. Subsidiary companies Village Roadshow Pictures and VR Television also produce feature films and TV series mainly for the US market, notably, the features *Over the Hill* and *The Power of One*, and the soap *Paradise Beach*.

Grundys is probably the best-known company outside Australia, and has been strategically engaged in internationalization for longer than probably any other Australian television production group. Until the company was sold to the British conglomerate Pearson in early 1995, it was based in the tax haven of Bermuda, where the parent company Grundy Worldwide Ltd was registered. The organization has been structured around four international divisions—Light Entertainment, Drama, Distribution, and Corporate—based in different territories (the USA, Europe, and Australasia). While Europe as a whole generates more production throughput, Australia remains the largest single country for production operations. In the 1990s Grundys was producing around fifty hours of television a week worldwide, and has made significant advances recently in East Asia and South America.

International 'Careers' of Australian Programmes

In order to focus our discussion of industrial and cultural factors which enhance or inhibit the export 'career' of Australian television, we now turn to a number of brief case-studies which assess individual programmes' success or failure in a variety of territories. Long-form series drama (*Neighbours*, *Paradise Beach*, *The Flying Doctors*) is emphasized, as this is the hardest genre to make a success of because it calls for an extended exposure to detailed cultural representations and a strong, ongoing involvement with character and situation. But Australia's only international television service (Australia Television) is also discussed, for it raises different cross-cultural and industry issues.

Cultural *Neighbours*?

Arguably the most outstanding example of Australian series export is the *Neighbours* 'phenomenon' in Britain, running from 1986 to the present day. Australian drama has been seen on British television screens for many years, including, since the late 1970s, serial drama such as *A Country Practice*, *The Sullivans*, *The Flying Doctors*, *Richmond Hill*, and *Prisoner: Cell Block H*. *Neighbours* began on BBC 1 in October 1986, strip-scheduled at the same time in the early afternoon from Monday to Friday. Its unanticipated success led to the day's episode being rescreened in the early evening, allowing it to capture a far greater proportion of young viewers and leading to runaway popularity. By 1988 it had become the most popular children's and young adults' programme on British television and it has remained in the ten most-watched programmes in Britain for several years. In an effort to counter it, the ITV network similarly strip-scheduled *Home and Away* from 1990 to immediately follow *Neighbours* in the early evening each night of the week. By early 1989 no less than fifteen hours a week of Australian soap opera was scheduled on British television, an amount far greater than the five hours of US drama, and greater even than the ten hours of local long-form drama (Craven 1989).

This provided a platform for a number of Australian programmes, produced a wide range of social response, and helped foster the development of new and more organic co-production arrangements between the British and Australian industries. By 1994 there were signs that the 'Australian cycle' had waned somewhat, with the ratings for *Neighbours* slipping and with a greater degree of industry resistance to foreign programmes dominating key parts of the schedules. However, the UK remains by far the most significant export market for the Australian television industry.

Much effort has been expended to explain the factors underlying this success. It was clear from journalistic commentary that the most public and popularized mode of explanation for the success of soaps like *Neighbours* or *Home and Away* in Britain rested on speculations about the mythological content and serial format of the programmes (speculations which closely resemble Liebes and Katz's (1990) findings, discussed in Chapter 1). The soaps are seen as filling a need in the public imagination once occupied by medieval morality plays and preaching, as providing models of behaviour directly relevant to their particular audiences. The serial format allows the consequences of such behaviour to be followed and also allows for varying means, times, and degrees of involvement and several points of association with and 'reading' of character.

A viewer survey (Wober and Fazal 1994) also provided interesting conclusions relevant to the question of consumption of non-domestic material. There was some evidence bearing out one of the *East of Dallas* team's dictums (Silj 1988) that a moderate foreignness (or what one British critic called the soaps' 'slight foreignness' (Marin 1989)) engendered more involvement and enjoyment among some viewers. This idea is expanded by Marin in these terms: 'characters outside our class system . . . can speak to us more freely than any well-defined character in an English soap, whose very definition would risk provoking all the class antagonisms which are so easily aroused here.' The 'morality tale' element put forward by critics for the appeal of soaps, which parallels so closely Liebes and Katz's findings, needs to be framed within this sense of slight foreignness. That is, the exotic or foreign elements—that 'Australians get into each other's lives and homes more than British people do', that there is a pleasing degree of 'old-fashioned' verbal cliché in the scripting, that overall the most widely noticed characteristic is an inference about life in Australia (that social interaction is more fluid)—carry with them a sense of attractive difference which is read in the act of viewing as a commentary on British life.

Textual and audience reception examinations (see also Gillespie 1993) of the success of Australian television in Britain can only be partial explanations, however. What they miss is a sense of the 'sharp end' of the social intertext created around Australian soaps, any ideological evaluation of their impact in the industrial circumstances of British television in the late 1980s. A case can be made (see Copley 1991) for *Neighbours*, and at least some of the other high-rating Australian drama, fitting all too well into the dual trajectories of deregulation and re-regulation of British television in the late 1980s. On the one hand, it was cheaply and readily available soap that answered a need for the BBC to respond, in an increasingly constrained financial environment, to attacks on its élitism and the challenges of the new commercialism. On the other, it was a clean, morally unproblematic soap, well suited to the moral re-regulation that proceeded apace with structural deregulation and the skew toward commercialism.

Often, the press rated the appeal of *Neighbours* against the 'bad' models of soap: 'not high life like *Dallas*, not low life like *EastEnders*, just everyday life' (*Trader*, 6 April 1987). The 'moral crusade' which elements of the press mounted around their constructed opposition between *Neighbours* and *EastEnders* demonstrates the degree to which Silj's (1988) 'sedimentation of other social practices' peculiar to a host country can dramatically affect the reception of popular imported television material. The most intriguing aspects of audience response to *Neighbours* may lie in the fantasy projections the soap fortuitously generates in a particular host society with historically close ties to Australia.

These aspects of the social intertext of *Neighbours* were complemented by programme scheduling. Both industry commentators (e.g. Wober and Fazal 1994) and some journalists regard such factors as a necessary and even partially sufficient recipe for success. Kate Bowles (in Taylor 1993: 13) argues against the 'common mythology' that 'open plan housing, beautiful people and hot weather' in *Neighbours* and *Home and Away* are the key ingredients. It was their placement in the schedules—stripped in the late afternoons as well as, with *Neighbours*, the early afternoons—that laid the basis for their fantasmic Australianness to become a featured factor. Indeed, it was supremely good timing that *Neighbours* became the first such programme to be stripped across the weekdays in Britain; the leading edge of a scheduling revolution within the commercialization that both BBC and ITV have pursued strongly since the mid-1980s. (The second programme to be similarly stripped was *Home and Away*.)

'Playing at being American': *Paradise Beach*

A contrasting case, this time of failure in the USA, was *Paradise Beach*. This relatively short-lived serial was screened in 1993–4 on the Australian Nine Network and in several major markets through a similar time period. It represents a good example of contemporary terms of 'playing at being American', in Caughie's (1990) two-edged sense of the term. The production and marketing strategy for *Paradise Beach* was unique in contemporary Australian serial television, in that while it was unequivocally an Australian production (both for regulatory purposes and for maximizing opportunities for local success), it was aimed primarily at the US market and other markets (being presold to BSkyB satellite television in Britain, South America, and parts of Europe—mostly sight unseen, a testament to the distribution profile of the participants in the venture) (Shoebridge 1993: 10). It appeared to bring together an exceptionally strong production, distribution, and exhibition alliance. *Paradise Beach* was co-produced by Village Roadshow Productions, with its studio complex at the Gold Coast offering complete production facilities, the Nine Network (the strongest-rating network needing successful local drama and an equity partner in the Warner Roadshow Movieworld Studios), and New World International/Genesis, a large US distribution company specializing in mostly US soap opera for the US syndication and international markets (*Baywatch*, *Santa Barbara*, *The Bold and the Beautiful*).

Paradise Beach was launched virtually simultaneously in Australia and the USA, and followed soon after in other territories. It was heavily promoted in Australia, filling an early evening slot, and received its highest exposure at the premiere screening, but dropped quickly in the ratings. In the USA, it was cleared by Genesis/New World for 85 per cent of the syndication market in a test campaign during the northern summer of 1993, an unprecedented exposure for a foreign-made serial. Paralleling the theme of the programme ('It's where teenagers from everywhere converge to cut loose, find the perfect wave, and fall hopelessly in love'), it was aimed at its target teen audience at the end of school for the academic year. However, it did not survive the summer, being pulled from US schedules before it had run the length of its test campaign.

Why did *Paradise Beach* fail? From a purely financial perspective, it did not fail. The experienced partners knew the programme was an experiment and structured its costs so that it was virtually certain of returning modest profits even if it failed to secure ongoing screentime in the way it ultimately did. However, as a strategy that could be built on by further Australian, or for that matter any foreign, but English-language, serial production aimed for long-term acceptance in international markets, it was a signal failure. This may be in part due to the very factor which guaranteed its bottom-line security—its extreme low-budget, instrumental production protocols. This approach to production virtually guaranteed an exceedingly negative critical reception in Australia, as well as elsewhere (for a derisively dismissive New Zealand account, see Wichtel 1993). This cannot be discounted as a factor in the fate of the programme locally (and even more so overseas), especially when serial programming needs to build audience by word of mouth and peer influence.

In some ways, the unprecedentedly hostile critical reaction was misplaced, as the cost structure and schedule slots (both locally and overseas) for *Paradise Beach* suggest the pertinent comparisons should be with daytime soap opera, as Schembri and Malone (1994: 32) have argued. However, such a reaction was to some extent invited by Village raising high expectations for the product: it was to be a cross between *Baywatch*, *Beverly Hills 90210*, and local product like *Neighbours* (all of them prime time, higher budget, and/or established long-term successes). Given Australia's tradition of producing high-quality serial drama for prime time slots, but hardly any for the daytime, the comparisons invited by the publicity made *Paradise Beach* an easy, if probably misplaced, target for critics.

Other, middle-range factors also intervened against the serial. The US market for pre-prime time soaps had declined considerably. The marketplace has become so fragmented and the average attention span so short that there had not been a successful new launch of a soap opera for many years in the USA. Currently, no strip soap in the USA runs after 3 p.m. As well, a crucial ancillary marketing outlet, the soap opera press (including the three main magazines *Soap Opera Weekly*, *Soap Opera Digest*, and *Soap Opera*, along with teen magazines like *Sixteen*, *Tiger Beat*, and *Sassy*) did not promote the programme. Again, decisions on the 'rightness', the cultural relevance, of *Paradise Beach* probably defeated the expectation that the specialist press would jump at the opportunity to get behind one of the very few new soaps aimed at teenagers in several years.

The programme, by positioning itself so closely to successful teenage prime time soaps, placed enormous pressure on itself to capture the very short life-span of teenage argot and fashion. The only way the programme's US distributors (McNamara *et al*. 1994) saw for such difficulties to be overcome would be for US scriptwriters to have been imported to oversee and generate storylining and dialogue. Such importation, of course, would have defeated the objective of qualifying *Paradise Beach* for the Australian drama quota.

The distributor's comments (McNamara *et al*. 1994) on

writing and technical style also went into fundamental issues of televisual culture. On the one hand, the storyliners tended to 'burn through story' much quicker than in US soaps. Events and emotional reactions that could have been milked far more were tossed off in off-camera asides, for example. Like much Australian audiovisual culture, the programme consistently dedramatized action. Dramatic angles and opportunities occurred off camera for cultural reasons as much to avoid expensive effects or complicated set ups. Therefore, narrative pacing was unfamiliar—the storylining was too fast (the slowness of US soaps is so that audience can miss episodes and not lose the continuity); but the emotional temperature was too low.

What the ultimate failure of *Paradise Beach* suggests is that, at least in terms of acceptance of foreign long-form drama in US broadcast television, the English language is not necessarily an advantage (Spanish-language soaps have more success in cable). In the soap format, it seems, US broadcast television material will always be the virtually absolute benchmark for audience acceptance. The Australian long-form successes in the USA have not been live-action adult or teen drama. Rather, they have been sci-tech (*Beyond 2000*) and children's animation (*Blinky Bill*). The first of these demonstrated that its genre could be exploited on an international basis, while the other was a tried-and-tested children's formula from the highly credentialled Yoram Gross Studios. This underscores the virtual impossibility of seeing foreign long-form drama on US broadcast television. Soap operas, more than any other format, must be allowed to build an audience through stable scheduling and committed marketing, for their 'dispersed narrative structure and incremental characterization make of them an acquired taste' (Crofts 1995: 98), all the more when they are foreign.

Social Values in a Serious Culture: *The Flying Doctors* in The Netherlands

A case very different from the commercializing UK and the supremely commercial USA is provided by the success of *The Flying Doctors* in The Netherlands, the only country in

Europe, besides the UK, where Australian programmes have established themselves as part of mainstream popular culture. *The Flying Doctors* began in 1987. For the seven years up to 1993 when the programme was cancelled in Australia, it formed the backbone of the public channel VARA's Saturday night schedule where it regularly won the 8.00 p.m. or 8.30 p.m. time-slot. Because of its popularity with Dutch audiences, VARA began repeats of the programme from the opening episode at 6.30 p.m. In 1992 it was voted the most popular imported programme by the Dutch public.

A number of factors in Dutch television and society combine to account for the success of this Australian series, but perhaps the most important is the unique nature of Holland's public service tradition and the way in which *The Flying Doctors* harmonizes with it. The Netherlands had an exclusively public service television system until the advent of private broadcaster RTL4 in 1989. However, its model of public service is quite unlike any other in the world, being based not on 'internal diversity' but on 'external diversity' (Nieuwenhuis 1992: 204). This comes about because the bodies responsible for broadcasting are not the actual broadcasters (transmitters of programmes) but organizations which are offshoots of the so-called 'pillars' of Dutch social institutions. Each pillar had its own broadcasting organization and was given airtime on the state run channel in proportion to the size of its membership. The traditional broadcasting organizations were VARA (socialists), KRO (Catholics), NCRV (Protestant), VPRO (liberal Protestants) and AVRO. The idea was that diversity would be ensured by virtue of each of these organizations choosing programming material that reflected their various ideological positions.

Although the system was never controlled centrally as in other comparable countries, a Reithian philosophy did to a considerable extent permeate all the broadcasting organizations, notably VARA, the socialist grouping, where a philosophy developed which attempted to wed popularity and progressiveness (Ang 1991: 130). VARA is the main purchaser of Australian material in The Netherlands and this broadcasting philosophy animates the taste regime through which its acquisitions staff choose programmes, including Australian programmes. VARA's Head of Acquisitions regards the BBC as the quality benchmark, and prefers, for instance, *Law and Order* over *LA Law* amongst US programming 'because it has more of a documentary flavour' (van Essen 1992). *The Flying Doctors* fulfilled the conditions of being both sufficiently progressive, in VARA's sense of the term (which can be read as pro-social and -communal values, but without the élitism often attributed to classical Reithianism), and popular in the sense that it has a very large and very devoted following amongst audiences. While the stability of this unique system of institutionalized ideological pluralism has been radically challenged by the rapid success of the new commercial broadcasters like RTL4, VARA has maintained a residual commitment to a form of progressiveness that can be imputed to series like *Flying Doctors*.

The reasons why Australian productions such as *The Flying Doctors* have made more of an impact in The Netherlands than in other European countries such as France, Germany, and Italy include the fact that the Dutch are very used to seeing programmes in English and programmes from the UK. In Holland, unlike in France, Germany, and Italy, programmes are subtitled rather than dubbed. Dutch audiences speak English in very large numbers, and they are used to British styles of comedy and drama. Being a small-to-medium size country, Holland has a somewhat higher level of imported content than the bigger European countries, and it has had a higher level of British imports than other countries. So there is a propensity to be open to British programming, and to the extent that Australian and British drama styles are similar, and more similar to each other than to American styles, then there is a particular preparedness in Dutch audiences for Australian drama.

However, the 'exoticism' of the Australian outback in *Flying Doctors* also appeals, as in other countries where the programme has done well. It is also a relatively 'safe' programme concept, with whatever progressiveness that can be imputed to the programme found in the 'warmth' of its portrayal of social solidarity and the communitarian values of 'helping people' in crisis. This contrasts with US programming which, according to a senior Dutch public-service executive, dwells on racial and social conflict which 'wouldn't wash with the Dutch audience' (Tolen-Worth 1992). And a leading Dutch independent producer accounted for *Flying Doctors*' popularity in the following terms: 'It's about helping people. We love hospital series. But there is also something Australian about *The Flying Doctors* that appeals. It is very down to earth—that basic earthiness. It shows good people, a healthy people, and an attractive Australian way of life' (von Bochove 1992).

Like most successful domestic serials around the world, but unusually for an imported programme, *Flying Doctors* has spawned its own fan club in the country. Its magazine contains episode summaries, photos of personalities and places from the show, *Flying Doctor* quizzes, and even copies of letters between Dutch fans and the actual Flying Doctor Service operating out of Broken Hill to which fans send donations of money. The show has also spawned a series of novelizations of *Flying Doctor* episodes which are jointly published by the Australian production company, Crawfords, and VARA, and appear in both hard and soft cover, with lavish colour illustrations of the stars of the show, at popular magazine outlets.

While much of this literature concerns the traditional preoccupations of soap opera fans everywhere, other themes which recur in these magazines and books are pleasure in the sense of community that viewers perceive at Cooper's Crossing, and respect for the devotion to duty in the face of danger and hardship that is part of the image of the Flying Doctor Service in Australia as well as overseas. It would be easy to draw the conclusion that the programme represents wish-fulfilment about values lost in modern urban living, but this alone does not account for why *The Flying Doctors* has done better in The Netherlands than in any other export market. The answer may well lie in the way it fulfils the particular set of broadcasting values of 'progressiveness and popularity' which have dominated the Dutch system until recently.

An Ersatz Asian Nation? The ABC in Asia

While Australia has a long tradition of broadcasting within the regions of Asia and the Pacific through the short-wave radio service Radio Australia, the most significant additional development in Australian public broadcasting within the region since the establishment of Radio Australia more than fifty years ago is the Australian Broadcasting Corporation's Australia Television (ATV), launched in February 1993. In the 1990s Australian public debate and public policy are undergoing rapid, perhaps fundamental, paradigm shifts in its current 'Asianization' push. Australia's new regional television initiative is overtly driven by diplomatic and trade imperatives. Six out of the ten largest markets for Australian trade are in the regions of Asia, while Australian trade with Japan is now equivalent to the whole volume of trade with the European Union. These trends are set to consolidate strongly in the years ahead.

Australia Television was initiated with a direct government allocation, with a significant portion of its running costs over time expected to be met from corporate sponsorship. It is a single-channel television service carried on Indonesia's Palapa B2P satellite. Expansion plans include transmitting on China's Apstar satellites (while continuing to transmit on Palapa), effectively giving the service the ability to be received throughout Asia, North Africa, the Middle East, and parts of Europe and Russia. It broadcasts from early morning to late evening across four time zones, and schedules mostly selected ABC domestic programmes, including children's, language education, drama, documentary, arts, and comedy.

The flagship programme of the service, and the only major programme made specifically for it, is the nightly *ATV News* bulletin (see Cunningham and Ritchie 1994). There are significant correlations between Australian government policies toward the region and the overall stance of the news. While there may be direct instances of state and internal ABC pressure on ATV journalists and problematic policies of pre- or self-censorship through detailed editorial notions of not offending cultural sensitivities in the region, the stance of *ATV*

News is one that seeks strategically to advance Australia's own national-development needs to integrate itself diplomatically (in both senses) in the region.

The diplomatic 'mission' of *ATV News* is also influenced by the fact that, at least in the medium term, the audience for Australia Television will be almost entirely élites of various countries with which Australia seeks enhanced trading, educational, cultural, and political ties; in particular Indonesia, Singapore, Taiwan, Hong Kong, and Malaysia—English-speaking élites for whom positive international presentations of national and regional issues may be of special importance (a fact that is highlighted strongly in the service's promotional publicity). This is a posture that could be called 'reverse orientalism'. Edward Said (1991) has shown the degree to which the West constructed a myth of non-Western peoples as the threatening 'other' on the basis of oppositions like rational versus irrational and developed versus undeveloped. Reverse orientalism overcompensates for this history, creating a, perhaps premature, identification with Asia by Australian Westerners.

Perhaps most interestingly, Australia is represented in *ATV News* as being *already* an Asian country. Stories which acknowledge it as a country just beginning to come to terms with the rights of its indigenous population, and as one which is still perceived in Asia in terms of the history of its operation of the White Australia Policy, are mostly absent. Australia, rather, is already multicultural, willing to assimilate with other cultures, and has religious and racial tolerance. ATV regularly features stories which represent Australia politically as a nation sharing the same interests and goals as its Asian neighbours, particularly the development and health of ASEAN (Association of South East Asian Nations). While 'Asianization' may well be an overriding cause of state here, it is hardly reflected in Asian nations' and peoples' perceptions of Australia, as any sample of Asian media coverage will indicate. *ATV News* works to qualify these perceptions, in particular, through stories about successful immigration from the region to Australia.

The tensions faced by *ATV News*, and the service generally, include the contradiction that, while it is one amongst several of the signals that could be construed by Asian opinion-formers as 'subverting' their national goals in the region, its rationale for Australia is precisely one of 'national development' as part of Asia. And its ability in the longer term to deliver on a key part of its mission—to 'naturalize' the Australian perspective as regional in its significance—will ultimately depend on establishing the credibility of its journalistic credentials. These credentials will have to be fashioned in a context of a sponsored service whose longer-term financial health will depend increasingly on attracting corporate support both in Australia and in the countries receiving the signal. The ABC's marketing document for the service, 'Beaming Across Asia', talks of an audience comprising 'the growing business and government élite in a region providing dynamic export opportunities for Australia'. This projected audience provides more than an attraction for potential sponsors to gain access to an influential market segment; it also nominates those élites that are in a position to influence Australia's integration into the region.

On the evidence of its early period of operation, the service exhibits aspects of development journalism, but Western-style development journalism; a style characterized by a posture of reverse orientalism. This is not necessarily a result of state direction, but arises from shared intent between media and government élites. By its nature the service will attempt to provide a broader perspective than that which may be deemed appropriate for domestic consumption. This is appropriate and welcome, for Australian media have traditionally focused on European (especially British) and American models, styles, and content. However, the challenges it poses for journalists in a volatile cross-cultural mediascape will be significant. Means must be found to allow both Australia's economic aspirations in the region and its traditions of independent journalism to flourish. If the service can address the considerable cross-cultural challenges it faces, particularly the widespread perception in many Asian countries that Australia remains a racist western country, it has the potential in time to become an important ongoing voice projecting Australia's place in the region.

Conclusion: Benefits and Drawbacks of Internationalization

Australia is a small but significant international trader of television programming and an even smaller player in transborder satellite television. However, it exerts a presence on the world's film and television screens that is disproportionate to its population base, geographical position, and size of its domestic market. The underlying reasons for this have been outlined in the early part of this chapter. What are some of the effects of increased internationalization on the domestic policy and industrial landscape?

It is important not to exaggerate the export record and potential of the industry. By world standards the industry is of small-to-medium size and its export record slight in comparison with other Australian service industry exports. For example, education services netted Australia $A1 billion in 1992 compared with an estimated $A65 million for total audiovisual (film, television, and video). A recent government report (BIE 1994) says that in all audiovisual (which, for example, includes music industry inputs), export is only 4 per cent of total revenue. But these data need major refinement. Until 1994 there had been no specific data collection for audiovisual and the methods by which the available figures have been captured—as part of an overall industry survey—severely underestimates the dollars being earned from export. They do not take account of the presence of foreign companies' investments in Australian programmes, which accounted in 1992–3 for the largest single source of investment in Australian audiovisual product (Given 1993). Nor do they factor in revenues from off-shore production, which have put audiovisual in a leading bracket of export-oriented industries in Queensland nor the earnings of Australian companies producing programmes outside Australia; nor the developments in new media products which are being increasingly exported (DITARD 1994). With these lacunae in mind, many industry representatives have claimed, with justification, that the figures should be closer to $A200 million (more than treble the official figures).

Apart from the bald figures, it is undeniable that audiovisual product is the most visible in any export portfolio, and accrues to the country a considerable yet resolutely intangible symbolic profile internationally. *Return to Eden* has been the single most-quoted source of positive understanding of Australia in Indonesia (Milne 1993). A 1991 study of provincial French adolescents' perceptions of Australia (de Jabrun 1993) showed that the prime source for general information about Australia was film and television, and that teen music and *Neighbours* personalities Kylie Minogue and Jason Donovan far outscored all other mentioned Australian figures. As Ian Craven (1989) argues, *Neighbours* may be regarded as playing a constructive role in internationalizing perspectives on suburban rather than bush modalities of Australian life. The Australian Tourist Commission in 1991 studied the impact of soap operas running in Europe, looking for ways to broaden and renovate predominant images of Australia as an outback adventure location. It found that Germans visiting Australia were keen to meet small-town locals (influenced by *A Country Practice* or *The Flying Doctors*), while Italians showed a liking for beaches (*Home and Away*) (McCathie 1991).

An increasing international orientation has led the industry and commentators to question whether the 1990s has borne tidings of the 'end of the national project' in higher-budget drama. Graeme Turner has argued that signs in the policy, criticism, and production climate indicate that decision-makers, cultural intellectuals, and industry personnel all now doubt the contemporary viability of cultural nationalism—which served as the intellectual glue holding together state support for, and audience response to, the industry—as a binding rhetoric and policy frame (Turner 1994). For Tom O'Regan, the industry's financial troubles of the late 1980s meant that a country 'capable of producing not simply more, but better quality, television, well placed to manage *on its own terms* the popular audience oriented "internationalisation" taking place in the more profitable parts of the international television system' had missed the boat (1991: 107, original emphasis).

However, it is possible to see a greater international

orientation, combined with social policies of multiculturalism, recasting traditional cultural nationalism but by no means abandoning it. To be sure, this is an ambivalent project, influenced to a considerable degree by the *force majeure* of international co-production and sales. The only way high end Australian production can prosper is through increased international linkages. But, at its best, internationalization is facilitating this redefinition, not fudging it in imprecise transnational cultural artifices. Whereas feature film co-productions are often characterized by no on-screen sense of one or more of the partner countries (for example, *Black Robe*, *The Prisoner of St Petersburg*), most television co-productions entered into by Australian participants do achieve some degree of on-screen partnership, caused no doubt by the need for all partners to engage popular audiences domestically.

This recasting means that the key interpretative categories used to analyse Australian drama production in the 1970s and 1980s (see Dermody and Jacka 1987; 1988*a*; 1988*b*) have to be remodelled. The key oppositions—which approximate the modernist and postmodernist elements of audiovisual culture outlined earlier—are no longer between what Dermody and Jacka called Industry-1 (cultural nationalism, art cinema and social realism, government protection) and Industry-2 (commercialism, international appeal at all costs, Hollywood imitations), but largely between forms of internationalism which advance local cultural development and those which do not. Jacka describes the shift as 'a drawing together of the warring factions within Australian film culture: the hitherto opposing forces of Industry-1 and Industry-2 are united by the recognition that the enemy is more without than within' (1993: 191).

While the earlier phase of greater international orientation in the mini-series in the 1980s, for example, relied on either fairly standard Australian ethnocentrism, using Asian-related stories as backdrops for Western characters (*A Long Way From Home: Barlow and Chambers*, 1988; *Bangkok Hilton*, 1989), or took the much-worn route of importing an American star to bolster potential sales for an Australian-based story (*The Last Frontier*, 1986), in the 1990s some major television events such as *The Leaving of Liverpool* (1992) and *The Magistrate* (1989) have shown the degree to which international co-production can advance an organic and critically revisionist, yet popular, sense of a multicultural contemporary Australia.

However, overall, it is clear that the programmes that travel best, and that have the best potential for export, are not necessarily the most innovative or most searching of Australian society. Saying this only confirms the truism that television is fundamentally a local medium. Humour (and thus comedy formats), most drama (relying as it does on some unavoidable specificities of character and place), and of course the vast bulk of news and current affairs remain stubbornly resistant to broad-based exploitation in a multiplicity of markets. What international acceptance such formats do find cannot be predicted with any degree of prior accuracy (and thus are resistant to broad policy and strategic settings).

The international marketplace of discrete programme trade is, unavoidably, a levelling arena, while transborder television has before it the considerable challenge of creatively overcoming 'cultural screens' as a central aspect of scheduling and marketing. It is in the areas of sport, nature documentary/natural history, some children's programming, and magazine style science and sci-tech that global television seeks sufficient purchase in universal thematics (the 'neutral' common values, settings, and aspirations Roland Barthes (1973) analysed in his 'Family of Man' essay) to offset the discount of cultural screens. It is in these formats, along with those serial drama forms that have established long-term acceptance internationally—what we would call 'volume television'—that the bulk of Australian trade is accomplished.

While Australian television programme-makers have engaged in significant export achievement, increasingly so over the last decade (and the trend is set upward), there are dangers in turning such activity over to a policy-led export drive, as current signs in the Australian policy environment indicate. A new national government cultural policy emphasizes industry and specifically export as one of its main elements. The Australian government's Department of Industry has focused on audiovisual as a potential growth area for export

(DITARD 1994). And the broadcast regulator, the ABA, is emphasizing the challenge of 'borderless markets' (see Johns 1993) in its consideration of changes to local content regulation.

Australian broadcasting policy, particularly in the area of providing a regulated 'safety net' for local television production, has been based explicitly on the central *cultural* rationale to ensure that Australians see themselves, their lives and society, reflected on their screens in reasonable amounts, and that this reflection take account of the pluralistic nature of the society. An *industry* policy of enhancing export will not necessarily match with this, or rather is not designed to do the same job. The current emphasis on industry policy has the potential to eclipse the original reasons for having a cultural policy for broadcasting.

Strong arguments have been mounted, both within the country and internationally, that Australia should change its currently strong local television regulation to a more Canadian-style system because of the industry growth that would flow from off-shore production being able to count within the local quota. There are, indeed, powerful reasons to underpin these developments with unequivocally supportive industry policies and initiatives, but these should not be confused with, or allowed to eclipse, a cultural policy for broadcasting. There are also inbuilt limits to growth of the industry, at least in the areas of traditional programme production—in general, it needs to have secured a local network licence before or while it seeks overseas markets. If the only objective was industry growth (irrespective of whether increased programme production found an audience here) then the argument for loosening content regulation would be hard to resist. But most overseas buyers look to local cultural resonance and viewer acceptance as a litmus test for consideration of the programme in their market.

While the dollar amounts involved in export and co-production should not be slighted in the least, the audiovisual sector will never be a Pied Piper leading the way out of Australia's endemic balance of payments deficits. Its function as a platform for greater international cultural understanding, profile, and acceptance will continue to be as important, in the widest sense of Australia's national interest as an internationalizing society, as the actual dollars earned as export income. Ultimately the arguments for audiovisual export will continue to be the same as arguments for support for audiovisual domestically—cultural first and then economic. This view found support from no less than the prime minister, Paul Keating, in 1992 when he suggested that cultural industries had a role to play in Australia's economic recovery, not just because they could contribute to wealth directly but because they could help to foster a 'sense of national purpose and national cohesion' that could give Australians the spirit to overcome their economic problems.

There are also some specific threats to the domestic industry arising from export. It may be that one of the factors leading to decreased licence fees from the networks for drama production lately is precisely the increased export success of Australian television, on the assumption that producers can top up with foreign earnings. And as Australian export activity becomes an expected norm, we might even see the re-emergence of the old 'infant industry' argument used against continued government support. That is, because the industry has matured into an international player, it does not need the iron lung of taxpayer support any longer. On balance, Australia's export profile is both unavoidable (for financial reasons) and welcome (for cultural reasons), but there are clouds to every silver lining.

References

ABA (Australian Broadcasting Authority) (1994), *Broadcasting Financial Results 1992–3* (Commonwealth of Australia, Sydney).

AFC (Australian Film Commission) (1992), *Get the Picture: Essential Data on Australian Film, Television and Video* (AFC, Sydney).

Ang, Ien (1991), *Desperately Seeking the Audience* (Routledge, London and New York).

Barthes, Roland (1973), *Mythologies* (Paladin, London).

BIE (Bureau of Industry Economics) (1994), *Audiovisual Industries in Australia: A Discussion Paper* (BIE, Canberra, April).

BTCE (Bureau of Transport and Communications Economics) (1991), *Economic Aspects of Broadcasting Regulation* (AGPS, Canberra).

CAUGHIE, JOHN (1990), 'Playing at Being American: Games and Tactics', in Patricia Mellencamp (ed.), *Logics of Television: Essays in Cultural Criticism* (Indiana University Press, Bloomington and Indianapolis), 44–58.

COPLEY, JASON (1991), 'The Road that Leads to Ramsey Street: Towards the Study of Soap Opera's Popularity in its Imported Context', unpublished BA Honours dissertation, Goldsmiths' College, University of London.

CRAVEN, IAN (1989), 'Distant Neighbours: Notes on Some Australian Soap Operas', *Australian Studies*, 3 (Dec.), 1–35.

CROFTS, STEPHEN (1995), 'Global Neighbours?', in Robert C. Allen (ed.), *To be Continued . . .* (Routledge, London and New York), 98–121.

CUNNINGHAM, STUART (1988), 'Kennedy-Miller: "House style" in Australian television', in Elizabeth Jacka and Susan Dermody (eds.), *The Imaginary Industry* (Australian Film, Television and Radio School, North Ryde, Sydney), 177–200.

—— (1992), *Framing Culture: Criticism and Policy in Australia* (Allen and Unwin, Sydney).

—— and TURNER, GRAEME (eds.) (1993), *The Media in Australia: Industries, Texts, Audiences* (Allen & Unwin, Sydney).

—— and RITCHIE, JOHN (1994), 'An Ersatz Asian Nation? The ABC in Asia', *Media Information Australia*, 71 (Feb.), 46–54.

DE BENS, ELS, KELLY, MARY, and BAKKE, MARIT (1992), 'Television Content: Dallasification of Culture?', in Karen Siune and Wolfgang Truetzschler (eds.), for the Euromedia Research Group, *Dynamics of Media Politics: Broadcast and Electronic Media in Western Europe* (Sage, London), 75–100.

DE JABRUN, MARY (1993), 'French Adolescents' Perceptions of Australia', in Don Grant and Graham Seal (eds.), *Australia in the World: Perceptions and Possibilities* (Black Swan Press, Perth), 102–7.

DERMODY, SUSAN, and JACKA, ELIZABETH (1987), *The Screening of Australia*, Volume 1: *Anatomy of a Film Industry* (Currency Press, Sydney).

—— and —— (1988*a*), *The Screening of Australia*, Volume 2: *Anatomy of a National Culture* (Currency Press, Sydney).

—— and —— (eds.) (1988*b*), *The Imaginary Industry: Australian Film in the Late Eighties* (Australian Film, Television and Radio School, North Ryde, Sydney).

DITARD (Department of Industry, Technology and Regional Development) (1994), *Media Developments in Asia and Implications for Australia: A Discussion Paper* (Audiovisual Task Force, DITARD, March).

GERRIE, ANTHEA (1992), 'Teaching the US to Suck Soap', *The Bulletin*, 9 (June), 98–100.

GILLESPIE, MARIE (1993), 'Soap Viewing, Gossip and Rumour amongst Punjabi Youth in Southall', in Philip Drummond, Richard Paterson, and Janet Willis (eds.), *National Identity and Europe: The Television Revolution* (BFI Publishing, London), 25–42.

GIVEN, JOCK (1993), 'Australian Content, Broadcasting and Export Opportunities', paper presented to the 1993 Australian Broadcasting Summit, 11 November.

GRANT, DON, and SEAL, GRAHAM (eds.) (1993), *Australia in the World: Perceptions and Possibilities* (Black Swan Press, Perth).

HILL, DAVID (1994), *Daily Variety* (10 Mar.).

JACKA, ELIZABETH (1991), *The ABC of Drama: 1975–1990* (Australian Film, Television and Radio School, North Ryde, Sydney).

—— (1993), 'Part 3: Film', in Stuart Cunningham and Graeme Turner (eds.), *The Media in Australia: Industries, Texts, Audiences* (Allen & Unwin, Sydney), 180–92.

JOHNS, BRIAN (1993), '"Borderless markets" Key Communications Challenge', *ABA Update*, 12 (Oct.), 1, 5–7, 9.

LEALAND GEOFF (1990), '"I'd just like to say how happy I am to be here in the seventh state of Australia": The Australianisation of New Zealand Television', *Sites*, 21 Spring), 100–12.

LIEBES, TAMAR, and KATZ, ELIHU (1990), *The Export of Meaning: Cross-Cultural Readings of Dallas* (Oxford University Press, New York).

LUMBY, CATHERINE, and O'NEIL, JOHN (1994), 'Tabloid Television', in Julianne Schultz (ed.), *Not Just Another Business: Journalists, Citizens and the Media* (Pluto Press and Ideas for Australia, Marrickville, Sydney), 149–66.

MCCATHIE, ANDREW (1991), 'Europe Tunes into "New-Look" Australia', *Financial Review* (3 Sept.), 32.

MCNAMARA, JAMES (Chief Executive Officer and President, New World Entertainment), DISERIO, THEA (Senior Vice-President, New World International), and OLDHAM, PHIL (Executive Vice President, Genesis Entertainment) (1994), interview with Stuart Cunningham, New York, March.

MARIN, MINETTE (1989), *The Daily Telegraph* (10 Mar.) 18, quoted in Wober and Fazal (1994).

MILLER, TOBY (1994), 'When Australia Became Modern', review of *National Fictions* (2nd edn.), *Continuum* 8/2: 206–14.

MILNE, JOHN (1993), 'Overcoming Australia's Regional Image Problem: A Personal View', in D. Grant and G. Seal (eds.), *Australia in the World: Perceptions and Possibilities* (Black Swan Press, Perth).

MILNER, ANDREW (1991), *Contemporary Cultural Theory* (Allen & Unwin, Sydney).

MOLLOY, SIMON, and BURGAN, BARRY (1993), *The Economics of Film and Television in Australia* (Australian Film Commission, Sydney).

MORAN, ALBERT (1985), *Images and Industry: Television Drama Production in Australia* (Currency Press, Sydney).

NIEUWENHUIS, A. J. (1992), 'Media Policy in the Netherlands: Beyond the Market', *European Journal of Communication*, 7/2: 195–218.

O'REGAN, TOM (1991), 'The Rise and Fall of Entrepreneurial TV: Australian TV, 1986–90', *Screen*, 32/1 (Spring), 94–108. Reprinted in Graeme Turner (ed.), *Nation, Culture, Text: Australian Cultural and Media Studies* (Routledge, London, 1993), 91–105.

—— (1993), *Australian Television Culture* (Allen & Unwin, Sydney).

PAPANDREA, FRANCO (1994), 'Effectiveness of Australian Content Regulation for Television Programs', paper presented to the conference Media Futures: Policy and Performance, July.

ROWE, DAVID (1994), 'The Federal Republic of *Sylvania Waters*', *Metro Magazine*, 98 (Winter), 14–23.

SAID, EDWARD (1991), *Orientalism: Western Concepts of the Orient* (Penguin, Harmondsworth).

SCHEMBRI, PETER, and MALONE, JACKIE (1994), '*Paradise Beach* Reconsidered', *Cinema Papers*, 97/98 (Apr.), 30–3.

SHAWCROSS, WILLIAM (1992), *Rupert Murdoch: Ringmaster of the Information Circus* (Random House, Sydney).

SHOEBRIDGE, NEIL (1993), 'Village Goes Global with Low-Risk TV', *Business Review Weekly* (7 May), 10–11.

SILJ, ALESSANDRO (1988), *East of Dallas: The European Challenge to American Television* (British Film Institute, London).

SMITH, ROFF (1992), 'I am 68. I live in the Bahamas. I am Australia's biggest TV star. Who am I?' *Sunday Age* (26 July), Agenda 1, 2.

TAYLOR, CATHERINE (1993), 'Squeaky-clean Soap, Export Quality', *The Australian* (28 May), 13.

TOLEN-WORTH, LOUISE (Head of Program Buying, NOS) (1992), interview with Elizabeth Jacka, Hilversum, November.

TURNER, GRAEME (1994), 'The End of the National Project? Australian Cinema in the 1990s', in Wimal Dissanayake (ed.), *Colonialism and Nationalism in Asian Cinema* (Indiana University Press, Bloomington), 202–16.

VAN ESSEN, RIA (Head of Acquisitions, VARA) (1992), interview with Elizabeth Jacka, Hilversum, October.

VON BOCHOVE, HEDY (Production Head, JE Productions) (1992), interview with Elizabeth Jacka, Aalsmeer, October.

WICHTEL, DIANA (1993), 'Ain't it a Beach', *Listener* (New Zealand) (28 Aug.), 71.

WOBER, MALLORY, and FAZAL, S. (1994), 'Neighbours at Home and Away: British Viewers' Perceptions of Australian Soap Operas', *Media Information Australia*, 71 (Feb.), 78–88.

Index

Index